THE
VALET'S TRAGEDY

AND OTHER STUDIES

ANDREW LANG

1st WORLD
LIBRARY
Literary Society

The Valet's Tragedy

Andrew Lang

© 1st World Library – Literary Society, 2004
PO Box 2211
Fairfield, IA 52556
www.1stworldlibrary.org
First Edition

LCCN: 2003099599

ISBN: 1-59540-003-6

Purchase *"The Valets Tragedy"*
as a traditional bound book at:
www.1stWorldLibrary.org/purchase.asp?ISBN=1-59540-003-6

1st World Library Literary Society is a nonprofit
organization dedicated to promoting literacy by:

- Creating a free internet library accessible from any
computer worldwide.
- Hosting writing competitions and offering book
publishing scholarships.

Readers interested in supporting literacy
through sponsorship, donations or
membership please contact:
literacy@1stworldlibrary.org
Check us out at: www.1stworldlibrary.org

The Valet's Tragedy
contributed by Ed, Tim & Rodney
in support of
1st World Library Literary Society

*TO THE MARQUIS D'EGUILLES 'FOR THE
LOVE OF THE MAID AND OF CHIVALRY'*

CONTENTS

PREFACE

These studies in secret history follow no chronological order. The affair of James de la Cloche only attracted the author's attention after most of the volume was in print. But any reader curious in the veiled intrigues of the Restoration will probably find it convenient to peruse 'The Mystery of James de la Cloche' after the essay on 'The Valet's Master,' as the puzzling adventures of de la Cloche occurred in the years (1668-1669), when the Valet was consigned to lifelong captivity, and the Master was broken on the wheel. What would have been done to 'Giacopo Stuardo' had he been a subject of Louis XIV., "tis better only guessing.' But his fate, whoever he may have been, lay in the hands of Lord Ailesbury's 'good King,' Charles II., and so he had a good deliverance.

The author is well aware that whosoever discusses historical mysteries pleases the public best by being quite sure, and offering a definite and certain solution. Unluckily Science forbids, and conscience is on the same side. We verily do not know how the false Pucelle arrived at her success with the family of the true Maid; we do not know, or pretend to know, who killed Sir Edmund Berry Godfrey; or how Amy Robsart came by her death; or why the Valet was so important a prisoner. It is only possible to restate the cases, and remove, if we may, the errors and confusions which beset the problems. Such a tiny point as the year of Amy Robsart's marriage is stated variously by our historians. To ascertain the truth gave the author half a day's work, and, at last, he would have voted for the wrong year, had he not been aided by the superior acuteness of his friend, Mr. Hay Fleming. He feels morally certain that, in trying to set historians right about Amy Robsart, he must have committed some conspicuous blunders; these always attend such enterprises of rectification.

With regard to Sir Edmund Berry Godfrey, Mr. A. W. Crawley-Boevey points out to me that in an unpublished letter of Mr. Alexander Herbert Phaire in 1743-44 (Addit. MSS. British Museum 4291, fol. 150) Godfrey is spoken of in connection with his friend Valentine Greatrakes, the 'miraculous Conformist,' or 'Irish Stroker,' of the Restoration. 'It is a pity,' Mr. Phaire remarks, 'that Sir Edmund's letters, to the number of 104, are not in somebody's hands that would oblige the world by publishing them. They contain many remarkable things, and the best and truest secret history in King Charles II.'s reign.' Where are these letters now? Mr. Phaire does not say to whom they were addressed, perhaps to Greatrakes, who named his second son after Sir Edmund, or to Colonel Phaire, the Regicide. This Mr. Phaire of 1744 was of Colonel Phaire's family. It does not seem quite certain whether Le Fevre, or Lee Phaire, was the real name of the so-called Jesuit whom Bedloe accused of the murder of Sir Edmund.

Of the studies here presented, 'The Valet's Master,' 'The Mystery of Sir Edmund Berry Godfrey,' 'The False Jeanne d'Arc,' 'The Mystery of Amy Robsart,' and 'The Mystery of James de la Cloche,' are now published for the first time. Part of 'The Voices of Jeanne d'Arc,' is from a paper by the author in 'The Proceedings of the Society for Psychical Research.' 'The Valet's Tragedy' is mainly from an article in 'The Monthly Review,' revised, corrected, and augmented. 'The Queen's Marie' is a recast of a paper in 'Blackwood's Magazine'; 'The Truth about "Fisher's Ghost,"' and 'Junius and Lord Lyttelton's Ghost' are reprinted, with little change, from the same periodical. 'The Mystery of Lord Bateman' is a recast of an article in 'The Cornhill Magazine.' The earlier part of the essay on Shakespeare and Bacon appeared in 'The Quarterly Review.' The author is obliged to the courtesy of the proprietors and editors of these serials for permission to use his essays again, with revision and additions.*

*Essays by the author on 'The False Pucelle' and on 'Sir Edmund Berry Godfrey' have appeared in The Nineteenth Century (1895) and in The Cornhill Magazine, but these are not the papers here presented.

The author is deeply indebted to the generous assistance of Father Gerard and Father Pollen, S.J.; and, for making transcripts of unpublished documents, to Miss E. M. Thompson and Miss Violet Simpson.

Since passing the volume for the press the author has received from Mr. Austin West, at Rome, a summary of Armanni's letter about Giacopo Stuardo. He is led thereby to the conclusion that Giacopo was identical with the eldest son of Charles II. - James de la Cloche - but conceives that, at the end of his life, James was insane, or at least was a 'megalomaniac,' or was not author of his own Will.

I.

THE VALET'S TRAGEDY

1. THE LEGEND OF THE MAN IN THE IRON MASK

The Mystery of the Man in the Iron Mask is, despite a pleasant saying of Lord Beaconsfield's, one of the most fascinating in history. By a curious coincidence the wildest legend on the subject, and the correct explanation of the problem, were offered to the world in the same year, 1801. According to this form of the legend, the Man in the Iron Mask was the genuine Louis XIV., deprived of his rights in favour of a child of Anne of Austria and of Mazarin. Immured in the Isles Sainte-Marguerite, in the bay of Cannes (where you are shown his cell, looking north to the sunny town), he married, and begot a son. That son was carried to Corsica, was named de Buona Parte, and was the ancestor of Napoleon. The Emperor was thus the legitimate representative of the House of Bourbon.

This legend was circulated in 1801, and is referred to in a proclamation of the Royalists of La Vendee. In the same year, 1801, Roux Fazaillac, a Citoyen and a revolutionary legislator, published a work in which he asserted that the Man in the Iron Mask (as known in rumour) was not one man, but a myth, in which the actual facts concerning at least two men were blended. It is certain that Roux Fazaillac was right; or that, if he was wrong, the Man in the Iron Mask was an obscure valet, of French birth, residing in England, whose real name was Martin.

Before we enter on the topic of this poor menial's tragic history, it may be as well to trace the progress of the romantic legend, as it blossomed after the death of the Man, whose Mask was not of iron, but of black velvet. Later we shall show how the legend struck root and flowered, from the moment when the poor valet, Martin (by his prison pseudonym 'Eustache Dauger'), was immured in the French fortress of Pignerol, in Piedmont (August 1669).

The Man, IN CONNECTION WITH THE MASK, is first known to us from a kind of notebook kept by du Junca, Lieutenant of the Bastille. On September 18, 1698, he records the arrival of the new Governor of the Bastille, M. de Saint-Mars, bringing with him, from his last place, the Isles Sainte-Marguerite, in the bay of Cannes, 'an old prisoner whom he had at Pignerol. He keeps the prisoner always masked, his name is not spoken. . . and I have put him, alone, in the third chamber of the Bertaudiere tower, having furnished it some days before with everything, by order of M. de Saint-Mars. The prisoner is to be served and cared for by M. de Rosarges,' the officer next in command under Saint-Mars.*

*Funck-Brentano. Legendes et Archives de la Bastille, pp. 86, 87, Paris, 1898, p. 277, a facsimile of this entry.

The prisoner's death is entered by du Junca on November 19, 1703. To that entry we return later.

The existence of this prisoner was known and excited curiosity. On October 15, 1711, the Princess Palatine wrote about the case to the Electress Sophia of Hanover, 'A man lived for long years in the Bastille, masked, and masked he died there. Two musketeers were by his side to shoot him if ever he unmasked. He ate and slept in his mask. There must, doubtless, have been some good reason for this, as otherwise he was very well treated, well lodged, and had everything given to him that he wanted. He took the Communion masked; was very devout, and read perpetually.'

On October 22, 1711, the Princess writes that the Mask was an English nobleman, mixed up in the plot of the Duke of Berwick against William III. - Fenwick's affair is meant. He was imprisoned and masked that the Dutch usurper might never know what had become of him.*

* Op. cit. 98, note 1.

The legend was now afloat in society. The sub-commandant of the Bastille from 1749 to 1787, Chevalier, declared, obviously on the evidence of tradition, that all the Mask's furniture and clothes were destroyed at his death, lest they might yield a clue to his identity. Louis XV. is said to have told Madame de Pompadour that the Mask was 'the minister of an Italian prince.' Louis XVI. told Marie Antoinette (according to Madame de Campan) that the Mask was a Mantuan intriguer, the same person as Louis XV. indicated. Perhaps he was, it is one of two possible alternatives. Voltaire, in the first edition of his 'Siecle de Louis XIV.,' merely spoke of a young, handsome, masked prisoner, treated with the highest respect by Louvois, the Minister of Louis XIV. At last, in 'Questions sur l'Encyclopedie' (second edition), Voltaire averred that the Mask was the son of Anne of Austria and Mazarin, an elder brother of Louis XIV. Changes were rung on this note: the Mask was the actual King, Louis XIV. was a bastard. Others held that he was James, Duke of Monmouth - or Moliere! In 1770 Heiss identified him with Mattioli, the Mantuan intriguer, and especially after the appearance of the book by Roux Fazaillac, in 1801, that was the generally accepted opinion.

It MAY be true, in part. Mattioli MAY have been the prisoner who died in the Bastille in November 1703, but the legend of the Mask's prison life undeniably arose out of the adventure of our valet, Martin or Eustache Dauger.

2. THE VALET'S HISTORY

After reading the arguments of the advocates of Mattioli, I could not but perceive that, whatever captive died, masked, at the Bastille in 1703, the valet Dauger was the real source of most of the legends about the Man in the Iron Mask. A study of M. Lair's book 'Nicholas Foucquet' (1890) confirmed this opinion. I therefore pushed the inquiry into a source neglected by the French historians, namely, the correspondence of the English ambassadors, agents, and statesmen for the years 1668, 1669.* One result is to confirm a wild theory of my own to the effect that the Man in the Iron Mask (if Dauger were he) may have been as great a mystery to himself as to historical inquirers. He may not have known WHAT he was imprisoned for doing! More important is the probable conclusion that the long and mysterious captivity of Eustache Dauger, and of another perfectly harmless valet and victim, was the mere automatic result of the 'red tape' of the old French absolute monarchy. These wretches were caught in the toils of the system, and suffered to no purpose, for no crime. The two men, at least Dauger, were apparently mere supernumeraries in the obscure intrigue of a conspirator known as Roux de Marsilly.

*The papers are in the Record Office; for the contents see the following essay, 'The Valet's Master.'

This truly abominable tragedy of Roux de Marsilly is

'another story,' narrated in the following essay. It must suffice here to say that, in 1669, while Charles II. was negotiating the famous, or infamous, secret treaty with Louis XIV. - the treaty of alliance against Holland, and in favour of the restoration of Roman Catholicism in England - Roux de Marsilly, a French Huguenot, was dealing with Arlington and others, in favour of a Protestant league against France.

When he started from England for Switzerland in February 1669, Marsilly left in London a valet, called by him 'Martin,' who had quitted his service and was living with his own family. This man is the 'Eustache Dauger' of our mystery. The name is his prison pseudonym, as 'Lestang' was that of Mattioli. The French Government was anxious to lay hands on him, for he had certainly, as the letters of Marsilly prove, come and gone freely between that conspirator and his English employers. How much Dauger knew, what amount of mischief he could effect, was uncertain. Much or little, it was a matter which, strange to say, caused the greatest anxiety to Louis XIV. and to his Ministers for very many years. Probably long before Dauger died (the date is unknown, but it was more than twenty-five years after Marsilly's execution), his secret, if secret he possessed, had ceased to be of importance. But he was now in the toils of the French red tape, the system of secrecy which rarely released its victim. He was guarded, we shall see, with such unheard-of rigour, that popular fancy at once took him for some great, perhaps royal, personage.

Marsilly was publicly tortured to death in Paris on June 22, 1669. By July 19 his ex-valet, Dauger, had entered on his mysterious term of captivity. How the French got possession of him, whether he yielded to cajolery, or was betrayed by Charles II., is uncertain. The French ambassador at St. James's, Colbert (brother of the celebrated Minister), writes thus to M. de Lyonne, in Paris, on July 1, 1669:* 'Monsieur Joly has spoken to the man Martin' (Dauger), 'and has really persuaded him that, by going to France and telling all that he knows against Roux, he will play the part of a lad of honour and a good subject.'

*Transcripts from Paris MSS. Vol. xxxiii., Record Office.

But Martin, after all, was NOT persuaded!

Martin replied to Joly that HE KNEW NOTHING AT ALL, and that, once in France, people would think he was well acquainted with the traffickings of Roux, 'AND SO HE WOULD BE KEPT IN PRISON TO MAKE HIM DIVULGE WHAT HE DID NOT KNOW.' The possible Man in the Iron Mask did not know his own secret! But, later in the conversation, Martin foolishly admitted that he knew a great deal; perhaps he did this out of mere fatal vanity. Cross to France, however, he would not, even when offered a safe-conduct and promise of reward. Colbert therefore proposes to ask Charles to surrender the valet, and probably Charles descended to the meanness. By July 19, at all events, Louvois, the War Minister of Louis XIV., was bidding Saint- Mars, at Pignerol in Piedmont, expect from Dunkirk a prisoner of the very highest importance - a valet! This valet, now called 'Eustache Dauger,' can only have been Marsilly's valet, Martin, who, by one means or another, had been brought from England to Dunkirk. It is hardly conceivable, at least, that when a valet, in England, is 'wanted' by the French police on July 1, for political reasons, and when by July 19 they have caught a valet of extreme political importance, the two valets should be two different men. Martin must be Dauger.

Here, then, by July 19, 1669, we find our unhappy serving-man in the toils. Why was he to be handled with such mysterious rigour? It is true that State prisoners of very little account were kept with great secrecy. But it cannot well be argued that they were all treated with the extraordinary precautions which, in the case of Dauger, were not relaxed for twenty-five or thirty years. The King says, according to Louvois, that the safe keeping of Dauger is 'of the last importance to his service.' He must have intercourse with nobody. His windows must be where nobody can pass; several bolted doors must cut him off from the sound of human voices. Saint-Mars himself, the commandant, must feed the valet daily. 'YOU MUST NEVER, UNDER ANY PRETENCE, LISTEN TO WHAT HE MAY WISH TO TELL YOU. YOU MUST THREATEN HIM WITH DEATH IF HE SPEAKS ONE WORD EXCEPT ABOUT HIS ACTUAL NEEDS. He is only a valet, and does not need much furniture.'*

*The letters are printed by Roux Fazaillac, Jung, Lair, and others.

Saint-Mars replied that, in presence of M. de Vauroy, the chief officer of Dunkirk (who carried Dauger thence to Pignerol), he had threatened to run Dauger through the body if he ever dared to speak, even to him, Saint-Mars. He has mentioned this prisoner, he says, to no mortal. People believe that Dauger is a Marshal of France, so strange and unusual are the precautions taken for his security.

A Marshal of France! The legend has begun. At this
time (1669) Saint-Mars had in charge Fouquet, the
great fallen Minister, the richest and most dangerous
subject of Louis XIV. By-and-by he also held Lauzun,
the adventurous wooer of la Grande Mademoiselle.
But it was not they, it was the valet, Dauger, who
caused 'sensation.'

On February 20,1672, Saint-Mars, for the sake of
economy wished to use Dauger as valet to Lauzun.
This proves that Saint-Mars did not, after all, see the
necessity of secluding Dauger, or thought the King's
fears groundless. In the opinion of Saint-Mars, Dauger
did not want to be released, 'would never ask to be set
free.' Then why was he so anxiously guarded? Louvois
refused to let Dauger be put with Lauzun as valet. In
1675, however, he allowed Dauger to act as valet to
Fouquet, but with Lauzun, said Louvois, Dauger must
have no intercourse. Fouquet had then another prisoner
valet, La Riviere. This man had apparently been
accused of no crime. He was of a melancholy
character, and a dropsical habit of body: Fouquet had
amused himself by doctoring him and teaching him to
read.

In the month of December 1678, Saint-Mars, the
commandant of the prison, brought to Fouquet a sealed
letter from Louvois, the seal unbroken. His own reply
was also to be sealed, and not to be seen by Saint-
Mars. Louvois wrote that the King wished to know one
thing, before giving Fouquet ampler liberty. Had his
valet, Eustache Dauger, told his other valet, La
Riviere, what he had done before coming to Pignerol?
(de ce a quoi il a ete employe auparavant que d'etre a
Pignerol). 'His Majesty bids me ask you [Fouquet] this
question, and expects that you will answer without

considering anything but the truth, that he may know what measures to take,' these depending on whether Dauger has, or has not, told La Riviere the story of his past life.* Moreover, Lauzun was never, said Louvois, to be allowed to enter Fouquet's room when Dauger was present. The humorous point is that, thanks to a hole dug in the wall between his room and Fouquet's, Lauzun saw Dauger whenever he pleased.

*Lair, Nicholas Foucquet, ii. pp. 463, 464.

From the letter of Louvois to Fouquet, about Dauger (December 23, 1678), it is plain that Louis XIV. had no more pressing anxiety, nine years after Dauger's arrest, than to conceal WHAT IT WAS THAT DAUGER HAD DONE. It is apparent that Saint-Mars himself either was unacquainted with this secret, or was supposed by Louvois and the King to be unaware of it. He had been ordered never to allow Dauger to tell him: he was not allowed to see the letters on the subject between Louvois and Fouquet. We still do not know, and never shall know, whether Dauger himself knew his own secret, or whether (as he had anticipated) he was locked up for not divulging what he did not know.

The answer of Fouquet to Louvois must have satisfied Louis that Dauger had not imparted his secret to the other valet, La Riviere, for Fouquet was now allowed a great deal of liberty. In 1679, he might see his family, the officers of the garrison, and Lauzun - it being provided that Lauzun and Dauger should never meet. In March 1680, Fouquet died, and henceforth the two valets were most rigorously guarded; Dauger, because he was supposed to know something; La Riviere, because Dauger might have imparted the real or fancied secret to him. We shall return to these poor serving-men, but here it is necessary to state that, ten months before the death of their master, Fouquet, an important new captive had been brought to the prison of Pignerol.

This captive was the other candidate for the honours of the Mask, Count Mattioli, the secretary of the Duke of Mantua. He was kidnapped on Italian soil on May 2, 1679, and hurried to the mountain fortress of Pignerol, then on French ground. His offence was the betraying of the secret negotiations for the cession of the town and fortress of Casal, by the Duke of Mantua, to Louis XIV. The disappearance of Mattioli was, of course, known to the world. The cause of his enlevement, and the place of his captivity, Pignerol, were matters of newspaper comment at least as early as 1687. Still earlier, in 1682, the story of Mattioli's arrest and seclusion in Pignerol had been published in a work named 'La Prudenza Trionfante di Casale.'* There was thus no mystery, at the time, about Mattioli; his crime and punishment were perfectly well known to students of politics. He has been regarded as the mysterious Man in the Iron Mask, but, for years after his arrest, he was the least mysterious of State prisoners.

*Brentano, op. cit. p. 117.

Here, then, is Mattioli in Pignerol in May 1679. While Fouquet then enjoyed relative freedom, while Lauzun schemed escapes or made insulting love to Mademoiselle Fouquet, Mattioli lived on the bread and water of affliction. He was threatened with torture to make him deliver up some papers compromising to Louis XIV. It was expressly commanded that he should have nothing beyond the barest necessaries of life. He was to be kept dans la dure prison. In brief, he was used no better than the meanest of prisoners. The awful life of isolation, without employment, without books, without writing materials, without sight or sound of man save when Saint-Mars or his lieutenant brought food for the day, drove captives mad.

In January 1680 two prisoners, a monk* and one Dubreuil, had become insane. By February 14, 1680, Mattioli was daily conversing with God and his angels. 'I believe his brain is turned,' says Saint-Mars. In March 1680, as we saw, Fouquet died. The prisoners, not counting Lauzun (released soon after), were now five: (1) Mattioli (mad); (2) Dubreuil (mad); (3) The monk (mad); (4) Dauger, and (5) La Riviere. These two, being employed as valets, kept their wits. On the death of Fouquet, Louvois wrote to Saint-Mars about the two valets. Lauzun must be made to believe that they had been set at liberty, but, in fact, they must be most carefully guarded IN A SINGLE CHAMBER. They were shut up in one of the dungeons of the 'Tour d'en bas.' Dauger had recently done something as to which Louvois writes: 'Let me know how Dauger can possibly have done what you tell me, and how he got the necessary drugs, as I cannot suppose that you supplied him with them' (July 10, 1680).**

*A monk, who may have been this monk, appears in the following essay.

**Lair, Nicholas Foucquet, ii. pp. 476, 477.

Here, then, by July 1680, are the two valets locked in one dungeon of the 'Tour d'en bas.' By September Saint-Mars had placed Mattioli, with the mad monk, in another chamber of the same tower. He writes:

'Mattioli is almost as mad as the monk,' who arose from bed and preached naked. Mattioli behaved so rudely and violently that the lieutenant of Saint-Mars had to show him a whip, and threaten him with a flogging. This had its effect. Mattioli, to make his peace, offered a valuable ring to Blainvilliers. The ring was kept to be restored to him, if ever Louis let him go free - a contingency mentioned more than once in the correspondence.

Apparently Mattioli now sobered down, and probably was given a separate chamber and a valet; he certainly had a valet at Pignerol later. By May 1681 Dauger and La Riviere still occupied their common chamber in the 'Tour d'en bas.' They were regarded by Louvois as the most important of the five prisoners then at Pignerol. They, not Mattioli, were the captives about whose safe and secret keeping Louis and Louvois were most anxious. This appears from a letter of Louvois to Saint-Mars, of May 12, 1681. The gaoler, Saint-Mars, is to be promoted from Pignerol to Exiles. 'Thither,' says Louvois, 'the king desires to transport SUCH OF YOUR PRISONERS AS HE THINKS TOO IMPORTANT TO HAVE IN OTHER HANDS THAN YOURS.' These prisoners are 'THE TWO IN THE LOW CHAMBER OF THE TOWER,' the two valets, Dauger and La Riviere.

From a letter of Saint-Mars (June 1681) we know that Mattioli was not one of these. He says: 'I shall keep at Exiles two birds (merles) whom I have here: they are only known as THE GENTRY OF THE LOW ROOM IN THE TOWER; MATTIOLI MAY STAY ON HERE AT PIGNEROL WITH THE OTHER PRISONERS' (Dubreuil and the mad monk). It is at this point that Le Citoyen Roux (Fazaillac), writing in the Year IX. of the Republic (1801), loses touch with the secret.* Roux finds, in the State Papers, the arrival of Eustache Dauger at Pignerol in 1669, but does not know who he is, or what is his quality. He sees that the Mask must be either Mattioli, Dauger, the monk, one Dubreuil, or one Calazio. But, overlooking or not having access to the letter of Saint-Mars of June 1681, Roux holds that the prisoners taken to Les Exiles were the monk and Mattioli. One of these must be the Mask, and Roux votes for Mattioli. He is wrong. Mattioli beyond all doubt remained at Pignerol.

*Recherches Historiques, sur l'Homme au Masque de Fer, Paris. An IX.

Mountains of argument have been built on these words, deux merles, 'two gaol-birds.' One of the two, we shall see, became the source of the legend of the Man in the Iron Mask. 'How can a wretched gaol-bird (merle) have been the Mask?' asks M. Topin. 'The rogue's whole furniture and table-linen were sold for 1 pound 19 shillings. He only got a new suit of clothes every three years.' All very true; but this gaol-bird and his mate, by the direct statement of Louvois, are 'the prisoners too important to be entrusted to other hands than yours' - the hands of Saint-Mars - while Mattioli is so unimportant that he may be left at Pignerol under Villebois.

The truth is, that the offence and the punishment of Mattioli were well known to European diplomatists and readers of books. Casal, moreover, at this time was openly ceded to Louis XIV., and Mattioli could not have told the world more than it already knew. But, for some inscrutable reason, the secret which Dauger knew, or was suspected of knowing, became more and more a source of anxiety to Louvois and Louis. What can he have known? The charges against his master, Roux de Marsilly, had been publicly proclaimed. Twelve years had passed since the dealings of Arlington with Marsilly. Yet, Louvois became more and more nervous.

In accordance with commands of his, on March 2, 1682, the two valets, who had hitherto occupied one chamber at Exiles as at Pignerol, were cut off from all communication with each other. Says Saint-Mars, 'Since receiving your letter I have warded the pair as strictly and exactly as I did M. Fouquet and M. Lauzun, who cannot brag that he sent out or received any intelligence. Night and day two sentinels watch their tower; and my own windows command a view of the sentinels. Nobody speaks to my captives but myself, my lieutenant, their confessor, and the doctor, who lives eighteen miles away, and only sees them when I am present.' Years went by; on January 1687 one of the two captives died; we really do not know which with absolute certainty. However, the intensified secrecy with which the survivor was now guarded seems more appropriate to Dauger; and M. Funck-Brentano and M. Lair have no doubt that it was La Riviere who expired. He was dropsical, that appears in the official correspondence, and the dead prisoner died of dropsy.

As for the strange secrecy about Dauger, here is an example. Saint-Mars, in January 1687, was appointed to the fortress of the Isles Sainte-Marguerite, that sun themselves in the bay of Cannes. On January 20 he asks leave to go to see his little kingdom. He must leave Dauger, but HAS FORBIDDEN EVEN HIS LIEUTENANT TO SPEAK TO THAT PRISONER.

This was an increase of precaution since 1682. He wishes to take the captive to the Isles, but how? A sedan chair covered over with oilcloth seems best. A litter might break down, litters often did, and some one might then see the passenger.

Now M. Funck-Brentano says, to minimise the importance of Dauger, 'he was shut up like so much luggage in a chair hermetically closed with oilcloth, carried by eight Piedmontese in relays of four.'

Luggage is not usually carried in hermetically sealed sedan chairs, but Saint-Mars has explained why, by surplus of precaution, he did not use a litter. The litter might break down and Dauger might be seen. A new prison was built specially, at the cost of 5,000 livres, for Dauger at Sainte-Marguerite, with large sunny rooms. On May 3, 1687, Saint-Mars had entered on his island realm, Dauger being nearly killed by twelve days' journey in a closed chair. He again excited the utmost curiosity. On January 8, 1688, Saint-Mars writes that his prisoner is believed by the world to be either a son of Oliver Cromwell, or the Duc de Beaufort,* who was never seen again, dead or alive, after a night battle in Crete, on June 25, 1669, just before Dauger was arrested. Saint-Mars sent in a note of the TOTAL of Dauger's expenses for the year 1687. He actually did not dare to send the ITEMS, he says, lest they, if the bill fell into the wrong hands, might reveal too much!

*The Duc de Beaufort whom Athos releases from prison in Dumas's Vingt Ans Apres.

Meanwhile, an Italian news-letter, copied into a Leyden paper, of August 1687, declared that Mattioli had just been brought from Pignerol to Sainte-Marguerite. There was no mystery about Mattioli, the story of his capture was published in 1682, but the press, on one point, was in error: Mattioli was still at Pignerol. The known advent of the late Commandant of Pignorol, Saint-Mars, with a single concealed prisoner, at the island, naturally suggested the erroneous idea that the prisoner was Mattioli. The prisoner was really Dauger, the survivor of the two valets.

From 1688 to 1691 no letter about Dauger has been published. Apparently he was then the only prisoner on the island, except one Chezut, who was there before Dauger arrived, and gave up his chamber to Dauger while the new cells were being built. Between 1689 and 1693 six Protestant preachers were brought to the island, while Louvois, the Minister, died in 1691, and was succeeded by Barbezieux. On August 13, 1691, Barbezieux wrote to ask Saint-Mars about 'the prisoner whom he had guarded for twenty years.' The only such prisoner was Dauger, who entered Pignerol in August 1669. Mattioli had been a prisoner only for twelve years, and lay in Pignerol, not in Sainte-Marguerite, where Saint-Mars now was. Saint-Mars replied: 'I can assure you that nobody has seen him but myself.'

By the beginning of March 1694, Pignerol had been bombarded by the enemies of France; presently Louis XIV. had to cede it to Savoy. The prisoners there must be removed. Mattioli, in Pignerol, at the end of 1693, had been in trouble. He and his valet had tried to smuggle out letters written on the linings of their pockets. These were seized and burned. On March 20, 1694, Barbezieux wrote to Laprade, now commanding at Pignerol, that he must take his three prisoners, one by one, with all secrecy, to Sainte-Marguerite. Laprade alone must give them their food on the journey. The military officer of the escort was warned to ask no questions. Already (February 26, 1694) Barbezieux had informed Saint-Mars that these prisoners were coming. 'They are of more consequence, one of them at least, than the prisoners on the island, and must be put in the safest places.' The 'one' is doubtless Mattioli. In 1681 Louvois had thought Dauger and La Riviere more important than Mattioli, who, in March 1694, came from Pignerol to Sainte-Marguerite. Now in April 1694 a prisoner died at the island, a prisoner who, like Mattioli, HAD A VALET. We hear of no other prisoner on the island, except Mattioli, who had a valet. A letter of Saint-Mars (January 6, 1696) proves that no prisoner THEN had a valet, for each prisoner collected his own dirty plates and dishes, piled them up, and handed them to the lieutenant

M. Funck-Brentano argues that in this very letter (January 6, 1696) Saint-Mars speaks of 'les valets de messieurs les prisonniers.' But in that part of the letter Saint-Mars is not speaking of the actual state of things at Sainte-Marguerite, but is giving reminiscences of Fouquet and Lauzun, who, of course, at Pignerol, had valets, and had money, as he shows. Dauger had no money. M. Funck-Brentano next argues that early in 1694 one of the preacher prisoners, Melzac, died, and cites M. Jung ('La Verite sur le Masque de Fer,' p. 91). This is odd, as M. Jung says that Melzac, or Malzac, 'DIED IN THE END OF 1692, OR EARLY IN 1693.' Why, then, does M. Funck-Brentano cite M. Jung for the death of the preacher early in 1694, when M. Jung (conjecturally) dates his decease at least a year earlier?* It is not a mere conjecture, as, on March 3, 1693, Barbezieux begs Saint-Mars to mention his

Protestant prisoners under nicknames. There are three, and Malzac is no longer one of them. Malzac, in 1692, suffered from a horrible disease, discreditable to one of the godly, and in October 1692 had been allowed medical expenses. Whether they included a valet or not, Malzac seems to have been non-existent by March 1693. Had he possessed a valet, and had he died in 1694, why should HIS valet have been 'shut up in the vaulted prison'? This was the fate of the valet of the prisoner who died in April 1694, and was probably Mattioli.

* M. Funck-Brentano's statement is in Revue Historique, lvi. p. 298. 'Malzac died at the beginning of 1694,' citing Jung, p. 91. Now on P. 91 M. Jung writes, 'At the beginning of 1694 Saint-Mars had six prisoners, of whom one, Melzac, dies.' But M. Jung (pp. 269, 270) later writes, 'It is probable that Melzac died at the end of 1692, or early in 1693,' and he gives his reasons, which are convincing. M. Funck-Brentano must have overlooked M. Jung's change of opinion between his P. 91 and his pp. 269, 270.

Mattioli, certainly, had a valet in December 1693 at Pignerol. He went to Sainte-Marguerite in March 1694. In April 1694 a prisoner with a valet died at Sainte-Marguerite. In January 1696 no prisoner at Sainte-Marguerite had a valet. Therefore, there is a strong presumption that the 'prisonnier au valet' who died in April 1694 was Mattioli.

After December 1693, when he was still at Pignerol, the name of Mattioli, freely used before, never occurs in the correspondence. But we still often hear of 'l'ancien prisonnier,' 'the old prisoner.' He was, on the face of it, Dauger, by far the oldest prisoner. In 1688,

Saint-Mars, having only one prisoner (Dauger), calls him merely 'my prisoner.' In 1691, when Saint-Mars had several prisoners, Barbezieux styles Dauger 'your prisoner of twenty years' standing.' When, in 1696-1698, Saint-Mars mentions 'mon ancien prisonnier,' 'my prisoner of long standing,' he obviously means Dauger, not Mattioli - above all, if Mattioli died in 1694. M. Funck-Brentano argues that 'mon ancien prisonnier' can only mean 'my erstwhile prisoner, he who was lost and is restored to me' - that is, Mattioli. This is not the view of M. Jung, or M. Lair, or M. Loiseleur.

Friends of Mattioli's claims rest much on this letter of Barbezieux to Saint-Mars (November 17, 1697): 'You have only to watch over the security of all your prisoners, WITHOUT EVER EXPLAINING TO ANY ONE WHAT IT IS THAT YOUR PRISONER OF LONG STANDING DID.' That secret, it is argued, MUST apply to Mattioli. But all the world knew what Mattioli had done! Nobody knew, and nobody knows, what Eustache Dauger had done. It was one of the arcana imperii. It is the secret enforced ever since Dauger's arrest in 1669. Saint-Mars (1669) was not to ask. Louis XIV. could only lighten the captivity of Fouquet (1678) if his valet, La Riviere, did not know what Dauger had done. La Riviere (apparently a harmless man) lived and died in confinement, the sole reason being that he might perhaps know what Dauger had done. Consequently there is the strongest presumption that the 'ancien prisonnier' of 1697 is Dauger, and that 'what he had done' (which Saint-Mars must tell to no one) was what Dauger did, not what Mattioli did. All Europe knew what Mattioli had done; his whole story had been published to the world in 1682 and 1687.

On July 19, 1698, Barbezieux bade Saint-Mars come to assume the command of the Bastille. He is to bring his 'old prisoner,' whom not a soul is to see. Saint-Mars therefore brought his man MASKED, exactly as another prisoner was carried masked from Provence to the Bastille in 1695. M. Funck-Brentano argues that Saint-Mars was now quite fond of his old Mattioli, so noble, so learned.

At last, on September 18, 1698, Saint-Mars lodged his 'old prisoner' in the Bastille, 'an old prisoner whom he had at Pignerol,' says the journal of du Junca, Lieutenant of the Bastille. His food, we saw, was brought him by Rosarges alone, the 'Major,' a gentleman who had always been with Saint-Mars. Argues M. Funck-Brentano, all this proves that the captive was a gentleman, not a valet. Why? First, because the Bastille, under Louis XIV., was 'une prison de distinction.' Yet M. Funck-Brentano tells us that in Mazarin's time 'valets mixed up with royal plots' were kept in the Bastille. Again, in 1701, in this 'noble prison,' the Mask was turned out of his room to make place for a female fortune-teller, and was obliged to chum with a profligate valet of nineteen, and a 'beggarly' bad patriot, who 'blamed the conduct of France, and approved that of other nations, especially the Dutch.' M. Funck-Brentano himself publishes these facts (1898), in part published earlier (1890) by M. Lair.* Not much noblesse here! Next, if Rosarges, a gentleman, served the Mask, Saint-Mars alone (1669) carried his food to the valet, Dauger. So the service of Rosarges does not ennoble the Mask and differentiate him from Dauger, who was even more nobly served, by Saint-Mars.

*Legendes de la Bastille, pp. 86-89. Citing du Junca's

Journal, April 30, 1701.

On November 19, 1703, the Mask died suddenly (still in his velvet mask), and was buried on the 20th. The parish register of the church names him 'Marchialy' or 'Marchioly,' one may read it either way; du Junca, the Lieutenant of the Bastille, in his contemporary journal, calls him 'Mr. de Marchiel.' Now, Saint-Mars often spells Mattioli, 'Marthioly.'

This is the one strength of the argument for Mattioli's claims to the Mask. M. Lair replies, 'Saint-Mars had a mania for burying prisoners under fancy names,' and gives examples. One is only a gardener, Francois Eliard (1701), concerning whom it is expressly said that, as he is a State prisoner, his real name is not to be given, so he is registered as Pierre Maret (others read Navet, 'Peter Turnip'). If Saint-Mars, looking about for a false name for Dauger's burial register, hit on Marsilly (the name of Dauger's old master), that MIGHT be miswritten Marchialy. However it be, the age of the Mask is certainly falsified; the register gives 'about forty- five years old.' Mattioli would have been sixty-three; Dauger cannot have been under fifty-three.

There the case stands. If Mattioli died in April 1694, he cannot be the Man in the Iron Mask. Of Dauger's death we find no record, unless he was the Man in the Iron Mask, and died, in 1703, in the Bastille. He was certainly, in 1669 and 1688, at Pignerol and at Sainte-Marguerite, the centre of the mystery about some great prisoner, a Marshal of France, the Duc de Beaufort, or a son of Oliver Cromwell. Mattioli was no mystery, no secret. Dauger is so mysterious that probably the secret of his mystery was unknown to himself. By 1701, when obscure wretches were shut up with the Mask, the secret, whatever its nature, had ceased to be of moment. The captive was now the mere victim of cruel routine. But twenty years earlier, Saint-Mars had said that Dauger 'takes things easily, resigned to the will of God and the King.'

To sum up, on July 1, 1669, the valet of the Huguenot intriguer, Roux de Marsilly, the valet resident in England, known to his master as 'Martin,' was 'wanted' by the French secret police. By July 19, a valet, of the highest political importance, had been brought to Dunkirk, from England, no doubt. My hypothesis assumes that this valet, though now styled 'Eustache Dauger,' was the 'Martin' of Roux de Marsilly. He was kept with so much mystery at Pignerol that already the legend began its course; the captive valet was said to be a Marshal of France! We then follow Dauger from Pignerol to Les Exiles, till January 1687, when one valet out of a pair, Dauger being one of them, dies. We presume that Dauger is the survivor, because the great mystery still is 'what he HAS DONE,' whereas the other valet had done nothing, but may have known Dauger's secret. Again, the other valet had long been dropsical, and the valet who died in 1687 died of dropsy.

In 1688, Dauger, at Sainte-Marguerite, is again the source and centre of myths; he is taken for a son of Oliver Cromwell, or for the Duc de Beaufort. In June 1692, one of the Huguenot preachers at Sainte-Marguerite writes on his shirt and pewter plate, and throws them out of window.* Legend attributes these acts to the Man in the Iron Mask, and transmutes a pewter into a silver plate. Now, in 1689-1693, Mattioli was at Pignerol, but Dauger was at Sainte-Marguerite, and the Huguenot's act is attributed to him. Thus

Dauger, not Mattioli, is the centre round which the myths crystallise: the legends concern HIM, not Mattioli, whose case is well known, and gives rise to no legend. Finally, we have shown that Mattioli probably died at Sainte-Marguerite in April 1694. If so, then nobody but Dauger can be the 'old prisoner' whom Saint-Mars brought, masked, to the Bastille, in September 1698, and who died there in November 1703. However, suppose that Mattioli did not die in 1694, but was the masked man who died in the Bastille in 1703, then the legend of Dauger came to be attributed to Mattioli: these two men's fortunes are combined in the one myth.

* Saint-Mars au Ministre, June 4, 1692.

The central problem remains unsolved,

WHAT HAD THE VALET, EUSTACHE DAUGER, DONE? *

* One marvels that nobody has recognised, in the mask, James Stuart (James de la Cloche), eldest of the children of Charles II. He came to England in 1668, was sent to Rome, and 'disappears from history.' See 'The Mystery of James de la Cloche.'

II.

THE VALET'S MASTER

The secret of the Man in the Iron Mask, or at least of one of the two persons who have claims to be the Mask, was 'WHAT HAD EUSTACHE DAUGER DONE?' To guard this secret the most extraordinary precautions were taken, as we have shown in the foregoing essay. And yet, if secret there was, it might have got wind in the simplest fashion. In the 'Vicomte de Bragelonne,' Dumas describes the tryst of the Secret-hunters with the dying Chief of the Jesuits at the inn in Fontainebleau. They come from many quarters, there is a Baron of Germany and a laird from Scotland, but Aramis takes the prize. He knows the secret of the Mask, the most valuable of all to the intriguers of the Company of Jesus.

Now, despite all the precautions of Louvois and Saint-Mars, despite sentinels for ever posted under Dauger's windows, despite arrangements which made it impossible for him to signal to people on the hillside at Les Exiles, despite the suppression even of the items in the accounts of his expenses, his secret, if he knew it, could have been discovered, as we have remarked, by the very man most apt to make mischievous use of it - by Lauzun. That brilliant and reckless adventurer could see Dauger, in prison at Pignerol, when he pleased, for he had secretly excavated a way into the rooms of his fellow-prisoner, Fouquet, on whom Dauger attended as valet. Lauzun was released soon after Fouquet's death. It is unlikely that he bought his liberty by the knowledge of the secret, and there is nothing to suggest that he used it (if he possessed it) in any other way.

The natural clue to the supposed secret of Dauger is a study of the career of his master, Roux de Marsilly. As official histories say next to nothing about him, we may set forth what can be gleaned from the State Papers in our Record Office. The earliest is a letter of Roux de Marsilly to Mr. Joseph Williamson, secretary of Lord Arlington (December 1668). Marsilly sends Martin (on our theory Eustache Dauger) to bring back from Williamson two letters from his own correspondent in Paris. He also requests Williamson to procure for him from Arlington a letter of protection, as he is threatened with arrest for some debt in which he is not really concerned. Martin will explain. The next paper is endorsed 'Received December 28, 1668, Mons. de Marsilly.' As it is dated December 27, Marsilly must have been in England. The contents of this piece deserve attention, because they show the terms on which Marsilly and Arlington were, or, at least, how Marsilly conceived them.

(1) Marsilly reports, on the authority of his friends at Stockholm, that the King of Sweden intends, first to intercede with Louis XIV. in favour of the French Huguenots, and next, if diplomacy fails, to join in arms with the other Protestant Powers of Europe.

(2) His correspondent in Holland learns that if the King of England invites the States to any 'holy resolution,'

they will heartily lend forces. No leader so good as the English King - Charles II! Marsilly had shown ARLINGTON'S LETTER to a Dutch friend, who bade him approach the Dutch ambassador in England. He has dined with that diplomatist. Arlington had, then, gone so far as to write an encouraging letter. The Dutch ambassador had just told Marsilly that he had received the same news, namely, that, Holland would aid the Huguenots, persecuted by Louis XIV.

(3) Letters from Provence, Languedoc, and Dauphine say that the situation there is unaltered.

(4) The Canton of Zurich write that they will keep their promises and that Berne IS ANXIOUS TO PLEASE THE KING OF GREAT BRITAIN, and that it is ready to raise, with Zurich, 15,000 men. They are not afraid of France.

(5) Zurich fears that, if Charles is not represented at the next Diet, Bale and Saint Gal will be intimidated, and not dare to join the Triple Alliance of Spain, Holland, and England. The best plan will be for Marsilly to represent England at the Diet of January 25, 1669, accompanied by the Swiss General Balthazar. This will encourage friends 'TO GIVE HIS BRITTANIC MAJESTY THE SATISFACTION WHICH HE DESIRES, and will produce a close union between Holland, Sweden, the Cantons, and other Protestant States.'

This reads as if Charles had already expressed some 'desire.'

(6) Geneva grumbles at a reply of Charles 'through a bishop who is their enemy,' the Bishop of London, 'a

persecutor of our religion,' that is, of Presbyterianism. However, nothing will dismay the Genevans, 'si S. M. B. ne change.'

Then comes a blank in the paper. There follows a copy of a letter as if FROM CHARLES II. HIMSELF, to 'the Right High and Noble Seigneurs of Zurich.' He has heard of their wishes from Roux de Marsilly, whom he commissions to wait upon them. 'I would not have written by my Bishop of London had I been better informed, but would myself have replied to your obliging letter, and would have assured you, as I do now, that I desire. . . .'

It appears as if this were a draft of the kind of letter which Marsilly wanted Charles to write to Zurich, and there is a similar draft of a letter for Arlington to follow, if he and Charles wish to send Marsilly to the Swiss Diet. The Dutch ambassador, with whom Marsilly dined on December 26, the Constable of Castille, and other grandees, are all of opinion that he should visit the Protestant Swiss, as from the King of England. The scheme is for an alliance of England, Holland, Spain, and the Protestant Cantons, against France and Savoy.

Another letter of Marsilly to Arlington, only dated Jeudi, avers that he can never repay Arlington for his extreme kindness and liberality. 'No man in England is more devoted to you than I am, and shall be all my life.'*

* State Papers, France, vol. 125, 106.

On the very day when Marsilly drafted for Charles his own commission to treat with Zurich for a Protestant alliance against France, Charles himself wrote to his sister, Madame (Henriette d'Orleans). He spoke of his secret treaty with France. 'You know how much secrecy is necessary for the carrying on of the business, and I assure you that nobody does, nor shall, know anything of it here, but myself and that one person more, till it be fit to be public.'* (Is 'that one person' de la Cloche?)

* Madame, by Julia Cartwright, p. 275.

Thus Marsilly thought Charles almost engaged for the Protestant League, while Charles was secretly allying himself with France against Holland. Arlington was probably no less deceived by Charles than Marsilly was.

The Bishop of London's share in the dealing with Zurich is obscure.

It appears certain that Arlington was not consciously deceiving Marsilly. Madame wrote, on February 12, as to Arlington, 'The man's attachment to the Dutch and his inclination towards Spain are too well known.'* Not till April 25, 1669, does Charles tell his sister that Arlington has an inkling of his secret dealings with France; how he knows, Charles cannot tell.** It is impossible for us to ascertain how far Charles himself deluded Marsilly, who went to the Continent early in spring, 1669. Before May 15/25 1669, in fact on April 14, Marsilly had been kidnapped by agents of Louis XIV., and his doom was dight.

* Madame, by Julia Cartwright, p. 281.

** Ibid. p. 285.

Here is the account of the matter, written to --- by Perwich in Paris:

W Perwich to ---

Paris, May 25, '69.

Honored Sir,

The Cantons of Switzerland are much troubled at the French King's having sent 15 horsemen into Switzerland from whence the Sr de Maille, the King's resident there, had given information of the Sr Roux de Marsilly's being there negociating the bringing the Cantons into the Triple League by discourses much to the disadvantage of France, giving them very ill impressions of the French King's Government, who was BETRAYED BY A MONK THAT KEPT HIM COMPANY and intercepted by the said horsemen brought into France and is expected at the Bastille. I believe you know the man. . . . I remember him in England.

Can this monk be the monk who went mad in prison at Pignerol, sharing the cell of Mattioli? Did he, too, suffer for his connection with the secret? We do not know, but the position of Charles was awkward. Marsilly, dealing with the Swiss, had come straight from England, where he was lie with Charles's minister, Arlington, and with the Dutch and Spanish ambassadors. The King refers to the matter in a letter to his sister of May 24, 1669 (misdated by Miss Cartwright, May 24, 1668.)*

'You have, I hope, received full satisfaction by the last

post in the matter of Marsillac [Marsilly], for my Ld. Arlington has sent to Mr. Montague [English ambassador at Paris] his history all the time he was here, by which you will see how little credit he had here, and that particularly my Lord Arlington was not in his good graces, because he did not receive that satisfaction, in his negotiation, he expected, and that was only in relation to the Swissers, and so I think I have said enough of this matter.'

* Madame, by Julia Cartwright, p. 264.

Charles took it easily!

On May 15/25 Montague acknowledged Arlington's letter to which Charles refers; he has been approached, as to Marsilly, by the Spanish resident, 'but I could not tell how to do anything in the business, never having heard of the man, or that he was employed by my Master [Charles] in any business. I have sent you also a copy of a letter which an Englishman writ to me that I do not know, in behalf of Roux de Marsilly, but that does not come by the post,' being too secret.*

* State Papers, France, vol. 126.

France had been well informed about Marsilly while he was in England. He then had a secretary, two lackeys, and a valet de chambre, and was frequently in conference with Arlington and the Spanish ambassador to the English Court. Colbert, the French ambassador in London, had written all this to the French Government, on April 25, before he heard of Marsilly's arrest.*

* Bibl. Nat., Fonds Francais, No. 10665.

The belief that Marsilly was an agent of Charles appears to have been general, and, if accepted by Louis XIV., would interfere with Charles's private negotiations for the Secret Treaty with France. On May 18 Prince d'Aremberg had written on the subject to the Spanish ambassador in Paris. Marsilly, he says, was arrested in Switzerland, on his way to Berne, with a monk who was also seized, and, a curious fact, Marsilly's valet was killed in the struggle. This valet, of course, was not Dauger, whom Marsilly had left in England. Marsilly 'doit avoir demande la protection du Roy de la Grande Bretagne en faveur des Religionaires (Huguenots) de France, et passer en Suisse AVEC QUELQUE COMMISSION DE SA PART.' D'Aremberg begs the Spanish ambassador to communicate all this to Montague, the English ambassador at Paris, but Montague probably, like Perwich, knew nothing of the business any more than he knew of Charles's secret dealings with Louis through Madame.*

* State Papers, France, vol. 126.

To d'Aremberg's letter is pinned an unsigned English note, obviously intended for Arlington's reading.

'Roux de Marsilly is still in the Bastille though they have a mind to hang him, yet they are much puzzled what to do with him. De Lionne has beene to examine him twice or thrice, but there is noe witnes to prove anything against him. I was told by one that the French king told it to, that in his papers they find great mention of the DUKE OF BUCKS: AND YOUR NAME, and speak as if he were much trusted by you. I have enquired what this Marsilly is, and I find by one Mr. Marsilly that I am acquainted withall, and a man of quality, that this man's name is onely Roux, and borne at Nismes and having been formerly a soldier in his troope, ever since has taken his name to gain more credit in Switserland where hee, Marsilly, formerly used to bee employed by his Coll: the Mareschall de Schomberg who invaded Switserland '

We next find a very curious letter, from which it appears that the French Government inclined to regard Marsilly as, in fact, an agent of Charles, but thought it wiser to trump up against him a charge of conspiring against the life of Louis XIV. On this charge, or another, he was executed, while the suspicion that he was an agent of English treachery may have been the real cause of the determination to destroy him. The Balthazar with whom Marsilly left his papers is mentioned with praise by him in his paper for Arlington, of December 27, 1668. He is the General who should have accompanied Marsilly to the Diet.

The substance of the letter (given in full in Note I.) is to the following effect. P. du Moulin (Paris, May 19/29, 1669) writes to Arlington. Ever since Ruvigny, the late French ambassador, a Protestant, was in England, the French Government had been anxious to kidnap Roux de Marsilly. They hunted him in England, Holland, Flanders, and Franche-Comte. As we know from the case of Mattioli, the Government of Louis XIV. was unscrupulously daring in breaking the laws of nations, and seizing hostile personages in foreign territory, as Napoleon did in the affair of the Duc d'Enghien. When all failed, Louis bade Turenne capture Roux de Marsilly wherever he could find him. Turenne sent officers and gentlemen abroad, and, after four months' search, they found Marsilly in Switzerland. They took him as he came out of the house of his friend, General Balthazar, and carried him to Gex. No papers were found on him, but he asked his captors to send to Balthazar and get 'the commission he had from England,' which he probably thought would give him the security of an official diplomatic position. Having got this document, Marsilly's captors took it to the French Ministers. Nothing could be more embarrassing, if this were true, to Charles's representative in France, Montague, and to Charles's secret negotiations, also to Arlington, who had dealt with Marsilly. On his part, the captive Marsilly constantly affirmed that he was the envoy of the King of England. The common talk of Paris was that an agent of Charles was in the Bastille, 'though at Court they pretend to know nothing of it.' Louis was overjoyed at Marsilly's capture, giving out that he was conspiring against his life. Monsieur told Montague that he need not beg for the life of a would-be murderer like Marsilly. But as to this idea, 'they begin now to mince it at Court,' and Ruvigny assured du Moulin 'that they had no such thoughts.' De Lyonne had seen Marsilly and observed that it was a blunder to seize him. The French Government was nervous, and Turenne's secretary had been 'pumping' several ambassadors as to what they thought of Marsilly's capture on foreign territory. One ambassador replied with spirit that a crusade by all Europe against France, as of old against the Moslems, would be necessary. Would Charles, du Moulin asked, own or disown Marsilly?

Montague's position was now awkward. On May 23, his account of the case was read, at Whitehall, to the Foreign Committee in London. (See Note II. for the document.) He did not dare to interfere in Marsilly's behalf, because he did not know whether the man was an agent of Charles or not. Such are the inconveniences of a secret royal diplomacy carried on behind the backs of Ministers. Louis XV. later pursued this method with awkward consequences.* The French Court, Montague said, was overjoyed at the capture of Marsilly, and a reward of 100,000 crowns, 'I am told very privately, is set upon his head.' The French ambassador in England, Colbert, had reported that Charles had sent Marsilly 'to draw the Swisses into the Triple League' against France. Montague had tried to reassure Monsieur (Charles's brother-in-law), but was himself entirely perplexed. As Monsieur's wife, Charles's sister, was working with Charles for the secret treaty with Louis, the State and family politics were clearly in a knot. Meanwhile the Spanish ambassador kept pressing Montague to interfere in favour of Marsilly. After Montague's puzzled note had been read to the English Foreign Committee on May 23, Arlington offered explanations. Marsilly came to England, he said, when Charles was entering into negotiations for peace with Holland, and when France seemed likely to oppose the peace. No proposition was made to him or by him. Peace being made, Marsilly was given money to take him out of the country. He wanted the King to renew his alliance with the Swiss cantons, but was told that the cantons must first expel the regicides of Charles I. He undertook to arrange this, and some eight months later came back to England. 'He was coldly used, and I was complained of for not using so important a man well enough.'

* Cf. Le Secret du Roi, by the Duc de Broglie.

As we saw, Marsilly expressed the most effusive gratitude to Arlington, which does not suggest cold usage. Arlington told the complainers that Marsilly was 'another man's spy,' what man's, Dutch, Spanish, or even French, he does not explain. So Charles gave Marsilly money to go away. He was never trusted with anything but the expulsion of the regicides from Switzerland. Arlington was ordered by Charles to write a letter thanking Balthazar for his good offices.

These explanations by Arlington do not tally with Marsilly's communications to him, as cited at the beginning of this inquiry. Nothing is said in these about getting the regicides of Charles I. out of Switzerland: the paper is entirely concerned with bringing the Protestant Cantons into anti-French League with England, Holland, Spain, and even Sweden. On the other hand, Arlington's acknowledged letter to Balthazar, carried by Marsilly, may be the 'commission' of which Marsilly boasted. In any case, on June 2, Charles gave Colbert, the French ambassador, an audience, turning even the Duke of York out of the room. He then repeated to Colbert the explanations of Arlington, already cited, and Arlington, in a separate interview, corroborated Charles. So Colbert wrote to Louis (June 3, 1669); but to de Lyonne, on the same day, 'I trust that you will extract from Marsilly much matter for the King's service. IT SEEMED TO ME THAT MILORD D'ARLINGTON WAS UNEASY ABOUT IT [EN AVAIT DE L'INQUIETUDE]. . . . There is here in England one Martin' (Eustace Dauger), 'who has been that wretch's valet, and who left him in discontent.' Colbert then proposes to examine Martin, who may know a good deal, and to send him into France. On June 10, Colbert writes to Louis that he expects to see Martin.*

* Bibl. Nat., Fonds Francais, No. 10665.

On June 24, Colbert wrote to Louis about a conversation with Charles. It is plain that proofs of a murder-plot by Marsilly were scanty or non-existent, though Colbert averred that Marsilly had discussed the matter with the Spanish Ministers. 'Charles knew that he had had much conference with Isola, the Spanish ambassador.' Meanwhile, up to July 1, Colbert was trying to persuade Marsilly's valet to go to France, which he declined to do, as we have seen. However, the luckless lad, by nods and by veiled words, indicated that he knew a great deal. But not by promise of security and reward could the valet be induced to return to France. 'I might ask the King to give up Martin, the valet of Marsilly, to me,' Colbert concludes, and, by hook or by crook, he secured the person of the wretched man, as we have seen. In a postscript, Colbert says that he has heard of the execution of Marsilly.

By July 19, as we saw in the previous essay, Louvois was bidding Saint-Mars expect, at Pignerol from Dunkirk, a prisoner of the highest political importance, to be guarded with the utmost secrecy, yet a valet. That valet must be Martin, now called Eustache Dauger, and his secret can only be connected with Marsilly. It may have been something about Arlington's negotiations through Marsilly, as compromising Charles II. Arlington's explanations to the Foreign Committee were certainly incomplete and disingenuous. He, if not Charles, was more deeply engaged with Marsilly than he ventured to report. But Marsilly himself avowed that he did not know why he was to be executed.

Executed he was, in circumstances truly hideous. Perwich, June 5, wrote to an unnamed correspondent in England: 'They have all his papers, which speak much of the Triple Alliance, but I know not whether they can lawfully hang him for this, having been naturalised in Holland, and taken in a privileged country' (Switzerland). Montague (Paris, June 22, 1669) writes to Arlington that Marsilly is to die, so it has been decided, for 'a rape which he formerly committed at Nismes,' and after the execution, on June 26, declares that, when broken on the wheel, Marsilly 'still persisted that he was guilty of nothing, nor did know why he was put to death.'

Like Eustache Dauger, Marsilly professed that he did not know his own secret. The charge of a rape, long ago, at Nismes, was obviously trumped up to cover the real reason for the extraordinary vindictiveness with which he was pursued, illegally taken, and barbarously slain. Mere Protestant restlessness on his part is hardly an explanation. There was clearly no evidence for the charge of a plot to murder Louis XIV., in which Colbert, in England, seems to have believed. Even if the French Government believed that he was at once an agent of Charles II., and at the same time a would-be assassin of Louis XIV., that hardly accounts for the intense secrecy with which his valet, Eustache Dauger, was always surrounded. Did Marsilly know of the Secret Treaty, and was it from him that Arlington got his first inkling of the royal plot? If so, Marsilly would probably have exposed the mystery in Protestant interests. We are entirely baffled.

In any case, Francis Vernon, writing from Paris to Williamson (?) (June 19/29 1669), gave a terrible account of Marsilly's death. (For the letter, see Note V.) With a broken piece of glass (as we learn from another source), Marsilly, in prison, wounded himself in a ghastly manner, probably hoping to die by loss of blood. They seared him with a red-hot iron, and hurried on his execution. He was broken on the wheel, and was two hours in dying (June 22). Contrary to usage, a Protestant preacher was brought to attend him on the scaffold. He came most reluctantly, expecting insult, but not a taunt was uttered by the fanatic populace. 'He came up the scaffold, great silence all about.' Marsilly lay naked, stretched on a St. Andrew's cross. He had seemed half dead, his head hanging limp, 'like a drooping calf.' To greet the minister of his own faith, he raised himself, to the surprise of all, and spoke out loud and clear. He utterly denied all share in a scheme to murder Louis. The rest may be read in the original letter (Note V.).

So perished Roux de Marsilly; the history of the master throws no light on the secret of the servant. That secret, for many years, caused the keenest anxiety to Louis XIV. and Louvois. Saint-Mars himself must not pry into it. Yet what could Dauger know? That there had been a conspiracy against the King's life? But that was the public talk of Paris. If Dauger had guilty knowledge, his life might have paid for it; why keep him a secret prisoner? Did he know that Charles II. had been guilty of double dealing in 1668-1669? Probably Charles had made some overtures to the Swiss, as a blind to his private dealings with Louis XIV., but, even so, how could the fact haunt Louis XIV. like a ghost? We leave the mystery much darker than we found it, but we see reason good why diplomatists should have murmured of a crusade against the cruel and brigand Government which sent soldiers to kidnap, in neighbouring states, men who did not know their own crime.

To myself it seems not improbable that the King and

Louvois were but stupidly and cruelly nervous about what Dauger MIGHT know. Saint- Mars, when he proposed to utilise Dauger as a prison valet, manifestly did not share the trembling anxieties of Louis XIV. and his Minister; anxieties which grew more keen as time went on. However, 'a soldier only has his orders,' and Saint-Mars executed his orders with minute precision, taking such unheard-of precautions that, in legend, the valet blossomed into the rightful king of France.

*   *   *

APPENDIX.

ORIGINAL PAPERS IN THE CASE OF ROUX DE MARSILLY.*

Note I. Letter of Mons. P. du Moulin to Arlington.**

Paris, May ye 19/29, 1669.

My Lord,

Ever since that Monsieur de Ruvigny was in England last, and upon the information he gave, this King had a very great desire to seize if it were possible this Roux de Marsilly, and several persons were sent to effect it, into England, Holland, Flanders, and Franche Comte: amongst the rest one La Grange, exempt des Gardes, was a good while in Holland with fifty of the guards dispersed in severall places and quarters; But all having miscarried the King recommended the thing to Monsieur de Turenne who sent some of his gentlemen and officers under him to find this man out and to endeavour to bring him alive. These men after foure months search found him att last in Switzerland, and having laid waite for him as he came out from Monsr Balthazar's house (a commander well knowne) they took him and carryed him to Gex before they could be intercepted and he rescued. This was done only by a warrant from Monsieur de Turenne but as soone as they came into the french dominions they had full powers and directions from this court for the bringing of him hither. Those that tooke him say they found no papers about him, but that he desired them to write to Monsr Balthazar to desire him to take care of his papers and to send him THE COMMISSION HE HAD FROM ENGLAND and a letter being written to that effect it was signed by the prisoner and instead of sending it as they had promised, they have brought it hither along with them. THEY DO ALL UNANIMOUSLY REPORT THAT HE DID CONSTANTLY AFFIRME THAT HE WAS IMPLOYED BY THE KING OF GREAT BRITTAIN AND DID ACT BY HIS COMMISSION; so that the general discourse here in towne is that one of the King of England's agents is in the Bastille; though att Court they pretend to know nothing of it and would have the world think they are persuaded he had no relacion to his Majesty. Your Lordship hath heard by the publique newes how overjoyed this King was att the bringing of this prisoner, and how farr he expressed his thanks to the cheife person employed in it, declaring openly that this man had long since conspired against his life, and agreable to this, Monsieur, fearing that Mylord Ambr. was come to interpose on the prisoner's behalfe asked him on Friday last att St. Germains whether that was the cause of his coming, and told him that he did not think he would speake for a man that attempted to kill the King. The same report hath been hitherto in everybody's mouth but they begin now to mince it att court, and Monsieur de Ruvigny would have persuaded me yesterday, they had no such thoughts. The truth is I am apt to believe they begin now to be ashamed of it: and I am informed from a very good hand that Monsieur de Lionne who hath been at the Bastille to speake with the prisoner hath confessed since that he can find no ground for this pretended attempting to the King's life, and that upon the whole he was of opinion that this man had much better been left alone than taken, and did look upon what he had done as the intemperancy of an ill-settled braine. And to satisfy your Lordship that they are nettled here, and are concerned to know what may be the issue of all this, Monsieur de Turenne's secretary was on Munday last sent to several forreigne Ministers to pump them and to learne what their thoughts were concerning this violence committed in the Dominions of a sovereign and an allye whereupon he was told by one of them that such proceedings would bring Europe to the necessity of entering into a Croisade against them, as formerly against the infidels. If I durst I would acquaint your Lordship with the reflexions of all publique ministers here and of other unconcerned persons in relation to his Majesty's owning or disowning this man; but not knowing the particulars of his case, nor the grounds his Ma'ty may go upon, I shall forbeare entering upon this discourse. ... .

Your Lordships' etc.

P. Du MOULIN.

* State Papers, France, vol. 126.

** Ibid.

Note II. Paper endorsed 'Mr. Montague originally in Cypher. Received May 19, '69. Read in foreigne Committee, 23 May. Roux de Marsilli.'*

I durst not venture to sollicite in Monsr Roux Marsilly's behalfe because I doe not know whether the King my Master hath imployed him or noe; besides he is a man, as I have beene told by many people here of worth, that has given out that hee is resolved to kill the French king at one time or other, and I think such men are as dangerous to one king as to another: hee is brought to the Bastille and I believe may be proceeded against and put to death, in very few daies. There is great joy in this Court for his being taken, and a hundred thousand crownes, I am told very privately, set upon his head; the French Ambassador in England watcht him, and hee has given the intelligence here of his being employed by the King, and sent into Switzerland by my Master to draw the Swisses into the Triple League. Hee aggravates the business as much as hee can to the prejudice of my Master to value his owne service the more, and they seeme here to wonder that the King my Master should have imployed or countenanced a man that had so base a design against the King's Person, I had a great deal of discourse with Monsieur about it, but I did positively say that he had noe relation to my knowledge to the King my Master, and if he should have I make a question or noe whither in this case the King will owne him. However, my Lord, I had nothing to doe to owne or meddle in a buisines that I was so much a stranger to. . . .

This Roux Marsilly is a great creature of the B. d'Isola's, wch makes them here hate him the more. The Spanish Resident was very earnest with mee to have done something in behalfe of Marsilly, but I positively refused.

* State Papers, France, vol. 126.

Note III. [A paper endorsed 'Roux de Marsilli. Read in for. Committee, 23d May.']*

Roux de Marsilly came hither when your Majesty had made a union with Holland for making the Peace betwixt the two Crownes and when it was probable the opposition to the Peace would bee on the side of France.

Marsilly was heard telling of longe things but noe proposition made to him or by him.

Presently the Peace was made and Marsilly told more plainly wee had no use of him. A little summe of money was given him to returne as he said whither he was to goe in Switzerland. Upon which hee wishing his Ma'ty would renew his allience wth the Cantons hee was answerd his M'ty would not enter into any comerce with them till they had sent the regicides out of their Country, hee undertooke it should bee done. Seven or eight months after wth out any intimation given him from hence or any expectation of him, he comes hither, but was so coldly used I was complained off for not using so important a man well enough. I answerd I saw noe use the King could make of him, because he had no credit in Switzerlande and for any thing else I thought him worth nothing to us, but above all because I knew by many circumstances HEE WAS ANOTHER MAN'S SPY and soe ought not to be paid by his Majesty. Notwithstanding this his Ma'ty being moved from compassion commanded hee should have some money given him to carry him away and that I should write to Monsieur Balthazar thanking him in the King's name for the good offices hee rendered in advancing a good understanding betwixt his Ma'ty and the Cantons and desiring him to continue them in all occasions.

The man was always looked upon as a hot headed and indiscreete man, and soe accordingly handled, hearing him, but never trusting him with anything but his own offered and undesired endeavours to gett the Regicides sent out of Switzerland.

*State Papers, France, vol. 126.

Note IV. Letter of W. Perwich to ---.*

Paris: June 5, 1669.

Honored Sir,

Roux Marsilly has prudently declared hee had some what of importance to say but it should bee to the King himselfe wch may be means of respiting his processe and as he hopes intercession may bee made for him; but people talk so variously of him that I cannot tell whether hee ought to bee owned by any Prince; the Suisses have indeed the greatest ground to reclayme him as being taken in theirs. They have all his papers which speak much of the Triple Alliance; if they have no other pretext of hanging him I know not whether they can lawfully for this, hee having been naturallised in Holland and taken in a priviledged Country. . . .

*State Papers, France, vol. 126.

Note V. Francis Vernon to [Mr. Williamson?].*

Paris: June 19/29 1669.

Honored Sir,

My last of the 26th Currt was soe short and soe abrupt that I fear you can peck butt little satisfaction out of it.

I did intend to have written something about Marsilly but that I had noe time then. In my letter to my Lord Arlington I writt that Friday 21 Currt hee wounded himself wch he did not because hee was confronted with Ruvigny as the Gazettes speake. For he knew before hee should dye, butt he thought by dismembering himself that the losse of blood would carry him out of the world before it should come to bee knowne that he had wounded himselfe. And when the Governor of the Bastille spied the blood hee said It was a stone was come from him which caused that effusion. However the governor mistrusted the worst and searcht him to see what wound he had made. So they seared him and sent word to St. Germaines which made his execution be hastened. Saturday about 1 of the clock hee was brought on the skaffold before the Chastelet and tied to St. Andrew's Crosse all wch while he acted the Dying man and scarce stirred, and seemed almost breathlesse and fainting. The Lieutenant General presst him to confesse and ther was a doctor of the Sorbon who was a counsellr of the Castelet there likewise to exhort him to disburthen his mind of any thing which might be upon it. Butt he seemed to take no notice and lay panting.

Then the Lieutenant Criminel bethought himself that the only way to make him speake would bee to sende for a ministre soo hoo did to Monsr Daillie butt hee because the Edicts don't permitt ministres to come to condemned persons in publique butt only to comfort them in private before they goe out of prison refused to come till hee sent a huissier who if hee had refused the second time would have brought him by force. At this second summons hee came butt not without great expectations to bee affronted in a most notorious manner beeing the first time a ministre came to appeare on a scaffold and that upon soe sinister an occasion. Yet when he came found a great presse of people. All made way, none lett fall soe much as a taunting word. Hee came up the Scaffold, great silence all about. Hee found him lying bound stretched on St Andrew's Crosse, naked ready for execution. Hee told him hee was sent for to exhort him to die patiently and like a Christian. Then immediately they were all surprized to see him hold up his head wch he lett hang on one side before like a drooping calfe and speake as loud and clear as the ministre, to whom he said with a chearful air hee was glad to see him, that hee need not question butt that hee would dye like a Christian and patiently too. Then hee went and spoke some places of Scripture to encourage him which he heard with great attention. They afterward came to mention some things to move him to contrition, and there hee tooke an occasion to aggravate the horrour of a Crime of attempting against the King's person. Hee said hee did not know what hee meant. For his part hee never had any evill intention against the Person of the King.

The Lieutenant Criminel stood all the while behind Monsieur Daillie and hearkened to all and prompted Monsr Daillie to aske him if hee had said there were 10 Ravillacs besides wch would doe the King's businesse. Hee protested solemnly hee never said any such words or if hee did hee never remembred, butt if hee had it was with no intention of Malice. Then Monsieur Daillie turned to the people and made a discourse in vindication of those of the Religion that it was no Principle of theirs attempts on the persons of King[s] butt only loyalty and obedience. This ended hee went away; hee staid about an hour in all, and immediately as soon as he was gone, they went to their worke and gave him eleven blows with a barre and laid him on the wheele. Hee was two houres dying. All about Monsr Daillie I heard from his own mouth for I went to wait on him because it was reported hee had said something concerning the King of England butt hee could tell mee nothing of that. There was a flying report that he should say going from the Chastelet - The Duke of York hath done mee a great injury - The Swisses they say resented his [Marsilly's] taking and misst butt half an hour to take them which betrayed him [the monk] after whom they sent. When he was on the wheele hee was heard to say Le Roy est grand tyrant, Le Roy me traitte d'un facon fort barbare. All that you read concerning oaths and dying en enrage is false all the oaths hee used being only asseverations to Monsr Daillie that he was falsely accused as to the King's person.

Sr I am etc

FRANS. VERNON.

* State Papers, France, vol. 126.

Note VI. The Ambassador Montague to Arlington.*

Paris: June 22, 1669.

My Lord,

The Lieutenant criminel hath proceeded pretty farre with Le Roux Marsilly. The crime they forme their processe on beeing a rape which he had formerly committed at Nismes soe that he perceiving but little hopes of his life, sent word to the King if hee would pardon him he could reveale things to him which would concerne him more and be of greater consequence to him, than his destruction.

*State Papers, France, vol. 126.

Note VII. The same to the same.

Paris: June 26, '69.

My Lord,

I heard that Marsilly was to be broke on the wheel and I gave order then to one of my servants to write Mr. Williamson word of it, soe I suppose you have heard of it already: they hastened his execution for feare he should have dyed of the hurt he had done himself the day before; they sent for a minister to him when he was upon the scaffold to see if he would confesse anything, but he still persisted that he was guilty of nothing nor DID NOT KNOW WHY HE WAS PUT TO DEATH. . . .

III.

THE MYSTERY OF SIR EDMUND
BERRY GODFREY

When London was a pleasanter place than it is to-day, when anglers stretched their legs up Tottenham Hill on their way to fish in the Lee; when the 'best stands on Hackney river' were competed for eagerly by bottom fishers; when a gentleman in St. Martin's Lane, between the hedges, could 'ask the way to Paddington Woods;' when a hare haunted Primrose Hill and was daily pursued by a gallant pack of harriers; enfin, between three and four on the afternoon of October 17, 1678, two common fellows stepped into the White House tavern in the fields north of Marylebone, a house used as a club by a set of Catholic tradesmen. They had been walking in that region, and, as the October afternoon was drawing in, and rain was falling, they sought refuge in the White House. It would appear that they had not the means of assuaging a reasonable thirst, for when they mentioned that they had noticed a gentleman's cane, a scabbard, a belt, and some add a pair of gloves, lying at the edge of a deep dry ditch, overgrown with thick bush and bramble, the landlord offered the new comers a shilling to go and fetch the articles.* But the rain was heavy, and probably the men took the shilling out in ale, till about five o'clock, when the weather held up for a while.

* A rather different account by the two original finders, Bromwell and Walters, is in L'Estrange's Brief History, iii. pp. 97, 98. The account above is the landlord's. Lords' MSS., Hist. MSS. Com., xi. pp. 2, 46, 47.

The delay was the more singular if, as one account avers, the men had not only observed the cane and scabbard outside of the ditch, on the bank, but also a dead body within the ditch, under the brambles.* By five o'clock the rain had ceased, but the tempestuous evening was dark, and it was night before Constable Brown, with a posse of neighbours on foot and horseback, reached the ditch. Herein they found the corpse of a man lying face downwards, the feet upwards hung upon the brambles; thus half suspended he lay, and the point of a sword stuck out of his back, through his black camlet coat.** By the lights at the inn, the body was identified as that of Sir Edmund Berry Godfrey, a Justice of the Peace for Westminster, who had been missing since Saturday October 12. It is an undeniable fact that, between two and three o'clock, before the body was discovered and identified, Dr. Lloyd, Dean of St. Asaph's, and Bishop Burnet, had heard that Godfrey had been found in Leicester Fields, with his own sword in his body. Dr. Lloyd mentioned his knowledge in the funeral sermon of the dead magistrate. He had the story from a Mr. Angus, a clergyman, who had it from 'a young man in a grey coat,' in a bookseller's shop near St. Paul's, about two o'clock in the afternoon. Angus hurried to tell Bishop Burnet, who sent him on to Dr. Lloyd.*** Either the young man in the grey coat knew too much, or a mere rumour, based on a conjecture that Godfrey had fallen on his own sword, proved to be accurate by accident; a point to be remembered. According to Roger Frith, at two o'clock he heard Salvetti, the ambassador of the Duke of Tuscany, say: 'Sir E. Godfrey is dead. . . the young Jesuits are grown desperate; the old ones would do no such thing.' This again may have been a mere guess by Salvetti.****

*Pollock, Popish Plot, pp. 95, 96.

**Brown in Brief History, iii. pp. 212-215, 222.

***L'Estrange, Brief History, iii. pp. 87-89.

****Lords' MSS. p. 48, October 24.

In the circumstances of the finding of the body it would have been correct for Constable Brown to leave it under a guard till daylight and the arrival of surgical witnesses, but the night was threatening, and Brown ordered the body to be lifted; he dragged out the sword with difficulty, and had the dead man carried to the White House Inn. There, under the candles, the dead man, as we said, was recognised for Sir Edmund Berry Godfrey, a very well-known justice of the peace and wood and coal dealer. All this occurred on Thursday, October 17, and Sir Edmund had not been seen by honest men and thoroughly credible witnesses, at least, since one o'clock on Saturday, October 12. Then he was observed near his house in Green Lane, Strand, but into his house he did not go.

Who, then, killed Sir Edmund?

The question has never been answered, though three guiltless men were later hanged for the murder. Every conceivable theory has been tried; the latest is that of

Mr. Pollock: Godfrey was slain by 'the Queen's confessor,' Le Fevre, 'a Jesuit,' and some other Jesuits, with lay assistance.* I have found no proof that Le Fevre was either a Jesuit or confessor of the Queen.

* Pollock, The Popish Plot, Duckworth, London, 1903.

As David Hume says, the truth might probably have been discovered, had proper measures been taken at the moment. But a little mob of horse and foot had trampled round the ditch in the dark, disturbing the original traces. The coroner's jury, which sat long and late, on October 18 and 19, was advised by two surgeons, who probably, like the rest of the world, were biassed by the belief that Godfrey had been slain 'by the bloody Papists.' In the reign of mad terror which followed, every one was apt to accommodate his evidence, naturally, to that belief. If they did not, then, like the two original finders, Bromwell and Walters, they might be thrown, heavily ironed, into Newgate.*

* Lords' MSS. P. 47, note 1.

But when the Popish Plot was exploded, and Charles II. was firm on his throne, still more under James II., every one was apt to be biassed in the opposite direction, and to throw the guilt on the fallen party of Oates, Bedloe, Dugdale, and the other deeply perjured and infamous informers. Thus both the evidence of 1678-1680, and that collected in 1684-1687, by Sir Roger L'Estrange, J.P. (who took great trouble and was allowed access to the manuscript documents of the earlier inquiries), must be regarded with suspicion.*

* L'Estrange, Brief History of the Times, London, 1687.

The first question is cui bono? who had an interest in Godfrey's death? Three parties had an interest, first, the Catholics (IF Godfrey knew their secrets); next, the managers of the great Whig conspiracy in favour of the authenticity of Oates's Popish Plot; last, Godfrey himself, who was of an hereditary melancholy (his father had suicidal tendencies), and who was involved in a quandary whence he could scarcely hope to extricate himself with life and honour.

Of the circumstances of Godfrey's quandary an account is to follow. But, meanwhile, the theory of Godfrey's suicide (though Danby is said to have accepted it) was rejected, probably with good reason (despite the doubts of L'Estrange, Hume, Sir George Sitwell, and others), by the coroner's jury.*

* Sitwell, The First Whig, Sacheverell.

Privately printed, 1894, Sir George's book - a most interesting volume, based on public and private papers - unluckily is introuvable. Some years have passed since I read a copy which he kindly lent me.

The evidence which determined the verdict of murder was that of two surgeons. They found that the body had been severely bruised, on the chest, by kicks, blows of a blunt weapon, or by men's knees. A sword-thrust had been dealt, but had slipped on a rib; Godfrey's own sword had then been passed through the left pap, and out at the back. There was said to be no trace of the shedding of fresh living blood on the clothes of Godfrey, or about the ditch. What blood appeared was old, the surgeons averred, and malodorous, and flowed after the extraction of the sword.

L'Estrange (1687) argues at great length, but on evidence collected later, and given under the Anti-Plot bias, that there was much more 'bloud' than was allowed for at the inquest. But the early evidence ought to be best. Again, the surgeons declared that Godfrey had been strangled with a cloth (as the jury found), and his neck dislocated. Bishop Burnet, who viewed the body, writes (long after the event): 'A mark was all round his neck, an inch broad, which showed he was strangled. . . . And his neck was broken. All this I saw.'*

* Burnet, History of his own Time, ii. p. 741. 1725.

L'Estrange argued that the neck was not broken (giving an example of a similar error in the case of a dead child), and that the mark round the neck was caused by the tightness of the collar and the flow of blood to the neck, the body lying head downwards. In favour of this view he produced one surgeon's opinion. He also declares that Godfrey's brothers, for excellent reasons of their own, refused to allow a thorough post-mortem examination. 'None of them had ever been opened,' they said. Their true motive was that, if Godfrey were a suicide, his estate would be forfeited to the Crown, a point on which they undoubtedly showed great anxiety.

Evidence was also given to prove that, on Tuesday and Wednesday, October 15 and 16, Godfrey's body was not in the ditch. On Tuesday Mr. Forsett, on Wednesday Mr. Harwood had taken Mr. Forsett's harriers over the ground, in pursuit of the legendary hare. They had seen no cane or scabbard; the dogs had found no corpse. L'Estrange replied that, as to the cane, the men could not see it if they were on the further side of the bramble-covered ditch. As to the dogs, they later hunted a wood in which a dead body lay for six weeks before it was found. L'Estrange discovered witnesses who had seen Godfrey in St. Martin's Lane on the fatal Saturday, asking his way to Paddington Woods, others who had seen him there or met him returning thence. Again, either he or 'the Devil in his clothes' was seen near the ditch on Saturday afternoon. Again, his clerk, Moore, was seen hunting the fields near the ditch, for his master, on the Monday afternoon. Hence L'Estrange argued that Godfrey went to Paddington Woods, on Saturday morning, to look for a convenient place of suicide: that he could not screw his courage to the sticking place; that he wandered home, did not enter his house, roamed out again, and, near Primrose Hill, found the ditch and 'the sticking place.' His rambles, said L'Estrange, could neither have been taken for business nor pleasure. This is true, if Godfrey actually took the rambles, but the evidence was not adduced till several years later; in 1678 the witnesses would have been in great danger. Still, if we accept L'Estrange's witnesses for Godfrey's trip to Paddington and return, perhaps we ought not to reject the rest.*

* Brief History, iii. pp. 252, 300, 174, 175; State Trials, viii. pp. 1387, 1392, 1393, 1359-1389.

On the whole, it seems that the evidence for murder, not suicide, is much the better, though even here absolute certainty is not attained. Granting Godfrey's constitutional hereditary melancholy, and the double quandary in which he stood, he certainly had motives for suicide. He was a man of humanity and courage, had bravely faced the Plague in London, had withstood the Court boldly on a private matter (serving a writ, as Justice, on the King's physician who owed him money in his capacity as a coal dealer), and he was lenient in applying the laws against Dissenters and Catholics.

To be lenient was well; but Godfrey's singular penchant for Jesuits, and especially for the chief Catholic intriguer in England, was probably the ultimate cause of his death, whether inflicted by his own hand or those of others.

2.

We now study Godfrey's quandary. On June 23, 1678, the infamous miscreant Titus Oates had been expelled from the Jesuit College of St. Omer's, in France. There he may readily have learned that the usual triennial 'consult' of English Jesuits was to be held in London on April 24, but WHERE it was held, namely in the Duke of York's chambers in St. James's Palace, Oates did not know, or did not say. The Duke, by permitting the Jesuits to assemble in his house, had been technically guilty of treason in 'harbouring' Jesuits, certainly a secret of great importance, as he was the head and hope of the Catholic cause, and the butt of the Whigs, who were eager to exclude him from the succession. Oates had scraps of other genuine news. He returned to London after his expulsion from St. Omer's, was treated with incautious kindness by Jesuits there, and, with Tonge, constructed his monstrous fable of a Popish plot to kill the King and massacre the Protestant public. In August, Charles was apprised of the plot, as was Danby, the Lord Treasurer; the Duke of York also knew, how much he knew is uncertain. The myth was little esteemed by the King.

On September 6, Oates went to Godfrey, and swore

before him, as a magistrate, to the truth of a written deposition, as to treason. But Godfrey was not then allowed to read the paper, nor was it left in his hands; the King, he was told, had a copy.* The thing might have passed off, but, as King James II. himself writes, he (being then Duke of York) 'press'd the King and Lord Treasurer several times that the letters' (letters forged by Oates) 'might be produced and read, and the business examined into at the Committee of Foreign Affairs.'** Mr. Pollock calls the Duke's conduct tactless. Like Charles I., in the mystery of 'the Incident,' he knew himself guiltless, and demanded an inquiry.

* Kirkby, Complete Narrative, pp. 2, 3, cited by Mr. Pollock. At the time, it was believed that Godfrey saw the depositions. **Clarke's Life of James II. i. p. 518. Cited from the King's original Memoirs.

On September 28, Oates was to appear before the Council. Earlier on that day he again visited Godfrey, handed to him a copy of his deposition, took oath to its truth, and carried another copy to Whitehall. As we shall see, Oates probably adopted this course by advice of one of the King's ministers, Danby or another. Oates was now examined before the King, who detected him in perjury. But he accused Coleman, the secretary of the Duchess of York, of treasonable correspondence with La Chaise, the confessor of Louis XIV.: he also said that, on April 24, he himself was present at the Jesuit 'consult' in the White Horse Tavern, Strand, where they decided to murder the King! This was a lie, but they HAD met on ordinary business of the Society, on April 24, at the palace of the Duke of York. Had the Jesuits, when tried, proved this, they would not have saved their lives, and Oates would merely have sworn that they met AGAIN, at the White Horse.

Godfrey, having Oates's paper before him, now knew that Coleman was accused. Godfrey was very intimate with many Jesuits, says Warner, who was one of them, in his manuscript history.* With Coleman, certainly a dangerous intriguer, Godfrey was so familiar that 'it was the form arranged between them for use when Godfrey was in company and Coleman wished to see him,' that Coleman should be announced under the name of Mr. Clarke.**

* Pollock, p. 91, note 1.

** Ibid. p. 151, note 3. Welden's evidence before the Lords' Committee, House of Lords MSS., p. 48. Mr. Pollock rather overstates the case. We cannot be certain, from Welden's words, that Coleman habitually used the name 'Clarke' on such occasions.

It is extraordinary enough to find a rigid British magistrate engaged in clandestine dealings with an intriguer like Coleman, who, for the purpose, receives a cant name. If that fact came out in the inquiry into the plot, Godfrey's doom was dight, the general frenzy would make men cry for his blood. But yet more extraordinary was Godfrey's conduct on September 28. No sooner had he Oates's confession, accusing Coleman, in his hands, than he sent for the accused. Coleman went to the house of a Mr. (or Colonel) Welden, a friend of Godfrey's, and to Godfrey it was announced that 'one Clarke' wished to see him there. 'When they were together at my house they were reading papers,' said Welden later, in evidence.* It cannot be doubted that, after studying Oates's deposition, Godfrey's first care was to give Coleman full warning. James II. tells us this himself, in his memoirs. 'Coleman being known to depend on the Duke, Sir Edmund Bury (sic) Godfrey made choice of him, to send to his Highness an account of Oates's and Tongue's depositions as soon as he had taken them,' that is, on September 28.** Apparently the Duke had not the precise details of Oates's charges, as they now existed, earlier than September 28, when they were sent to him by Godfrey.

* See previous note (Pollock, p. 151, note 3.)

** Life of James II. i, p. 534.

It is Mr. Pollock's argument that, when Godfrey and Coleman went over the Oates papers, Coleman would prove Oates's perjury, and would to this end let out that, on April 24, the Jesuits met, not as Oates swore, at a tavern, but at the Duke of York's house, a secret fatal to the Duke and the Catholic cause. The Jesuits then slew Godfrey to keep the secret safe.*

* Pollock, p. 153.

Now, first, I cannot easily believe that Coleman would blab this secret (quite unnecessarily, for this proof of Oates's perjury could not be, and was not, publicly adduced), unless Godfrey was already deep in the Catholic intrigues. He may have been, judging by his relations with Coleman. If Godfrey was not himself engaged in Catholic intrigues, Coleman need only tell him that Oates was not in England in April, and could not have been, as he swore he was, at the 'consult.' Next, Godfrey was not the man (as Mr. Pollock supposes) to reveal his knowledge to the world, from a sense of duty, even if the Court 'stifled the plot.' Mr. Pollock says: 'Godfrey was, by virtue of his position as justice of the peace, a Government official. . . . Sooner or later he would certainly reveal it. . . . The secret. . . had come into the hands of just one of the men who could not afford, even if he might wish, to retain it '*

Mr. Pollock may conceive, though I do not find him saying so, that Godfrey communicated Oates's charges to Coleman merely for the purpose of 'pumping' him and surprising some secret. If so he acted foolishly.

* Pollock, p. 154.

In fact, Godfrey was already 'stifling the plot.' A Government official, he was putting Coleman in a posture to fly, and to burn his papers; had he burned all of them, the plot was effectually stifled. Next, Godfrey could not reveal the secret without revealing his own misprision of treason. He would be asked 'how he knew the secret.' Godfrey's lips were thus sealed; he had neither the wish nor the power to speak out, and so his knowledge of the secret, if he knew it, was innocuous to the Jesuits. 'What is it nearer?' Coleman was reported, by a perjured informer, to have asked.*

* State Trials, vii. 1319. Trial of Lord Stafford, 1680.

To this point I return later. Meanwhile, let it be granted that Godfrey knew the secret from Coleman, and that, though, since Godfrey could not speak without self-betrayal - though it was 'no nearer' - still the Jesuits thought well to mak sikker and slay him.

Still, what is the evidence that Godfrey had a mortal secret? Mr. Pollock gives it thus: 'He had told Mr. Wynnel that he was master of a dangerous secret, which would be fatal to him. "Oates," he said, "is sworn and is perjured."'* These sentences are not thus collocated in the original. The secret was not, as from Mr. Pollock's arrangement it appears to be, that Oates was perjured.

* Pollock, p. 150.

The danger lay, not in knowledge that Oates was perjured - all the Council knew the King to have discovered that. 'Many believed it,' says Mr. Pollock. 'It was not an uncommon thing to say.'* The true peril, on Mr. Pollock's theory, was Godfrey's possession of PROOF that Oates was perjured, that proof involving the secret of the Jesuit 'consult' of April 14, AT THE DUKE OF YORK'S HOUSE. But, by a singular oversight, Mr. Pollock quotes only part of what Godfrey said to Wynell (or Wynnel) about his secret. He does not give the whole of the sentence uttered by Wynell. The secret, of which Godfrey was master, on the only evidence, Wynell's, had nothing to do with the Jesuit meeting of April 24. Wynell is one of L'Estrange's later witnesses. His words are:

Godfrey: 'The (Catholic) Lords are as innocent as you or I. Coleman will die, but not the Lords.'

Wynell: 'If so, where are we then?'

Godfrey: 'Oates is sworn and is perjured.'

*   *   *

'Upon Wynell's asking Sir Edmund some time why he was so melancholy, his answer has been, "he was melancholy because he was master of a dangerous secret that would be fatal to him, THAT HIS SECURITY WAS OATE'S DEPOSITION, THAT THE SAID OATES HAD FIRST DECLARED IT TO A PUBLIC MINISTER, AND SECONDLY THAT HE CAME TO SIR EDMUND BY HIS (the Minister's) DIRECTION.'**

* Pollock, p. 152.

** L'Estrange, part iii. p. 187.

We must accept all of Mr. Wynell's statement or none; we cannot accept, like Mr. Pollock, only Godfrey's confession of owning a dangerous secret, without Godfrey's explanation of the nature of the danger. Against THAT danger (his knowing and taking no action upon what Oates had deposed) Godfrey's 'security' was Oates's other deposition, that his information was already in the Minister's hands, and that he had come to Godfrey by the Minister's orders. The invidiousness of knowing and not acting on Oates's 'dangerous secret,' Godfrey hoped, fell on the Minister rather than on himself. And it did fall on Danby, who was later accused of treason on this very ground, among others. Such is Wynell's evidence, true or false. C'est a prendre ou a laisser in bulk, and in bulk is of no value to Mr. Pollock's argument.

That Godfrey was in great fear after taking Oates's deposition, and dealing with Coleman, is abundantly attested. But of what was he afraid, and of whom? L'Estrange says, of being made actual party to the plot, and not of 'bare misprision' only, the misprision of not acting on Oates's information.* It is to prove this point that L'Estrange cites Wynell as quoted above. Bishop Burnet reports that, to him, Godfrey said 'that he believed he himself should be knocked on the head.'**

Knocked on the head by whom? By a frightened Protestant mob, or by Catholic conspirators? To Mr. Robinson, an old friend, he said, 'I do not fear them if they come fairly, and I shall not part with my life tamely.' Qu'ils viennent! as Tartarin said, but who are 'they'? Godfrey said that he had 'taken the depositions very unwillingly, and would fain have had it done by others. . . . I think I shall have little thanks for my pains. . . . Upon my conscience I believe I shall be the first martyr.'*** He could not expect thanks from the Catholics: it was from the frenzied Protestants that he expected 'little thanks.'

* L'Estrange, iii. p. 187.

** Burnet, ii. p. 740.

*** State Trials, vii. pp. 168, 169.

Oates swore, and, for once, is corroborated, that Godfrey complained 'of receiving affronts from some great persons (whose names I name not now) for being so zealous in this business.' If Oates, by 'great persons,' means the Duke of York, it was in the Duke's own cause that Godfrey had been 'zealous,' sending him warning by Coleman. Oates added that others threatened to complain to Parliament, which was to meet on October 21, that Godfrey had been 'too remiss.' Oates was a liar, but Godfrey, in any case, was between the Devil and the deep sea. As early as October 24, Mr. Mulys attested, before the Lords, Godfrey's remark, 'he had been blamed by some great men for not having done his duty, and by other great men for having done too much.' Mulys corroborates Oates.* If Godfrey knew a secret dangerous to the Jesuits (which, later, was a current theory), he might be by them silenced for ever. If his conduct, being complained of, was examined into by Parliament, misprision of treason was the lowest at which his offence could be rated. Never was magistrate in such a quandary. But we do not know, in the state of the evidence, which of his many perils he feared most, and his possession of 'a dangerous secret' (namely, the secret of the consult of April 24) is a pure hypothesis. It is not warranted, but refuted, by Godfrey's own words as reported by Wynell, when, unlike Mr. Pollock, we quote Wynell's whole sentence on the subject. (see previous exchange between Godfrey and Wynell.)

* Lords' MSS., P. 48.

3.

The theories of Godfrey's death almost defy enumeration. For suicide, being a man of melancholic temperament, he had reasons as many and as good as mortal could desire. That he was murdered for not being active enough in prosecuting the plot, is most improbable. That he was taken off by Danby's orders, for giving Coleman and the Duke of York early warning, is an absurd idea, for Danby could have had him on THAT score by ordinary process of law. That he was slain by Oates's gang, merely to clinch the fact that a plot there veritably was, is improbable. At the same time, Godfrey had been calling Oates a perjurer: he KNEW that Oates was forsworn. This was an unsafe thing for any man to say, but when the man was the magistrate who had read Oates's deposition, he invited danger. Such were the chances that Godfrey risked from the Plot party. The Catholics, on the other hand, if they were aware that Godfrey possessed the secret of the Jesuit meeting of April 24, and if they deemed him too foolish to keep the secret in his own interest, could not but perceive that to murder him was to play into the hands of the Whigs by clinching the belief in a Popish plot. Had they been the murderers, they would probably have taken his money and rings, to give the idea that he had been attacked and robbed by vulgar villains. If they 'were not the damnedest fools' (thus freely speaks L'Estrange), they would not have taken deliberate steps to secure the instant discovery of the corpse. Whoever pitched Godfrey's body into the bramble-covered ditch, meant it to be found, for his cane, scabbard, and so on were deliberately left outside of the ditch. Your wily Jesuit would have caused the body to disappear, leaving the impression that Godfrey had merely absconded, as he had the best reasons for doing. On the other hand, Oates's gang would not, if they first strangled Godfrey, have run his own sword through his body, as if he had committed suicide - unless, indeed, they calculated that this would be a likely step for your wily Jesuit to take, in the circumstances. Again, an educated 'Jesuit,' like Le Fevre, 'the Queen's confessor,' would know that the sword trick was futile; even a plain man, let alone a surgeon, could detect a wound inflicted on a corpse four or five days old.

Two other theories existed, first, that Godfrey hanged himself, and that his brothers and heirs did the sword trick, to suggest that he had not committed suicide by strangulation, but had been set on and stabbed with his own sword. In that case, of course, the brothers would have removed his rings and money, to prove that he had been robbed. The other theory, plausible enough, held that Godfrey was killed by Catholics, NOT because he took Oates's deposition (which he was bound to do), but because he officiously examined a number of persons to make discoveries. The Attorney-General at the trial of Godfrey's alleged murderers (February 1679), declared that Sir Edmund had taken such examinations: 'we have proof that he had some, , , perhaps some more than are now extant'* This theory, then, held that he was taken off to prevent his pursuing his zealous course, and to seize the depositions which he had already taken. When this was stated to Charles II., on November 7, 1678, by the perjured Bedloe, the King naturally remarked: 'The parties were still alive' (the deponents) 'to give the informations.' Bedloe answered, that the papers were to be seized 'in hopes the second informations taken from the parties would not have agreed with the first, and so the thing would have been disproved.'** This was monstrously absurd, for the slayers of Godfrey could not have produced the documents of which they had robbed him.

* State Trials, vii. p. 163.

** Pollock, p. 385.

The theory that Sir Edmund was killed because Coleman had told him too many secrets did not come to general knowledge till the trial of Lord Stafford in 1680. The hypothesis - Godfrey slain because, through Coleman, he knew too many Catholic secrets - is practically that of Mr. Pollock. It certainly does supply a motive for Godfrey's assassination. Hot-headed Catholics who knew, or suspected, that Godfrey knew too much, MAY have killed him for that reason, or for the purpose of seizing his papers, but it is improbable that Catholics of education, well aware that, if he blabbed, Godfrey must ruin himself, would have put their hands into his blood, on the mere chance that, if left alive, he might betray both himself and them.

4.

It is now necessary to turn backward a little and see what occurred immediately after the meeting of Coleman and Godfrey on September 28. On that day, Oates gave his lying evidence before the Council: he was allowed to go on a Jesuit drive, with warrants and officers; he caught several of the most important Jesuits. On September 29, the King heard his tale, and called him a 'lying knave.' None the less he was sent on another drive, and, says Mr. Pollock, 'before dawn most the Jesuits of eminence in London lay in gaol.' But Le Fevre, 'the Queen's confessor,' and the other 'Jesuits' whom Mr. Pollock suspects of Godfrey's murder, were not taken. Is it likely (it is, of course, possible) that they stayed on in town, and killed Godfrey twelve days later?

Meanwhile Coleman, thanks to Godfrey's warning, had most of September 28, the night of that day, and September 29, wherein to burn his papers and abscond. He did neither; if he destroyed some papers, he left others in his rooms, letters which were quite good enough to hang him for high treason, as the law stood. Apparently Coleman did not understand his danger. On Sunday night, September 29, a warrant for his apprehension was issued, and for the seizure of his papers. 'He came voluntarily in on Monday morning,' having heard of the warrant. This is not the conduct of a man who knows himself guilty. He met the charges with disdain, and made so good a case that, instead of being sent to Newgate, he was merely entrusted to a messenger, who was told 'to be very civil to Mr. Coleman.'

Charles II. went to the Newmarket Autumn Meeting, Coleman's papers were examined, and 'sounded so strange to the Lords' that they sent him to Newgate (October 1). The papers proved that Coleman, years before, had corresponded (as Oates had sworn) with the confessor of Louis XIV. and had incurred the technical guilt of treason. Either Coleman did not understand the law and the measure of his offence (as seems probable), or he thought his papers safely hidden. But the heather was on fire. The belief in Oates's impossible Plot blazed up, 'hell was let loose'*

* State Trials, vii. p. 29.

Coleman had thought himself safe, says James II., then Duke of York. 'The Duke perceiving' (from Godfrey's information of September 28) 'Oates had named Coleman, bade him look to himself, for he was sure to find no favour, and therefore, if he had any papers that might hurt him, to secure them immediately; but he, apprehending no danger, let them be seized, however kept close himself, and sent to advise with the Duke whether he should deliver himself up or not. The Duke replyd, "He knew best what was in his papers; if they contain'd any expression which could be wrested to an ill sence, he had best not appear, otherwise the surrendering himself would be an argument of innocency." He did accordingly,' and was condemned in November, and hanged.*

* Life of James II., i. p. 534.

King James's tale agrees with the facts of Coleman's

surrender. 'He came in voluntarily.' He did not appreciate the resources of civilisation at the service of the English law of treason: he had dabbled in intrigue without taking counsel's advice, and knowing for certain that Oates was an inconsistent liar, Coleman took his chance with a light heart. However, not only did some of his letters bring him (though he could not understand the fact) within the elastic law of treason; but Oates's evidence was accepted when conspicuously false; Coleman was not allowed to produce his diary and prove an alibi as to one of Oates's accusations, and a new witness, Bedloe, a perjurer who rivalled Oates, had sprung up out of the filth of London streets. So Coleman swung for it, as Godfrey, according to Wynell, had prophesied that he would.

Coleman's imprisonment began twelve days before Godfrey's disappearance. At Coleman's trial, late in November, a mere guess was given that Godfrey was slain to prevent him (a Protestant martyr) from blabbing Catholic secrets. This cause of Godfrey's taking off was not alleged by Bedloe. This man, a notorious cosmopolitan rogue, who had swindled his way through France and Spain, was first heard of in the Godfrey case at the end of October. He wrote to the Secretaries of State from Bristol (L'Estrange says from Newbury on his way to Bristol), offering information, as pardon and reward had been promised to contrite accomplices in the murder. He came to town, and, on November 7, gave evidence before the King. Bedloe gave himself out as a Jesuit agent; concerning the Plot he added monstrous inventions to those of Oates.

'As to Sir Edmund Godfrey; was promised 2,000 guineas to be in it by Le Fere' (Le Fevre, 'the Queen's confessor),' [by] 'my Lord Bellasis' gentleman, AND

THE YOUNGEST OF THE WAITERS IN THE
QUEENE'S CHAPEL, IN A PURPLE GOWN, and to
keep the people orderly'*

* See Pollock, pp. 384, 387. The report is from
Secretary Coventry's MSS., at Longleat. The evidence
as to Bedloe's deposition before the King (November
7) is in a confused state. Mr. Pollock prints (pp. 383,
384, cf. p. 110) a document from 'Brit. Mus. Addit.
MS. 11058, f. 244.' This is also given, with the same
erroneous reference, by Mr. Foley, in Records of the
English Province of the Society of Jesus, vol. v. p. 30,
note. The right reference is 11055. The document is
quite erroneously printed, with variations in error, by
Mr. Foley and Mr. Pollock. Bedloe really said that
Godfrey was lured into Somerset House Yard, not into
'some house yard' (Foley), or 'into a house yard'
(Pollock). Bedloe, so far, agreed with Prance, but, in
another set of notes on his deposition (Longleat MSS.,
Coventry Papers, xi. 272-274, Pollock, 384-387), he
made Somerset House the scene of the murder. There
are other errors. Mr. Pollock and Mr. Foley make
Bedloe accuse Father Eveley, S.J., in whom I naturally
recognised Father Evers or Every, who was then at
Tixall in Staffordshire. The name in the MS. is 'Welch,'
not Eveley. The MS. was manifestly written not before
September 12. It does not appear that Bedloe, on
November 7, knew the plot as invented by Oates, on
which compare Mr. Pollock, p. 110, who thinks that 'it
is quite possible that Charles II. deceived him,' Bishop
Burnet, 'intentionally,' on this head (Burnet, ii. 745-
746, 1725). By printing 'he acquainted' instead of 'he
acquainteth the Lords,' in the British Museum MS.,
and by taking the document, apparently, to be of
November 7, Mr. Pollock has been led to an incorrect
conclusion. I am obliged to Father Gerard, S.J., for a

correct transcript of the British Museum MS.; see also Note iii., 'The Jesuit Murderers,' at the end of this chapter, and Father Gerard's The Popish Plot and its Latest Historian (Longman's, 1903).

Bedloe here asserts distinctly that one accomplice was an official of the Queen's chapel, in her residence, Somerset House: a kind of verger, in a purple gown. This is highly important, for the man whom he later pretended to recognise as this accomplice was not a 'waiter,' did not 'wear a purple gown;' and, by his own account, 'was not in the chapel once a month.' Bedloe's recognition of him, therefore, was worthless. He said that Godfrey was smothered with a pillow, or two pillows, in a room in Somerset House, for the purpose of securing 'the examinations' that Godfrey had taken. 'Coleman and Lord Bellasis advised to destroy him.' His informant was Le Fevre. One Walsh (a 'Jesuit'), Le Fevre, Lord Bellasis's man, and 'the chapel keeper' did the deed. The chapel keeper carried him' (Godfrey) 'off.' 'HE DID NOT SEE HIM' (Godfrey) 'AFTER HE WAS DEAD.'

On the following day Bedloe told his tale at the bar of the House of Lords. He now, contradicting himself, swore THAT HE SAW GODFREY'S DEAD BODY IN SOMERSET HOUSE. He was offered 2,000 guineas to help to carry him off. This was done by chairmen, 'retainers to Somerset House,' on Monday night (October 14).*

* Pollock, p. 387, Lords' Journals, xiii. p. 343.

On that night, Bedloe saw Samuel Atkins, Mr. Pepys's clerk, beside the corpse, by the light of a dark lantern. Atkins had an alibi, so Bedloe shuffled, and would not swear to him.

On November 14, before the Lords' Committee, Bedloe again gave evidence. The 2,100 pounds were now 4,000 pounds offered to Bedloe, by Le Fevre, early in October, to kill a man. The attendant in the Queen's chapel was at the scene (a pure figment) of the corpse exposed under the dark lantern. The motive of the murder was to seize Godfrey's examinations, which he said he had sent to Whitehall. At a trial which followed in February 1679, Mr. Robinson, who had known Godfrey for some forty years, deposed that he had said to him, 'I understand you have taken several examinations.' 'Truly,' said he, 'I have.' 'Pray, Sir, have you the examinations about you, will you please to let me see them?' 'No, I have them not, I delivered them to a person of quality.'*

* State Trials, vii. 168.

This person of quality was not the Duke of York, for it may be noted that, on the day before his disappearance, Godfrey had, in fact, received back from the Lord Chief Justice the original copy of Oates's depositions. This copy was found in his house, after his death, and handed over by his brother to the Government.* To get the examinations was always the motive of the murder, with Bedloe. The hour of Godfrey's death was now 2 P.M.; now 3, or 4, or 5 P.M., on October 12. The body was hidden in various rooms of Somerset House, or under the high altar in the Queen's Chapel. The discrepancies never affected the faith given to Bedloe.

* Lords' MSS., Hist. MSS. Commission Report, xi. Appendix, part ii., pp. 2,3.

At the end of December came in a new accomplice-witness. This was an Irishman, Miles Prance, a silversmith, who had a business among Catholics, and worked for the Queen's Chapel. Unlike all the other informers, Prance had hitherto been an ordinary fellow enough, with a wife and family, not a swindling debauchee. He was arrested on December 21, on information given by John Wren, a lodger of his, with whom he had quarrelled. Wren had noticed that Prance lay out of his own house while Godfrey was missing, which Prance admitted to be true.*

* Op. cit. p. 51. Prance both said, and denied, that he slept out while Sir Edmund was missing. He was flurried and self-contradictory.

Bedloe, passing through a room in the House of Commons, saw Prance in custody, and at once pretended to recognise in him the 'chapel keeper,' 'under waiter,' or 'man in the purple gown,' whom he had seen by the light of a dark lantern, beside Godfrey's body, in a room of Somerset House, on October 14. 'There was very little light' on that occasion, Bedloe had said, and he finally refused, we saw, to swear to Atkins, who had an alibi. But, as to Prance, he said: 'This is one of the rogues that I saw with a dark lantern about the body of Sir Edmund, but he was then in a periwig.'* The periwig was introduced in case Prance had an alibi: Oates had used the same 'hedge,' 'a periwig doth disguise a man very much,' in Coleman's case.**

* L'Estrange, iii. pp. 52, 53, 65.

** State Trials, vii. 27.

What was Bedloe's recognition of Prance worth?
Manifestly nothing! He had probably seen Prance (not
as a 'waiter') in the Queen's Chapel. Now he found him
in custody. Cautious as regards Atkins, six weeks
earlier, Bedloe was emboldened now by a train of
successes. He had sworn away Coleman's life. His self-
contradictions had been blindly swallowed. If Prance
could prove an alibi, what was that to Bedloe? The
light of the dark lantern had been very bad; the rogue,
under that light, had worn a periwig, which 'doth
disguise a man very much.' Bedloe could safely say
that he had made an innocent error. Much worse
blunders had not impaired his credit; later he made
much worse blunders, undetected. He saw his chance
and took it.

Prance, who denied everything, was hurried to
Newgate, and thrown, without bed or covering, into the
freezing 'condemned hole,' where he lay perishing of
cold through the night of December 21, December 22,
and the night of that day. On December 23, he offered,
no wonder, to confess. He was examined by the Lords,
and (December 24) by the Council.

Prance knew, all the world knew, the details about
Godfrey's bruises; the state of his neck, and the sword-
thrusts. He knew that Bedloe had located the murder in
Somerset House. As proclamations for the men
accused by Bedloe had long been out, he MAY have
guessed that Le Fevre, Walsh, and Pritchard were
wanted for Godfrey's murder, and had been denounced
by Bedloe. But this is highly improbable, for nothing
about Godfrey's murder is hinted at in the proclamation
for Le Fevre, Walsh, and Pritchard.* We have no
reason, then, to suppose that Prance knew who the men
were that Bedloe had accused; consequently he had to

select other victims, innocent men of his acquaintance. But, as a tradesman of the Queen, Prance knew her residence, Somerset House, the courts, outer stairs, passages, and so on. He knew that Bedloe professed to have recognised him there in the scene of the dark lantern.

* Lords' Journals, xiii. p. 346; Lords' MSS., p. 59.

Prance had thus all the materials of a confession ready made, but not of a confession identical with Bedloe's. He was 'one of the most acute and audacious of the Jesuit agents,' says Mr. Pollock.* Yet Mr. Pollock argues that for Prance to tell the tale which he did tell, in his circumstances of cold and terror, required a most improbable 'wealth of mental equipment,' 'phenomenal powers of memory, imagination, and coolness,' if the tale was false.** Therefore Prance's story of the murder was true, except in the details as to the men whom he accused. On December 24, he was taken to the places which he described (certainly lying in his tale), and preserved consistency, though, after long search, he could not find one of the rooms in which he said that the corpse was laid.***

* Pollock,p.166.

** Ibid. p. 146.

*** Lords' Journals, xii. pp. 436-438.

As Prance, by Mr. Pollock's theory, was one of the most acute of Jesuit agents, and as he had all the materials, and all the knowledge necessary for a confession, he had, obviously, no difficulty in making up his evidence. Even by Mr. Pollock's showing, he was cool and intellectual enough; for, on that showing, he adapted into his narrative, very subtly, circumstances which were entirely false. If, as Mr. Pollock holds, Prance was astute enough to make a consistent patchwork of fact and lie, how can it be argued that, with the information at his command, he could not invent a complete fiction?

Again, Prance, by misstating dates wildly, hoped, says Mr. Pollock, to escape as a mere liar.* But, when Prance varied in almost every detail of time, place, motive, and person from Bedloe, Mr. Pollock does not see that his own explanation holds for the variations. If Prance wished to escape as a babbling liar, he could not do better than contradict Bedloe. He DID, but the Protestant conscience swallowed the contradictions. But again, if Prance did not know the details of Bedloe's confession, how could he possibly agree with it?

* Pollock, p. 160.

The most essential point of difference was that Bedloe accused 'Jesuits,' Le Fevre, Walsh, and Pritchard, who had got clean away. Prance accused two priests, who escaped, and three hangers on of Somerset House, Hill, Berry (the porter), and Green. All three were hanged, and all three confessedly were innocent. Mr. Pollock reasons that Prance, if guilty (and he believes him guilty), 'must have known the real authors' of the crime, that is, the Jesuits accused by Bedloe. 'He must have accused the innocent, not from necessity, but from choice, and in order to conceal the guilty.' 'He knew Bedloe to have exposed the real murderers, and . . . he wished to shield them.'* How did he know whom Bedloe had exposed? How could he even know the exact spot, a room in Somerset House, where Bedloe placed the murder? Prance placed it in Somerset YARD.

* Pollock, p. 148.

It is just as easy to argue, on Mr. Pollock's other line, that Prance varied from Bedloe in order that the inconsistencies might prove his own falsehood. But we have no reason to suppose that Prance did know the details of Bedloe's confession, as to the motive of the murder, the hour, the exact spot, and the names of the criminals. Later he told L'Estrange a palpable lie: Bedloe's confession had been shown to him before he made his own. If that were true, he purposely contradicted Bedloe in detail. But Mr. Pollock rejects the myth. Then how did Prance know the details given by Bedloe?* Ignorant of Bedloe's version, except in two or three points, Prance could not but contradict it. He thus could not accuse Bedloe's Jesuits. He did not name other men, as Mr. Pollock holds, to shield the Jesuits. Practically they did not need to be shielded. Jesuits with seven weeks' start of the law were safe enough. Even if they were caught, were guilty, and had the truth extracted from them, involving Prance, the truth about HIM would come out, whether he now denounced them or not. But he did not know that Bedloe had denounced them.

* Pollock, pp. 142, 143.

Mr. Pollock's theory of the relation of Bedloe to Godfrey's murder is this: Bedloe had no hand in the murder, and never saw the corpse. The crime was done in Somerset House, 'the Queen's confessor,' Father Le Fevre, S.J., having singular facilities for entering, with his friends, and carrying a dead body out 'through a private door' - a door not mentioned by any witnesses, nor proved to exist by the evidence of a chart. This Le Fevre, with Walsh, lived in the same house as Bedloe. From them, Bedloe got his information. 'It is easy to conjecture how he could have obtained it. Walsh and Le Fevre were absent from their rooms, for a considerable part of the nights of Saturday and Wednesday, October 12 and 16. Bedloe's suspicions must have been aroused, and, either by threats or cajolery, he wormed part of the secret out of his friends. He obtained a general idea of the way in which the murder had been committed and of the persons concerned in it. One of these was a frequenter of the Queen's chapel whom he knew by sight. He thought him to be a subordinate official there.'*

* Pollock, pp 157, 158.

On this amount of evidence Bedloe invented his many contradictions. Why he did not cleave to the facts imparted to him by his Jesuit friends, we do not learn. 'A general idea of the way in which the murder was committed' any man could form from the state of Godfrey's body. There was no reason why Walsh and Le Fevre 'should be absent from their rooms on a considerable part of the night of Saturday 12,' and so excite Bedloe's suspicions, for, on his versions, they slew Godfrey at 2 P.M., 5 P.M., or any hour between. No proof is given that they were in their lodgings, or in London, during the fortnight which followed Oates's three successful Jesuit drives of September 28-30. In all probability they had fled from London before Godfrey's murder. No evidence can I find that Bedloe's Jesuits were at their lodgings on October 12-16. They were not sought for there, but at Somerset House.*

Two sisters, named Salvin, were called before the Lords' Committee, and deposed that Bedloe and Le Fevre had twice been at their house when Walsh said mass there.**

* Lords' Journals, xiii. pp. 343 346.

** Ibid. p. 353.

That is all! Bedloe had some acquaintance with the men he accused; so had Prance with those he denounced. Prance's victims were innocent, and against Bedloe's there is not, so far, evidence to convict a cat on for stealing cream. He recognised Prance, therefore he really knew the murderers - that is all the argument.

Mr. Pollock's theory reposes on the belief, rejected by L'Estrange, that the Jesuits 'were the damnedest fools.' Suppose them guilty. The first step of a Jesuit, or of any gentleman, about to commit a deliberate deeply planned murder, is to secure an alibi. Le Fevre did not, or, when questioned (on Mr. Pollock's theory) by Bedloe, he would have put him off with his alibi. Again, 'a Jesuit,' 'the Queen's confessor,' does not do his murders in the Queen's house: no gentleman does. But, if Le Fevre did commit this solecism, he would have told Bedloe a different story; if he confessed to him at all. These things are elementary.

Prance's confession, as to the share of Hill, Berry, and Green in the murder, was admittedly false. On one point he stumbled always: 'Were there no guards at the usual places at the time of the carrying on this work?' he was asked by one of the Lords on December 24,1678. He mumbled, 'I did not take notice of any.'*

He never, on later occasions, could answer this question about the sentries. Prance saw no sentries, and there is nowhere any evidence that the sentries were ever asked whether they saw either Prance, Le Fevre, or Godfrey, in Somerset House or the adjacent Somerset Yard, on October 12. They were likely to know both the Queen's silversmith and 'the Queen's confessor,' and Godfrey they may have known. Prance and the sentries had, for each other, the secret of fern-seed, they walked invisible. This, of itself, is fatal to Prance's legend.

* Lords' Journals, xiii. p. 438.

No sooner had Prance confessed than he withdrew his confession. He prayed to be taken before the King, knelt, and denied all. Next day he did the same before the Council. He was restored to his pleasant quarters in Newgate, and recanted his recantation. He again withdrew, and maintained that his confession was false, before King and Council (December 30), 'He knows nothing in the world of all he has said.' The Lord Chancellor proposed 'to have him have the rack.'*

* State Papers, Domestic, Charles II., Dec. 30, 1678, Bundle 408.

Probably he 'did not have the rack,' but he had the promise of it, and nearly died of cold, ironed, in the condemned cell. 'He was almost dead with the disorder in his mind, and with cold in his body,' said Dr. Lloyd, who visited him, to Burnet. Lloyd got a bed and a fire for the wretch, who revived, and repeated his original confession.* Lloyd believed in his sincerity, says Burnet, writing many years later. In 1686, Lloyd denied that he believed.

* Burnet, ii. p. 773.

Prance's victims, Hill, Berry, and Green, were tried on February 5, 1679. Prance told his story. On one essential point he professed to know nothing. Where was Godfrey from five to nine o'clock, the hour when he was lured into Somerset House? He was dogged in fields near Holborn to somewhere unknown in St. Clement's. It is an odd fact that, though at the dinner hour, one o'clock, close to his own house, and to that of Mr. Welden (who had asked him to dine), Sir Edmund seems to have dined nowhere. Had he done so, even in a tavern, he must have been recognised. Probably Godfrey was dead long before 9 P.M. Mr. Justice Wild pressed Prance on this point of where Godfrey was; he could say nothing.* Much evidence (on one point absurd) was collected later by L'Estrange, and is accepted by North in his 'Examen,' to prove that, by some of his friends, Godfrey was reckoned 'missing' in the afternoon of the fatal Saturday.** But no such evidence was wanted when Hill, Berry, and Green were tried.*** The prosecution, with reckless impudence, mingled Bedloe's and Prance's contradictory lies, and accused Bedloe's 'Jesuits,' Walsh and Le Fevre, in company with Prance's priests, Gerald and Kelly.**** Bedloe, in his story before the jury, involved himself in even more contradictory lies than usual. but, even now, he did not say anything that really implicated the men accused by Prance, while Prance said not a word, in Court or elsewhere, about the men accused by Bedloe.*****

* State Trials, vii. 177.

** This is said in 1681 in A Letter to Miles Prance.

*** North, Examen, p. 201.

**** State Trials, vii, 178 (Speech of Serjeant Stringer).

***** Ibid. vii. 179 183.

Lord Chief Justice Scroggs actually told the jury that 'for two witnesses to agree as to many material circumstances with one another, that had never conversed together, is impossible. . . .They agree so in all things.'* The two witnesses did not agree at all, as we have abundantly seen, but, in the fury of Protestant fear, any injustice could be committed, and every kind of injustice was committed at this trial. Prance later pleaded guilty on a charge of perjury, and well he might. Bedloe died, and went to his own place with lies in his mouth.

* State Trials, vii. 216.

5.

If I held a brief against the Jesuits, I should make much of a point which Mr. Pollock does not labour. Just about the time when Prance began confessing, in London, December 24, 1678, one Stephen Dugdale, styled 'gentleman,' was arrested in Staffordshire, examined, and sent up to town. He was a Catholic, and had been in Lord Aston's service, but was dismissed for dishonesty. In the country, at Tixall, he knew a Jesuit named Evers, and through Evers he professed to know much about the mythical plot to kill the King, and the rest of the farrago of lies. At the trial of the five Jesuits, in June 1679, Dugdale told what he had told privately, under examination, on March 21, 1679.* This revelation was that Harcourt, a Jesuit, had written from town to Evers, a Jesuit at Tixall, by the night post of Saturday, October 12, 1678, 'This very night Sir Edmundbury (sic) Godfrey is dispatched.' The letter reached Tixall by Monday, October 14.

* Fitzherbert MSS; State Trials, vii. 338.

Mr. Pollock writes: 'Dugdale was proved to have spoken on Tuesday, October 15, 1678, of the death of a justice of the peace in Westminster, which does not go far.'* But if this is PROVED, it appears to go all the way; unless we can explain Dugdale's information without involving the guilty knowledge of Harcourt. The proof that Dugdale, on Tuesday, October 15, spoke at Tixall of Godfrey's death, two days before Godfrey's body was found near London, stands thus: at the trial of the Jesuits a gentleman, Chetwyn, gave evidence that, on the morning of Tuesday, October 15, a Mr. Sanbidge told him that Dugdale had talked at an alehouse about the slaying of a justice of peace of Westminster. Chetwyn was certain of the date, because on that day he went to Litchfield races. At Litchfield he stayed till Saturday, October 19, when he heard from London of the discovery of Godfrey's body.** Chetwyn asked Dugdale about this, when Dugdale was sent to town, in December 1678. Dugdale said he remembered the facts, but, as he did not report them to his examiners (a singular omission), he was not called as a witness at the trial of Berry, Green, and Hill. Chetwyn later asked Dugdale why he was not called, and said: 'Pray let me see the copy of your deposition sworn before the Council. He showed it me, and there was not a syllable of it, that I could see, BUT AFTERWARDS IT APPEARED TO BE THERE.'

* Pollock, p. 341, note 2.

** State Trials, vii. 339, 341,

Lord Chief Justice. 'That is not very material, if the thing itoolf bo true. '

Chetwyn. 'But its not being there made me remember it.'

Its later appearance, 'there,' shows how depositions were handled!

Chetwyn, in June 1679, says that he heard of Dugdale's words as to the murder, from Mr. Sanbidge, or Sambidge, or Sawbridge. At the trial of Lord Stafford (1680) Sanbidge 'took it upon his salvation' that Dugdale told him nothing of the matter, and vowed that Dugdale was a wicked rogue.* Mr. Wilson, the parish clergyman of Tixall, was said to have heard Dugdale speak of Godfrey's death on October 14. He also remembered no such thing. Hanson, a running-man, heard Dugdale talk of the murder of a justice of the peace at Westminster as early as the morning of Monday, October 14, 1678: the London Saturday post arrived at Tixall on Monday morning. Two gentlemen, Birch and Turton, averred that the news of the murder 'was all over the country' near Tixall, on Tuesday, October 15; but Turton was not sure that he did not hear first of the fact on Friday, October 18, which, by ordinary post from London, was impossible.

* State Trials, vii. 1406.

Such was the evidence to show that Dugdale spoke of Godfrey's death, in the country, two or three days before Godfrey's body was found. The fact can scarcely be said to be PROVED, considering the excitement of men's minds, the fallacies of memory, the silence of Dugdale at his first examination before the Council, Sanbidge's refusal to corroborate Chetwyn, and Wilson's inability to remember anything about a matter so remarkable and so recent. To deny, like Sanbidge, to be unable to remember, like Wilson, demanded some courage, in face of the frenzied terror of the Protestants. Birch confessedly took no notice of the rumour, when it first reached him, but at the trial of Green, Berry, and Hill, 'I told several gentlemen that I did perfectly remember before Thursday it was discoursed of in the country by several gentlemen where I lived.'* The 'several gentlemen' whom Birch 'told' were not called to corroborate him. In short, the evidence seems to fall short of demonstrative proof.

* State Trials. vii. 1455.

But, if it were all true, L'Estrange (and a writer who made the assertion in 1681) collected a good deal of evidence* to show that a rumour of Godfrey's disappearance, and probable murder by bloody Papists, was current in London on the afternoon of the day when he disappeared, Saturday, October 12.*** Mr. Pollock says that the evidence is 'not to be relied on,' and part of it, attributing the rumour to Godfrey's brothers, is absurd. THEY were afraid that Godfrey had killed himself, not that he was murdered by Papists. That 'his household could not have known that he would not return,' is not to the point. The people who raised the rumour were not of Godfrey's household. Nor is it to the point, exactly, that, being invited to dine on Saturday by Mr. Welden, who saw him on Friday night, 'he said he could not tell whether he should.'** For Wynell had expected to dine with him at Welden's to talk over some private business about house property.*** Wynell (the authority for Godfrey's being 'master of a dangerous secret') did expect to meet Godfrey at dinner, and, knowing the fears to which Godfrey often confessed, might himself have originated, by his fussy inquiries, the rumour that Sir Edmund was missing. The wild excitement of the town might add 'murdered by Papists,' and the rumour might really get into a letter from London of Saturday night, reaching Tixall by Monday morning. North says: 'It was in every one's mouth, WHERE IS GODFREY? HE HAS NOT BEEN AT HIS HOUSE ALL THIS DAY, THEY SAY HE IS MURDERED BY THE PAPISTS.'**** That such a pheemee^ might arise is very conceivable. In all probability the report which Bishop Burnet and Dr. Lloyd heard of the discovery of Godfrey's body, before it was discovered, was another rumour, based on a lucky conjecture. It is said that the report of the fall of Khartoum was current in Cairo on the day of the unhappy event. Rumour is correct once in a myriad times, and, in October 1678, London was humming with rumours. THIS report might get into a letter to Tixall, and, if so, Dugdale's early knowledge is accounted for; if knowledge he had, which I have shown to be disputable.

* Letter to Miles Prance, March, 1681. L'Estrange, Brief History, iii. pp. 195-201.

** Lords' MSS., p. 48; Pollock, p. 93, and note 2.

*** L'Estrange, Brief History, iii. pp. 188, 190, 195.

**** Examen, p. 201. Anglicised version of the author's original Greek text.

Dugdale's talk was thought, at the time, to clinch the demonstration that the Jesuits were concerned in Godfrey's murder, L'Estrange says, and he brings in his witnesses to prove, that the London rumour existed, and could reach the country by post. In fact, Chetwyn, on the evidence of Sanbidge, suggested this improvement of his original romance to Dugdale, and Sanbidge contradicted Chetwyn. He knew nothing of the matter. Such is the value of the only testimony against the Jesuits which deserves consideration.

We do not propose to unriddle this mystery, but to show that the most recent and industrious endeavour to solve the problem is unsuccessful. We cannot deny that Godfrey may have been murdered to conceal Catholic secrets, of which, thanks to his inexplicable familiarity with Coleman, he may have had many. But we have tried to prove that we do not KNOW him to have had any such Catholic secrets, or much beyond Oates's fables; and we have probably succeeded in showing that against the Jesuits, as Sir Edmund's destroyers, there is no evidence at all.

Had modern men of science, unaffected by political and religious bias, given evidence equivalent to that of the two surgeons, one might conceive that Godfrey was probably slain, as Macaulay thought, by hotheaded Catholics. But I confess to a leaning in favour of the picture of Godfrey sketched by L'Estrange; of the man confessing to hereditary melancholy; fretted and alarmed by the tracasseries and perils of his own position, alarming his friends and endangering himself by his gloomy hints; settling, on the last night of his life (Friday, October 11), with morbid anxiety, some details of a parish charity founded by himself; uncertain as to whether he can dine with Welden (at about one) next day; seen at that very hour near his own house, yet dining nowhere; said to have roamed, before that hour, to Paddington Woods and back again; seen vaguely, perhaps, wandering near Primrose Hill in the afternoon, and found dead five days later in the bush covered ditch near Primrose Hill, his own sword through his breast and back, his body in the attitude of one who had died a Roman death.

Between us and that conclusion - suicide caused by fear - nothing stands but the surgical evidence, and the grounds of that evidence are disputed.

Surgical evidence, however, is a fact 'that winna ding,' and I do not rely on the theory of suicide. But, if Godfrey was murdered by Catholics, it seems odd that nobody has suggested, as the probable scene, the Savoy, which lay next on the right to Somerset Yard. The Savoy, so well described by Scott in Peveril of the Peak, and by Macaulay, was by this time a rambling, ruinous, labyrinth of lanes and dilapidated dwellings, tenanted by adventurers and skulking Catholics. It was an Alsatia, says Macaulay, more dangerous than the Bog of Allen, or the passes of the Grampians. A courageous magistrate might be lured into the Savoy to stop a fight, or on any similar pretence; and, once within a rambling old dwelling of the Hospital, would be in far greater peril than in the Queen's guarded residence. Catholic adventurers might here destroy Godfrey, either for his alleged zeal, or to seize his papers, or because he, so great a friend of Catholics as he was, might know too much. The body could much more easily be removed, perhaps by water, from the Savoy, than from the guarded gates of Somerset House. Oates knew the Savoy, and said falsely that he had met Coleman there.* If murder was done, the

Savoy was as good a place for the deed as the Forest of Bondy.

* State Trials, vii. 28.

*　*　*

NOTE I.

CHARLES II. AND GODFREY'S DEATH.

The Duke of York, speaking of Bedloe's evidence before the Lords (November 8), says, 'Upon recollection the King remembered he was at Sommerset House himself, at the very time he swore the murder was committed: . . . his having been there at that time himself, made it impossible that a man should be assaulted in the Court, murder'd, and hurryd into the backstairs, when there was a Centry at every door, a foot Company on the Guard, and yet nobody see or knew anything of it.* Now evidence was brought that, at 5 P.M. on Saturday, October 12, the Queen decided to be 'not at home.' But Bedloe placed the murder as early as 2 P.M., sometimes, and between two o'clock and five o'clock the King may, as the Duke of York says, have been at Somerset House. Reresby, in his diary, for November 21, 1678, says that the King told him on that day that he was 'satisfied' Bedloe had given false evidence as to Godfrey's murder. The Duke of York probably repeats the King's grounds for this opinion. Charles also knew that the room selected by Bedloe as the scene of the deed was impossible.

Life of James II, i. pp. 527, 528.

NOTE II.

PRANCE AND THE WHITE HOUSE CLUB.

The body of Godfrey was found in a ditch near the White House Tavern, and that tavern was used as a club by a set of Catholic tradesmen. Was Prance a member? The landlord, Rawson, on October 24, mentioned as a member 'Mr. PRINCE, a silversmith in Holborn.' Mr. PRANCE was a silversmith in Covent Garden. On December 21, Prance said that he had not seen Rawson for a year; he was asked about Rawson. The members of the club met at the White House during the sitting of the coroner's inquest there, on Friday, October 18. Prance, according to the author of 'A Letter to Miles Prance,' was present. He may have been a member, he may have known the useful ditch where Godfrey's corpse was found, but this does not rise beyond the value of conjecture.*

* Lords' MSS. pp. 46, 47, 51.

NOTE III.

THE JESUIT MURDERERS.

There is difficulty in identifying as Jesuits the 'Jesuits' accused by Bedloe. The chief is 'Father Le Herry,'* called 'Le Ferry' by Mr. Pollock and Mr. Foley. He also appears as Le Faire, Lee Phaire, Le Fere, but usually Le Fevre, in the documents. There really was a priest styled Le Fevre. A man named Mark Preston was accused of being a priest and a Jesuit. When arrested he declared that he was a married layman with a family. He had been married in Mr. Langhorne's rooms, in the Temple, by Le Fevre, a priest, in 1667, or, at least, about eleven years before 1678.** I cannot find that Le Fevre was known as a Jesuit to the English members of the Society. He is not in Oates's list of conspirators. He does not occur in Foley's 'Records,' vol. v., a very painstaking work. Nor would he be omitted because accused of a crime, rather he would be reckoned as more or less of a martyr, like the other Fathers implicated by the informers. The author of 'Florus Anglo-Bavaricus'*** names 'Pharius' (Le Phaire), 'Valschius' (Walsh), and 'Atkinsus,' as denounced by Bedloe, but clearly knows nothing about them. 'Atkinsus' is Mr. Pepys's clerk, Samuel Atkins, who had an alibi. Valschius is Walsh, certainly a priest, but not to be found in Foley's 'Records' as a Jesuit.

* Brit. Mus. Addit. MS. 11055, 245.

** Lords' Journals, xiii. 331, 332. Lords' MSS., p. 99.

*** Liege, 1685, p. 137.

That Le Fevre was the Queen's confessor I find no proof. But she had a priest named Ferrera, who might be confused with Le Faire.* He was accused of calling a waterman to help to take two persons down the river on November 6, 1678. He was summoned before the Lords, but we do not know that he came. Ferrera MAY have been the Queen's confessor, he was 'one of the Queen's priests.' In 1670 she had twenty-eight priests as chaplains; twelve were Portuguese Capuchins, six were Benedictines, two, Dominicans, and the rest seculars.** Mrs. Prance admitted that she knew 'Mr.

Le Phaire, and that he went for a priest.'*** Of Le Fevre, 'Jesuit' and 'Queens confessor,' I know no more.

* Lords' MSS., p. 49.

** Maziere Brady, Episcopal Succession in England, p. 124 (1876).

*** Lords' MSS p. 52.

It appears that Mr. Pollock's authority for styling Le Fevre 'the Queen's confessor' is a slip of information appended to the Coventry notes, in the Longleat MSS., on Bedloe's deposition of November 7.* I do not know the authority of the writer of the slip. It is admitted that the authority of a slip pinned on to a letter of Randolph's is not sufficient to prove John Knox to have been one of the Riccio conspirators. The same slip appears to style Charles Walsh a Jesuit of the household of Lord Bellasis. This Walsh is unknown to Foley.

* Pollock, pp. 155, 157, note 2, in each case.

As to Father Pritchard, a Jesuit, Bedloe, in the British Museum MS., accuses 'Penthard, a layman.' He develops into Pridgeot, a Jesuit.* Later he is Father Pritchard, S.J. There was such a Jesuit, and, according to the Jesuit Annual Letter of 1680, he passed sixteen years in the South Wales Mission, and never once went to London. In 1680 he died in concealment.** It is clear that if Le Fevre was the Queen's confessor, the sentries at Somerset House could prove whether he was there on the day of Godfrey's murder. No such evidence was adduced. But if Le Fevre was not the Queen's confessor, he would scarcely have facilities for smuggling a dead body out of 'a private door. '

* Longleat MS., Pollock, p. 386.

** Foley, v. 875-877

IV.

THE FALSE JEANNE D'ARC.

Who that ever saw Jeanne d'Arc could mistake her for another woman? No portrait of the Maid was painted from the life, but we know the light perfect figure, the black hair cut short like a soldier's, and we can imagine the face of her, who, says young Laval, writing to his mother after his first meeting with the deliverer of France, 'seemed a thing all divine.' Yet even two of her own brothers certainly recognised another girl as the Maid, five years after her death by fire. It is equally certain that, eight years after the martyrdom of Jeanne, an impostor dwelt for several days in Orleans, and was there publicly regarded as the heroine who raised the siege in 1429. Her family accepted the impostor for sixteen years. These facts rest on undoubted evidence.

To unravel the threads of the story is a task very difficult. My table is strewn with pamphlets, papers, genealogies, essays; the authors taking opposite sides as to the question, Was Jeanne d'Arc burned at Rouen on May 30, 1431? Unluckily even the most exact historians (yea, even M. Quicherat, the editor of the five volumes of documents and notices about the Maid) (1841-1849) make slips in dates, where dates are all important. It would add confusion if we dwelt on these errors, or on the bias of the various disputants.

Not a word was said at the Trial of Rehabilitation in 1452-1456 about the supposed survival of the Maid. But there are indications of the inevitable popular belief that she was not burned. Long after the fall of Khartoum, rumours of the escape of Charles Gordon were current; even in our own day people are loth to believe that their hero has perished. Like Arthur he will come again, and from Arthur to James IV. of Scotland, from James IV. to the Duke of Monmouth, or the son of Louis XVI., the populace believes and hopes that its darling has not perished. We destroyed the Mahdi's body to nullify such a belief, or to prevent worship at his tomb. In the same way, at Rouen, 'when the Maid was dead, as the English feared that she might be said to have escaped, they bade the executioner rake back the fire somewhat that the bystanders might see her dead.'* An account of a similar precaution, the fire drawn back after the Maid's robes were burned away, is given in brutal detail by the contemporary diarist (who was not present), the Bourgeois de Paris.**

* Quicherat, iii. p. 191. These lines are not in MS. 5970. M. Save, in Jehanne des Armoises, Pucelle d'Orleans, p. 6 (Nancy, 1893), interpolates, in italics, words of his own into his translation of this text, which improve the force of his argument!

** Quicherat, iv. p. 471.

In spite of all this, the populace, as reflected in several chronicles, was uncertain that Jeanne had died. A 'manuscript in the British Museum' says: 'At last they burned her, or another woman like her, on which point many persons are, and have been, of different opinions.'*

* Save, p. 7, citing Bibliotheque de l'Ecole des Chartes, ii., Second Series.

This hopeful rumour of the Maid's escape was certain to arise, populus vult decipi.

Now we reach a point at which we may well doubt how to array the evidence. But probably the best plan is first to give the testimony of undoubted public documents from the Treasury Accounts of the town of Orleans. In that loyal city the day of the Maid's death had been duly celebrated by religious services; the Orleanese had indulged in no illusions. None the less on August 9, 1436, the good town pays its pursuivant, Fleur-de-lys, 'because he had brought letters to the town FROM JEHANNE LA PUCELLE'! On August 21 money is paid to 'Jehan du Lys, brother of Jehanne la Pucelle,' because he has visited the King, Charles VII., is returning to his sister, the Maid, and is in want of cash, as the King's order given to him was not fully honoured. On October 18 another pursuivant is paid for a mission occupying six weeks. He has visited the Maid at Arlon in Luxembourg, and carried letters from her to the King at Loches on the Loire. Earlier, in August, a messenger brought letters from the Maid, and went on to Guillaume Belier, bailiff of Troyes, in whose house the real Maid had lodged, at Chinon, in the dawn of her mission, March 1429. Thus the impostor was dealing, by letters, with some of the people who knew the Maid best, and was freely accepted by her brother Jehan.*

* Quicherat, v. pp. 326-327.

For three years the account-books of Orleans are silent about this strange Pucelle. Orleans has not seen her, but has had Jeanne's brother's word for her reappearance, and the word, probably, of the pursuivants sent to her. Jeanne's annual funeral services are therefore discontinued.

Mention of her in the accounts again appears on July 18, 1439. Money is now paid to Jaquet Leprestre for ten pints and a chopine of wine given to DAME JEHANNE DES ARMOISES. On the 29th, 30th, and on August 1, when she left the town, entries of payments for quantities of wine and food for Jehanne des Armoises occur, and she is given 210 livres 'after deliberation with the town council,' 'for the good that she did to the said town during the siege of 1429.'

The only Jehanne who served Orleans in the siege was Jehanne d'Arc. Here, then, she is, as Jehanne des Armoises, in Orleans for several days in 1439, feasted and presented with money by command of the town council. Again she returns and receives 'propine' on September 4.* The Leprestre who is paid for the wine was he who furnished wine to the real Maid in 1429.

* Quicherat, v. pp. 331-332.

It is undeniable that the people of Orleans must have seen the impostor in 1439, and they ceased to celebrate service on the day of the true Maid's death. Really it seems as if better evidence could not be that Jeanne des Armoises, nee Jeanne d'Arc, was alive in 1439. All Orleans knew the Maid, and yet the town council recognised the impostor.

She is again heard of on September 27, 1439, when the town of Tours pays a messenger for carrying to Orleans letters which Jeanne wrote to the King, and also letters from the bailli of Touraine to the King, concerning Jeanne. The real Jeanne could not write, but the impostor, too, may have employed a secretary.*

* Quicherat, v. p. 332.

In June 1441 Charles VII. pardoned, for an escape from prison, one de Siquemville, who, 'two years ago or thereabouts' (1439), was sent by the late Gilles de Raiz, Marechal de France, to take over the leadership of a commando at Mans, which had hitherto been under 'UNE APPELEE JEHANNE, QUI SE DISOIT PUCELLE.'* The phrase 'one styled Jehanne who called herself Pucelle' does not indicate fervent belief on the part of the King. Apparently this Jeanne went to Orleans and Tours after quitting her command at Mans in 1439. If ever she saw Gilles de Raiz (the notorious monster of cruelty) in 1439, she saw a man who had fought in the campaigns of the true Maid under her sacred banner, argent a dove on an azure field.**

* Quicherat, v. p. 333.

** She never used the arms given to her and her family by Charles VII.

Here public documents about the impostor fall silent. It is not known what she was doing between August 9, 1436, and September 1439. At the earlier date she had written to the town of Orleans; at the later, she was writing to the King, from Tours. Here an error must be avoided. According to the author of the 'Chronicle of the Constable of Alvaro de Luna,'* the impostor was, in 1436, sending a letter, and ambassadors, to the King of Spain, asking him to succour La Rochelle. The ambassadors found the King at Valladolid, and the

Constable treated the letter, 'as if it were a relic, with great reverence.'

* Madrid, 1784, p. 131.

The impostor flies high! But the whole story is false.

M. Quicherat held at first that the date and place may be erroneously stated, but did not doubt that the False Pucelle did send her ambassadors and letter to the King of Spain. We never hear that the true Maid did anything of the sort. But Quicherat changed his mind on the subject. The author of the 'Chronicle of Alvaro de Luna' merely cites a Coronica de la Poncella. That coronica, says Quicherat later, 'is a tissue of fables, a romance in the Spanish taste,' and in this nonsense occurs the story of the embassy to the Spanish King. That story does not apply to the False Pucelle, and is not true, a point of which students of Quicherat's great work need to be warned; his correction may escape notice.*

* Revue des Questions Historiques, April 1, 1881, pp. 553-566. Article by the Comte de Puymaigre.

We thus discard a strong trump in the hand of believers that the impostor was the real Maid; had a Pucelle actually sent ambassadors to Spain in 1436, their case would be stronger than it is.

Next, why is the false Pucelle styled 'Jeanne des Armoises' in the town accounts of Orleans in 1439?

This leads us to the proofs of the marriage of the false Pucelle, in 1436, with a Monsieur Robert des Armoises, a gentleman of the Metz country. The evidence is in a confused state. In the reign of Louis XIV. lived a Pere Vignier, a savant, who is said to have been a fraudulent antiquary. Whether this be true or not, his brother, after the death of Pere Vignier, wrote a letter to the Duc de Grammont, which was published in the 'Mercure Galant' of November, 1683 The writer says that his brother, Pere Vignier, found, at Metz, an ancient chronicle of the town, in manuscript, and had a copy made by a notary royal. The extract is perfectly genuine, whatever the reputation of the discoverer may be. This portion of the chronicle of the doyen of Saint-Thibaud de Metz exists in two forms, of which the latter, whoever wrote it, is intended to correct the former.

In the earlier shape the author says that, on May 20, 1436, the Pucelle Jeanne came to Metz, and was met by her brothers, Pierre, a knight, and Jehan, an esquire. Pierre had, in fact, fought beside his sister when both he and she were captured, at Compiegne, in May 1430. Jehan, as we have already seen, was in attendance on the false Maid in August 1436.

According to the Metz chronicle, these two brothers of the Maid, on May 20, 1436, recognised the impostor for their sister, and the account-books of Orleans leave no doubt that Jehan, at least, actually did accept her as such, in August 1436, four months after they met in May. Now this lasting recognition by one, at least, of the brothers, is a fact very hard to explain.

M. Anatole France offers a theory of the easiest. The brothers went to Lorraine in May 1436, to see the pretender. 'Did they hurry to expose the fraud, or did they not think it credible, on the other hand, that, with God's permission, the Saint had risen again? Nothing could seem impossible, after all that they had seen. . . . They acted in good faith. A woman said to them, "I am Jeanne, your sister." They believed, because they wished to believe.' And so forth, about the credulity of the age.

The age was not promiscuously credulous. In a RESURRECTION of Jeanne, after death, the age did not believe. The brothers had never seen anything of the kind, nor had the town council of Orleans. THEY had nothing to gain by their belief, the brothers had everything to gain. One might say that they feigned belief, in the hope that 'there was money in it;' but one cannot say that about the people of Orleans who had to spend money. The case is simply a puzzle.*

* Anatole France, 'La Fausse Pucelle,' Revue de Famille, Feb. 15, 1891. I cite from the quotation by M. P. Lanery d'Arc in Deux Lettres (Beauvais, 1894), a brochure which I owe to the kindness of the author.

After displaying feats of horsemanship, in male attire, and being accepted by many gentlemen, and receiving gifts of horses and jewels, the impostor went to Arlon, in Luxembourg, where she was welcomed by the lady of the duchy, Elizabeth de Gorlitz, Madame de Luxembourg. And at Arlon she was in October 1436, as the town accounts of Orleans have proved. Thence, says the Metz chronicle, the 'Comte de Warnon-bourg'(?) took her to Cologne, and gave her a cuirass. Thence she returned to Arlon in Luxembourg, and there married the knight Robert des Hermoises, or Armoises, 'and they dwelt in their own house at Metz, as long as they would.' Thus Jeanne became 'Madame des Hermoises,' or 'Ermaises,' or, in the town accounts of Orleans, in 1439, 'des Armoises.'

So says the Metz chronicle, in one form, but, in another manuscript version, it denounces this Pucelle as an impostor, who especially deceived tous les plus grands. Her brothers, we read (the real Maid's brothers), brought her to the neighbourhood of Metz. She dwelt with Madame de Luxembourg, and married 'Robert des Armoize.'* The Pere Vignier's brother, in 1683, published the first, but not the second, of these two accounts in the 'Mercure Galant' for November.

* Quicherat, v. pp. 321-324, cf. iv. 321.

In or about 1439, Nider, a witch-hunting priest, in his Formicarium, speaks of a false Jeanne at Cologne, protected by Ulrich of Wirtemberg, (the Metz chronicle has 'Comte de Warnonbourg'), who took the woman to Cologne. The woman, says Nider, was a noisy lass, who came eating, drinking, and doing conjuring feats; the Inquisition failed to catch her, thanks to Ulrich's protection. She married a knight, and presently became the concubine of a priest in Metz.* This reads like a piece of confused gossip.

* Quicherat, v. pp. 324-325.

Vignier's brother goes on to say (1683) in the 'Mercure Galant,' that his learned brother found the wedding contract of Jeanne la Pucelle and Robert des Armoises in the charter chest of the M. des Armoises of his own day, the time of Louis XIV. The brother of Vignier had himself met the son of this des Armoises, who corroborated the fact. But 'the original copy of this ancient manuscript vanished, with all the papers of Pere Vignier, at his death.'

Two months later, in the spring of 1684, Vienne de

Plancy wrote to the 'Mercure Galant,' saying that 'the late illustrious brother' of the Duc de Grammont was fully persuaded, and argued very well in favour of his opinion, that the actual Pucelle did not die at Rouen, but married Robert des Armoises. He quoted a genuine petition of Pierre du Lys, the brother of the real Maid, to the Duc d'Orleans, of 1443. Pierre herein says he has warred 'in the company of Jeanne la Pucelle, his sister, jusqu'a son absentement, and so on till this hour, exposing his body and goods in the King's service.' This, argued M. de Grammont, implied that Jeanne was not dead; Pierre does not say, feue ma soeur, 'my late sister,' and his words may even mean that he is still with her. ('Avec laquelle, jusques a son absentement, ET DEPUIS JUSQUES A PRESENT, il a expose son corps.')*

* The petition is in Quicherat, v. pp. 212-214. For Vienne-Plancy see the papers from the Mercure Galant in Jeanne d'Arc n'a point ete brulee a Rouen (Rouen, Lanctin, 1872). The tract was published in 100 copies only.

Though no copy of the marriage contract of Jeanne and des Armoises exists, Quicherat prints a deed of November 7, 1436, in which Robert des Armoises and his wife, 'La Pucelle de France,' acknowledge themselves to be married, and sell a piece of land. The paper was first cited by Dom Calmet, among the documents in his 'Histoire de Lorraine.' It is rather under suspicion.

There seems no good reason, however, to doubt the authenticity of the fact that a woman, calling herself Jeanne Pucelle de France, did, in 1436, marry Robert des Armoises, a man of ancient and noble family.

Hence, in the town accounts of Tours and Orleans, after October 1436, up to September 1439, the impostor appears as 'Mme. Jehanne des Armoises.' In August 1436, she was probably not yet married, as the Orleans accounts then call her 'Jehanne la Pucelle,' when they send their pursuivants to her; men who, doubtless, had known the true Maid in 1429-1430. These men did not undeceive the citizens, who, at least till September 1439, accepted the impostor. There is hardly a more extraordinary fact in history. For the rest we know that, in 1436-1439, the impostor was dealing with the King by letters, and that she held a command under one of his marshals, who had known the true Maid well in 1429-1430.

It appears possible that, emboldened by her amazing successes, the false Pucelle sought an interview with Charles VII. The authority, to be sure, is late. The King had a chamberlain, de Boisy, who survived till 1480, when he met Pierre Sala, one of the gentlemen of the chamber of Charles VIII. De Boisy, having served Charles VII., knew and told Sala the nature of the secret that was between that king and the true Maid. That such a secret existed is certain. Alain Chartier, the poet, may have been present, in March 1429, when the Maid spoke words to Charles VII. which filled him with a spiritual rapture. So Alain wrote to a foreign prince in July 1429. M. Quicherat avers that Alain was present: I cannot find this in his letter.* Any amount of evidence for the 'sign' given to the King, by his own statement, is found throughout the two trials, that of Rouen and that of Rehabilitation. Dunois, the famous Bastard of Orleans, told the story to Basin, Bishop of Lisieux; and at Rouen the French examiners of the Maid vainly tried to extort from her the secret.** In 1480, Boisy, who had been used to sleep in the bed of

Charles VII., according to the odd custom of the time, told the secret to Sala. The Maid, in 1429, revealed to Charles the purpose of a secret prayer which he had made alone in his oratory, imploring light on the question of his legitimacy.*** M. Quicherat, no bigot, thinks that 'the authenticity of the revelation is beyond the reach of doubt.'****

* Quicherat, Apercus Nouveaux, p. 62. Proces, v. p. 133.

** For the complete evidence, see Quicherat, Apercus, pp. 61-66.

*** Quicherat, v. p. 280, iv. pp. 258, 259, another and ampler account, in a MS. of 1500. Another, iv. p. 271: MS. of the period of Louis XII.

**** Apercus, p. 60, Paris, 1850.

Thus there was a secret between the true Maid and Charles VII. The King, of course, could not afford to let it be known that he had secretly doubted whether he were legitimate. Boisy alone, at some later date, was admitted to his confidence.

Boisy went on to tell Sala that, ten years later (whether after 1429 or after 1431, the date of the Maid's death, is uncertain), a pretended Pucelle, 'very like the first,' was brought to the King. He was in a garden, and bade one of his gentlemen personate him. The impostor was not deceived, for she knew that Charles, having hurt his foot, then wore a soft boot. She passed the gentleman, and walked straight to the King, 'whereat he was astonished, and knew not what to say, but, gently saluting her, exclaimed, "Pucelle, my dear, you are right welcome back, in the name of God, who knows the secret that is between you and me.'" The false Pucelle then knelt, confessed her sin, and cried for mercy. 'For her treachery some were sorely punished, as in such a case was fitting.'*

* Quicherat, v. p. 281. There is doubt as to whether Boisy's tale does not refer to Jeanne la Feronne, a visionary. Varlet de Vireville, Charles VII., iii. p. 425, note 1.

If any deserved punishment, the Maid's brothers did, but they rather flourished and prospered, as time went on, than otherwise.

It appears, then, that in 1439-1441 the King exposed the false Pucelle, or another person, Jeanne la Feronne. A great foe of the true Maid, the diarist known as the Bourgeois de Paris, in his journal for August 1440, tells us that just then many believed that Jeanne had not been burned at Rouen. The gens d'armes brought to Paris 'a woman who had been received with great honour at Orleans' - clearly Jeanne des Armoises. The University and Parlement had her seized and exhibited to the public at the Palais. Her life was exposed; she confessed that she was no maid, but a mother, and the wife of a knight (des Armoises?). After this follows an unintelligible story of how she had gone on pilgrimage to Rome, and fought in the Italian wars.* Apparently she now joined a regiment at Paris, et puis s'en alla, but all is very vaguely recorded.

* Quicherat, v. pp. 334, 335; c.f. Lefevre-Pontalis, Les Sources Allemands, 113-115. Fontemoing, Paris, 1903.

The most extraordinary circumstance remains to be

told. Apparently the brothers and cousins of the true Maid continued to entertain and accept the impostor! We have already seen that, in 1443, Pierre du Lys, in his petition to the Duc d'Orleans, writes as if he did not believe in the death of his sister, but that may be a mere ambiguity of language; we cannot repose on the passage.

In 1476 a legal process and inquest was held as to the descendants of the brother of the mother of Jeanne d'Arc, named Voulton or Vouthon. Among other witnesses was Henry de Voulton, called Perinet, a carpenter, aged fifty-two. He was grandson of the brother of the mother of Jeanne d'Arc, his grand-maternal aunt. This witness declared that he had often seen the two brothers du Lys, Jehan and Pierre, with their sister, La Pucelle, come to the village of Sermaise and feast with his father. They always accepted him, the witness, as their cousin, 'in all places where he has been, conversed, eaten, and drunk in their company.' Now Perinet is clearly speaking of his associations with Jeanne and her brothers AFTER HE HIMSELF WAS A MAN GROWN. Born in 1424, he was only five years old when the Maid left Domremy for ever. He cannot mean that, as a child of five, he was always, in various places, drinking with the Maid and her brothers. Indeed, he says, taking a distinction, that in his early childhood - 'son jeune aage' - he visited the family of d'Arc, with his father, at Domremy, and saw the Maid, qui pour lors estoit jeune fille.*

* De Bouteiller et de Braux, Nouvelles Recherches sur la Famille de Jeanne d'Arc, Paris, 1879, pp. 8, 9.

Moreover, the next witness, the cure of Sermaise, aged fifty-three, says that, twenty-four years ago (in 1452), a young woman dressed as a man, calling herself Jeanne la Pucelle, used to come to Sermaise, and that, as he heard, she was the near kinswoman of all the Voultons, 'and he saw her make great and joyous cheer with them while she was at Sermaise.'* Clearly it was about this time, in or before 1452, that Perinet himself was conversant with Jehan and Pierre du Lys, and with their sister, calling herself La Pucelle.

* Op. cit. p. 11.

Again, Jehan le Montigueue, aged about seventy, deposed that, in 1449, a woman calling herself Jeanne la Pucelle came to Sermaise and feasted with the Voultons, as also did (but he does not say at the same time) the Maid's brother, Jehan du Lys.* Jehan du Lys could, at least, if he did not accept her, have warned his cousins, the Voultons, against their pretended kinswoman, the false Pucelle. But for some three years at least she came, a welcome guest, to Sermaise, matched herself against the cure at tennis, and told him that he might now say that he had played against la Pucelle de France. This news gave him the greatest pleasure.

* Op. cit. pp. 4,5, MM. de Bouteiller and de Graux do not observe the remarkable nature of this evidence, as regards the BROTHERS of the Maid; see their Preface, p. xxx.

Jehan Guillaume, aged seventy-six, had seen both the self-styled Pucelle and the real Maid's brothers at the house of the Voultons. He did not know whether she was the true Maid or not.

It is certain, practically, that this PUCELLE, so merry

at Sermaise with the brothers and cousins of the Maid, was the Jeanne des Armoises of 1436-1439. The du Lys family could not successively adopt TWO impostors as their sister! Again, the woman of circ. 1449-1452 is not a younger sister of Jeanne, who in 1429 had no sister living, though one, Catherine, whom she dearly loved, was dead.

We have now had glimpses of the impostor from 1436 to 1440, when she seems to have been publicly exposed (though the statement of the Bourgeois de Paris is certainly that of a prejudiced writer), and again we have found the impostor accepted by the paternal and maternal kin of the Maid, about 1449-1452. In 1452 the preliminary steps towards the Rehabilitation of the true Maid began, ending triumphantly in 1456. Probably the families of Voulton and du Lys now, after the trial began in 1452, found their jolly tennis-playing sister and cousin inconvenient. She reappears, NOT at Sermaise, in 1457. In that year King Rene (father of Margaret, wife of our Henry VI.) gives a remission to 'Jeanne de Sermaises.' M. Lecoy de la March, in his 'Roi Rene' (1875) made this discovery, and took 'Jeanne de Sermaises' for our old friend, 'Jeanne des Ermaises,' or 'des Armoises.' She was accused of 'having LONG called herself Jeanne la Pucelle, and deceived many persons who had seen Jeanne at the siege of Orleans.' She has lain in prison, but is let out, in February 1457, on a five years' ticket of leave, so to speak, 'provided she bear herself honestly in dress, and in other matters, as a woman should do.'

Probably, though 'at present the wife of Jean Douillet,' this Jeanne still wore male costume, hence the reference to bearing herself 'honestly in dress.' She acknowledges nothing, merely says that the charge of imposture lui a ete impose, and that she has not been actainte d'aucun autre vilain cas.* At this date Jeanne cruised about Anjou and the town of Saumur. And here, at the age of forty-five, if she was of the same age as the true Maid, we lose sight for ever of this extraordinary woman. Of course, if she was the genuine Maid, the career of La Pucelle de France ends most ignobly. The idea 'was nuts' (as the Elizabethans said) to a good anti-clerical Frenchman, M. Lesigne, who, in 1889, published 'La Fin d'une Legende.' There would be no chance of canonising a Pucelle who was twice married and lived a life of frolic.

* Lecoy de la Marche, Le Roi Rene, ii. 281-283, 1875.

A more serious and discreet scholar, M. Gaston Save, in 1893, made an effort to prove that Jeanne was not burned at Rouen.* He supposed that the Duchess of Bedford let Jeanne out of prison and bribed the two priests, Massieu and Ladvenu, who accompanied the Maid to the scaffold, to pretend that they had been with her, not with a substituted victim. This victim went with hidden face to the scaffold, le visage embronche, says Percival de Cagny, a retainer of Jeanne's 'beau duc,' d'Alencon.** The townspeople were kept apart by 800 English soldiers.*** The Madame de Luxembourg who entertained the impostor at Arlon (1436) was 'perhaps' the same as she who entertained the real Jeanne at Beaurevoir in 1430. Unluckily THAT lady died in November 1430!

* Jehanne des Armoises, Pucelle d'Orleans, Nancy, 1893.

** Quicherat, iv. 36.

*** Quicherat, ii. 14, 19.

However, the Madame de Luxembourg who entertained the impostor was aunt, by marriage, of the Duke of Burgundy, the true Maid's enemy, and she had means of being absolutely well informed, so the case remains very strange. Strange, too, it is that, in the records of payment of pension to the true Maid's mother, from the town of Orleans, she is 'mere de la Pucelle' till 1452, when she becomes 'mere de feue la Pucelle,' 'mother of the LATE Pucelle.' That is to say, the family and the town of Orleans recognised the impostor till, in 1452, the Trial of Rehabilitation began. So I have inferred, as regards the family, from the record of the inquest of 1476, which, though it suited the argument of M. Save, was unknown to him.

His brochure distressed the faithful. The Abbe, Dr. Jangen, editor of 'Le Pretre,' wrote anxiously to M. P. Lanery d'Arc, who replied in a tract already cited (1894). But M. Lanery d'Arc did not demolish the sounder parts of the argument of M. Save, and he knew nothing of the inquest of 1476, or said nothing. Then arose M. Lefevre Pontalis.* Admitting the merits of M. Save's other works, he noted many errors in this tract. For example, the fire at Rouen was raked (as we saw) more or less (admodum) clear of the dead body of the martyr. But would it be easy, in the circumstances, to recognise a charred corpse? The two Mesdames de Luxembourg were distinguished apart, as by Quicherat. The Vignier documents as to Robert des Armoises were said to be impostures. Quicherat, however, throws no doubt on the deed of sale by Jehanne and her husband, des Armoises, in November 1436. Many errors in dates were exposed. The difficulty about the impostor's reception in Orleans, was recognised, and it is, of course, THE difficulty. M. Lefevre de Pontalis, however, urges that her brothers are not said to have been with her, 'and there is not a trace of their persistence in their error after the first months of the imposture.' But we have traces, nay proofs, in the inquest of 1476. The inference of M Save from the fact that the Pucelle is never styled 'the late Pucelle,' in the Orleans accounts, till 1452, is merely declared 'inadmissible.' The fact, on the other hand, is highly significant. In 1452 the impostor was recognised by the family; but in that year began the Trial of Rehabilitation, and we hear no more of her among the du Lys and the Voultons. M. Lefevre Pontalis merely mentions the inquest of 1476, saying that the impostor of Sermaise (1449-1452) may perhaps have been another impostor, not Jeanne des Armoises. The family of the Maid was not capable, surely, of accepting TWO impostors, 'one down, the other come on'! This is utterly incredible.

* Le Moyen Age, June 1895.

In brief, the family of Jeanne, in 1436,1449-1452, were revelling with Jeanne des Armoises, accepting her, some as sister, some as cousin. In 1439 the Town Council of Orleans not only gave many presents of wine and meat to the same woman, recognising her as their saviour in the siege of 1429, but also gave her 210 livres. Now, on February 7, 1430, the town of Orleans had refused to give 100 crowns, at Jeanne's request, to Heliote, daughter of her Scottish painter, 'Heuves Polnoir.'* They said that they could not afford the money. They were not the people to give 210 livres to a self-styled Pucelle without examining her personally. Moreover, the impostor supped, in August 1439, with Jehan Luillier, who, in June, 1429, had supplied the true Maid with cloth, a present from Charles d'Orleans. He was in Orleans during the siege of 1429, and gave evidence as to the actions of the Maid at the trial in 1456.** This man clearly did not detect or expose the impostor, she was again welcomed at Orleans six weeks after he supped with her. These facts must not be overlooked, and they have never been explained. So there we leave the most surprising and baffling of historical mysteries. It is, of course, an obvious conjecture that, in 1436, Jehan and Pierre du Lys may have pretended to recognise the impostor, in hopes of honour and rewards such as they had already received through their connection with the Maid. But, if the impostor was unmasked in 1440, there was no more to be got in that way.*** While the nature of the arts of the False Pucelle is inscrutable, the evidence as to the heroic death of the True Maid is copious and deeply moving. There is absolutely no room for doubt that she won the martyr's crown at Rouen.

* Quicherat, v. 155.

** Quicherat, v. pp. 112,113,331, iii. p. 23.

*** By 1452, Pierre du Lys had un grand hotel opposite the Ile des Boeufs, at Orleans, given to him for two lives, by Charles d'Orleans, in 1443. He was also building a town house in Orleans, and the chevalier Pierre was no snob, for he brought from Sermaise his carpenter kinsman, Perinet de Voulton, to superintend the erection. Nouvelles Recherches, pp. 19, 20.

V.

JUNIUS AND LORD LYTTELTON'S GHOST

'Sir,' said Dr. Johnson, 'it is the most extraordinary thing that has happened in my day.'

The most extraordinary thing that had happened in Dr. Johnson's day was the 'warning' to the noble peer generally spoken of as 'the wicked Lord Lyttelton.' The Doctor went on thus: 'I heard it with my own ears from his uncle, Lord Westcote. I am so glad to have every evidence of the spiritual world that I am willing to believe it.' Dr. Adams replied, 'You have evidence enough - good evidence, which needs no support.' Dr. Johnson growled out, 'I like to have more!'

Thus the Doctor was willing to believe what it suited him to believe, even though he had the tale at third or fourth hand; for Lord Westcote was not with the wicked Lord Lyttelton at the time of his death, on November 27, 1779. Dr. Johnson's observations were made on June 12, 1784.

To Lord Westcote's narrative we shall return.

As a study in Russian scandal, and the growth and development of stories, this anecdote of Lord Lyttelton deserves attention. So first we must glance at the previous history of the hero. Thomas Lord Lyttelton was born, says Mr. Coulton (in the 'Quarterly Review,' No. 179, p. 111), on January 30, 1744.* He was educated at Eton, where Dr. Barnard thought his boyish promise even superior to that of Charles James Fox. His sketches of scenery in Scotland reminded Mrs. Montagu of the vigour of Salvator Rosa, combined with the grace of Claude Lorraine! At the age of nineteen, already affianced to Miss Warburton, he went on the Grand Tour, and excelled the ordinary model of young debauchery abroad. Mr. James Boswell found a Circe at Siena, Lyttelton found Circes everywhere. He returned to England in 1765; and that learned lady, Mrs. Carter, the translator of Epictetus, 'admired his talents and elegant manners, as much as she detested his vices.' In 1768 he entered the House of Commons, and, in his maiden speech, implored the Assembly to believe that America was more important than Mr. Wilkes (and Liberty). Unseated for bribery in January 1769, he vanished from the public view, more or less, for a season; at least he is rarely mentioned in memoirs, and Coulton thinks that young Lyttelton was now engaged - in what does the reader suppose? In writing 'The Letters of Junius'!**

* The writer was not Croker, but Mr. Coulton, 'a Kentish gentleman,' says Lockhart, February 7, 1851, to his daughter Charlotte.

** If Lyttelton went to Italy on being ejected from Parliament, as Mr. Rigg says he did in the 'Dictionary of National Biography,' Coulton's theory will be hard to justify.

He was clever enough; his rank was like that assumed as his own by Junius; his eloquence (as he proved later in the House of Lords) was vituperative enough; he shared some of Junius's hatreds, while he proclaimed, like Junius, that the country was going to the dogs. Just as Junius was ending his Letters, the prodigal, Thomas Lyttelton, returned to his father's house; and Chatham wrote to congratulate the parent (February 15, 1772). On May 12, 1772, Junius published his last letter in 'The Public Advertiser;' and on June 26 Mr. Lyttelton married a widow, a Mrs. Peach. He soon left his wife, and was abroad (with a barmaid) when his father died in 1773. In January 1774 he took his seat in the Lords. Though Fox thought him a bad man, his first speech was in favour of securing to authors a perpetual copyright in their own works. He repeated his arguments some months later; so authors, at least, have reason for judging him charitably.

Mr. Carlyle would have admired Lyttelton. His politics (at one juncture) were 'The Dictatorship for Lord Chatham'! How does this agree with the sentiments of Junius? In 1767-69 Junius had exhausted on Chatham his considerable treasury of insult. He is 'a lunatic brandishing a crutch,' 'so black a villain,' 'an abandoned profligate,' and he exhibits 'THE UPSTART INSOLENCE OF A DICTATOR!' This goes not well with Lyttelton's sentiments in 1774. True, but by that date (iii. 305) Junius himself had discovered 'that if this country can be saved, it must be saved by Lord Chatham's spirit, by Lord Chatham's abilities.' Lyttelton and Junius are assuredly both of them ruffianly, scandal-loving, inconsistent, and patrician in the manner of Catiline. So far, the likeness is close.

About America Lyttelton wavered. On the whole, he recognised the need of fighting; and his main idea was that, as fight we must, we should organise our forces well, and fight with our heads as well as with our hands. He disdained the policy of the ostrich. The Americans were in active rebellion; it could not be blinked. He praised Chatham while he opposed him. He was 'fighting for his own hand.' Ministers felt the advantage of his aid; they knew his unscrupulous versatility, and in November 1775 bought Lyttelton with a lucrative sinecure - the post of Chief Justice of Eyre beyond the Trent. Coulton calls the place 'honourable;' we take another view. Lyttelton was bought and sold, but no one deemed Lyttelton a person of scrupulous conscience.

The public prospects darkened, folly was heaped on folly, blunder on blunder, defeat on defeat. On April 24, 1779, Horace Walpole says that Lord Lyttelton 'has again turned against the Court on obtaining the Seals'* November 25, 1779, saw Lyttelton go boldly into Opposition. He reviewed the whole state of the empire. He poured out a torrent of invective. As to his sinecure, he said, 'Perhaps he might not keep it long.' 'The noble Lords smile at what I say!'

* Is this a slip, or misprint, for 'on NOT obtaining the Seals'?

They need not have smiled. He spoke on Thursday, November 25; on Saturday, November 27, the place in Eyre was vacant, and Lord Lyttelton was a dead man.

The reader will keep in mind these dates. On Thursday, November 25, 1779, the first day of the session, Lyttelton overflows in a volcanic speech against the Court. He announces that his place may soon be vacant. At midnight on November 27 he is dead.

On all this, and on the story of the ghostly 'warning' to Lord Lyttelton, delivered in the night of Wednesday, November 24, Coulton builds a political romance. In his view, Lyttelton, expelled from Parliament, lavished his genius and exuded his spleen in the 'Letters of Junius.' Taking his seat in the Lords, he fights for his own hand, is bought and muzzled, wrenches off his muzzle, blazes into a fierce attack on the wrongs which he is weary of witnessing, the hypocrisy which he is tired of sharing, makes his will, sets his house in order, plays one last practical joke by inventing the story of the ghostly warning, surrounds himself with dissolute company, and at midnight on November 27 deliberately fulfils his own prediction, and dies by his own hand. It is a tale creditable to Coulton's fancy. A patrician of genius, a wit, a profligate, in fatigue and despair, closes his career with a fierce harangue, a sacrilegious jest, a debauch, and a draught of poison, leaving to Dr. Johnson a proof of 'the spiritual world,' and to mankind the double mystery of Junius and of the Ghost.

As to the identity of Junius, remembering the warning of Lord Beaconsfield, 'If you wish to be a bore, take up the "Letters of Junius,"' we shall drop that enigma; but as to the alleged suicide of Lord Lyttelton, we think we can make that seem extremely improbable. Let us return to the course of events, as stated by Coulton and by contemporaries.

The warning of death in three days, says Coulton, occurred (place not given) on the night of November 24, 1779. He observes: 'It is certain that, on the morning after that very day' (November 25), 'Lord Lyttelton had related, not to one person alone, but to several, and all of them people of credit, the particulars of a strange vision which he said had appeared to him the preceding night.' On Thursday, the 25th, as we saw, he spoke in the Lords. On Friday, the 26th, he went down to his house at Epsom, Pitt Place, where his party, says Coulton, consisted of Mr. (later Lord) Fortescue, Captain (later Admiral) Wolsley, Mrs. Flood, and the Misses Amphlett. Now, the town had no kind of doubt concerning the nature of Lord Lyttelton's relations with two, if not three, of the Misses Amphlett. His character was nearly as bad, where women were concerned, as that of Colonel Charteris. But Walpole, writing to Mann on November 28 (the day after Lord Lyttelton's death), says: 'Lord Lyttelton is dead suddenly. SUDDENLY, in this country, is always at first construed to mean BY A PISTOL. . . The story given out is, that he looked ill, AND HAD SAID HE SHOULD NOT LIVE THREE DAYS; that, however, he had gone to his house at Epsom. . . with a caravan of nymphs; and on Saturday night had retired before supper to take rhubarb, returned, supped heartily, went into the next room again, and died in an instant.'

Nothing here of a dream or ghost. We only hear of a prophecy, by Lyttelton, of his death.

Writing to Mason on Monday, November 29, Walpole avers that Lord Lyttelton was 'attended only by four virgins, whom he had picked up in the Strand.' Here Horace, though writing from Berkeley Square, within two days of the fatal 27th, is wrong. Lord Lyttelton had the Misses Amphlett, Captain Wolsley, Mr. Fortescue, and Mrs. Flood with him. According to Walpole, he felt unwell on Saturday night (the 27th), 'went to bed, rung his bell in ten minutes, and in one minute after the arrival of his servant expired!' 'He had said on Thursday that he should die in three days, HAD DREAMT SO, and felt that it would be so. On Saturday he said, "If I outlive to-day, I shall go on;" but enough of him.'

Walpole speaks of a DREAM, but he soon has other, if not better, information. Writing to Mason on December 11, he says that ghost stories from the north will now be welcome. 'Lord Lyttelton's vision has revived the taste; though it seems a little odd that an APPARITION should despair of getting access to his Lordship's bed, in the shape of a young woman, without being forced to use the disguise of a robin-redbreast.' What was an apprehension or prophecy has become a dream, and the dream has become an apparition of a robin-redbreast and a young woman.

If this excite suspicion, let us hasten to add that we have undesigned evidence to Lord Lyttelton's belief that he had beheld an APPARITION - evidence a day earlier than the day of his death. Mrs. Piozzi (then Mrs. Thrale), in her diary of Sunday, November 28, writes: 'Yesterday a lady from Wales dropped in and said that she had been at Drury Lane on Friday night. "How," I asked, "were you entertained?" "Very strangely indeed! Not with the play, though, but the discourse of a Captain Ascough, who averred that a friend of his, Lord Lyttelton, has SEEN A SPIRIT, who has warned him that he will die in three days. I have thought of nothing else since."'

Next day, November 29, Mrs. Piozzi heard of Lord Lyttelton's death.*

* Notes and Queries. Series V., vol. ii. p. 508. December 26,1874.

Here is proof absolute that the story, with apparition, if not with robin, was current THE DAY BEFORE LORD LYTTELTON'S DECEASE.

Of what did Lord Lyttelton die?

'According to one of the papers,' says Coulton, vaguely, 'the cause of death was disease of the heart.' A brief 'convulsion' is distinctly mentioned, whence Coulton concludes that the disease was NOT cardiac. On December 7, Mason writes to Walpole from York: 'Suppose Lord Lyttelton had recovered the breaking of his blood-vessel!'

Was a broken blood-vessel the cause of death? or have we here, as is probable, a mere inference of Mason's?

Coulton's account is meant to lead up to his theory of suicide. Lord Lyttelton mentioned his apprehension of death 'somewhat ostentatiously, we think.' According to Coulton, at 10 P.M. on Saturday, Lord Lyttelton, looking at his watch, said: 'Should I live two hours longer, I shall jockey the ghost.' Coulton thinks that it would have been 'more natural' for him to await the fatal hour of midnight 'in gay company' than to go to bed before twelve. He finishes the tale thus: Lord Lyttelton was taking rhubarb in his bedroom; he sent his valet for a spoon, and the man, returning, found him 'on the point of dissolution.'

'His family maintained a guarded and perhaps judicious silence on the subject,' yet Lord Westcote spoke of it to Dr. Johnson, and wrote an account of it, and so did Lord Lyttelton's widow; while Wraxall, as we shall see, says that the Dowager Lady Lyttelton painted a picture of the 'warning' in 1780.

Harping on suicide, Coulton quotes Scott's statement in 'Letters on Demonology:' 'Of late it has been said, and PUBLISHED, that the unfortunate nobleman had determined to take poison.' Sir Walter gives no authority, and Coulton admits that he knows of none. Gloomy but commonplace reflections in the so-called 'Letters' of Lyttelton do not even raise a presumption in favour of suicide, which, in these very Letters, Lyttelton says that he cannot defend by argument.* That Lyttelton made his will 'a few weeks before his death,' providing for his fair victims, may be accounted for, as we shall see, by the threatening state of his health, without any notion of self-destruction. Walpole, in his three letters, only speaks of 'a pistol' as the common construction of 'sudden death;' and that remark occurs before he has heard any details. He rises from a mere statement of Lord Lyttelton's, that he is 'to die in three days,' to a 'dream' containing that assurance, and thence to apparitions of a young woman and a robin-redbreast. The appearance of that bird, by the way, is, in the folk-lore of Surrey, an omen of death. Walpole was in a position to know all current gossip, and so was Mrs. Piozzi.

* Coulton's argument requires him to postulate the authenticity of many, at least, of these Letters, which were given to the world by the author of 'Doctor Syntax.'

We now turn to a narrative nearly contemporary, that written out by Lord Westcote on February 13, 1780. Lord Westcote examined the eldest Miss Amphlett, Captain (later Admiral) Charles Wolsley, Mrs. Flood, Lord Lyttelton's valet, Faulkner, and Stuckey, the servant in whose arms, so to speak, Lord Lyttelton died. Stuckey was questioned (note this) in the presence of Captain Wolsley and of MR. FORTESCUE. The late Lord Lyttelton permitted the Westcote narrative to be published in 'Notes and Queries' (November 21, 1874). The story, which so much pleased Dr. Johnson, runs thus: -

On Thursday, November 25, Mrs. Flood and the three Misses Amphlett were residing at Lord Lyttelton's house in Hill Street, Berkeley Square. Who IS this Mrs. Flood? Frederick Flood (1741-1824) married LADY Julia Annesley in 1782. The wife of the more famous Flood suits the case no better: his wife was LADY F. M. Flood; she was a Beresford. (The 'Dictionary of National Biography' is responsible for these facts.) At all events, on November 25, at breakfast, in Hill Street, Lord Lyttelton told the young ladies and their chaperon that he had had an extraordinary DREAM.

He seemed to be in a room which a bird flew into; the bird changed into a woman in white, who told him he should die in three days.

He 'did not much regard it, because he could in some measure account for it; for that a few days before he had been with Mrs. Dawson, when a robin-redbreast flew into her room.' On the morning of Saturday he told the same ladies that he was very well, and believed he should 'BILK THE GHOST.' The dream has become an apparition! On that day - Saturday - he, with the ladies, Fortescue, and Wolsley, went to Pitt Place; he went to bed after eleven, ordered rolls for breakfast, and, in bed, 'died without a groan,' as his servant was disengaging him from his waistcoat. During dinner he had 'a rising in his throat' (a slight sickness), 'a thing which had often happened to him before.' His physician, Dr. Fothergill, vaguely attributed his death to the rupture of some vessel in his side, where he had felt a pain in summer.

From this version we may glean that Lord Lyttelton was not himself very certain whether his vision occurred when he was awake or asleep. He is made to speak of a 'dream,' and even to account for it in a probable way; but later he talks of 'bilking the GHOST.' The editor of 'Notes and Queries' now tries to annihilate this contemporary document by third-hand evidence, seventy years after date. In 1851 or 1852 the late Dowager Lady Lyttelton, Sarah, daughter of the second Earl Spencer, discussed the story with Mr. Fortescue, a son of the Mr. Fortescue who was at Pitt Place, and succeeded to the family title six years later, in 1785. The elder Mr. Fortescue, in brief, is said to have averred that he had heard nothing of the dream or prediction till 'some days after;' he, therefore, was inclined to disbelieve in it. We have demonstrated, however, that if Mr. Fortescue had heard nothing, yet the tale was all over the town before Lord Lyttelton died. Nay, more, we have contemporary proof that Mr. Fortescue HAD heard of the affair! Lyttelton died at midnight on the Saturday, November 27. In her diary for the following Tuesday (November 30), Lady Mary Coke says that she has just heard the story of the 'dream' from Lady Bute, who had it from Mr. Ross, WHO HAD IT FROM MR. FORTESCUE!* Mr. Fortescue, then, must have told the tale as early as the Monday after the fatal Saturday night. Yet in old age he seems to have persuaded himself that the tale came later to his knowledge. Some irrelevant, late, and fourth-hand versions will be found in 'Notes and Queries,' but they merely illustrate the badness of such testimony.

* See The Letters and Journals of Lady Mary Coke, iii. 85. Note - She speaks of 'a dream.'

One trifle of contemporary evidence may be added: Mrs. Delany, on December 9, 1779, wrote an account of the affair to her niece - here a bird turns into a woman.

In pursuit of evidence, it is a long way from 1780 to 1816. In November of that year, T. J. wrote from Pitt Place, Epsom, in 'The Gentleman's Magazine;' but his letter is dated 'January 6.' T. J. has bought Pitt Place, and gives 'a copy of a document in writing, left in the house' (where Lyttelton died) 'as an heirloom which may be depended on.' This document begins, 'Lord Lyttelton's Dream and Death (see Admiral Wolsley's account).'

But where IS Admiral Wolsley's account? Is it in the archives of Sir Charles Wolseley of Wolseley? Or is THIS (the Pitt Place document) Admiral Wolsley's account? The anonymous author says that he was one of the party at Pitt Place on November 27,1779, with 'Lord Fortescue,' 'Lady Flood,' and the two Misses Amphlett. Consequently this account is written after 1785, when Mr. Fortescue succeeded to his title. Lord Lyttelton, not long returned from Ireland, had been suffering from 'suffocating fits' in the last month. And THIS, not the purpose of suicide, was probably his reason for executing his will. 'While in his house in Hill Street, Berkeley Square, he DREAMT three days before his death he saw a bird fluttering, and afterwards a woman appeared in white apparel, and said, "Prepare to meet your death in three days." He was alarmed and called his servant. On the third day, while at breakfast with the above-named persons, he said, "I have jockeyed the ghost, as this is the third day.'" Coulton places this incident at 10 P.M. on Saturday, and makes his lordship say, 'In two hours I shall jockey the ghost.' 'The whole party set out for Pitt Place,' which contradicts Coulton's statement that they set out on Friday, but agrees with Lord Westcote's. 'They had not long arrived when he was seized with a usual fit. Soon recovered. Dined at five. To bed at eleven.' Then we hear how he rebuked his servant for stirring his rhubarb 'with a tooth-pick' (a plausible touch), sent him for a spoon, and was 'in a fit' on the man's return. 'The pillow being high, his chin bore hard on his neck. Instead of relieving him, the man ran for help: on his return found him dead.'

This undated and unsigned document, by a person who professes to have been present, is not, perhaps, very accurate in dates. The phrase 'dreamt' is to be taken as the common-sense way of stating that Lord Lyttelton had a vision of some sort. His lordship, who spoke of 'jockeying the GHOST,' may have believed that he was awake at the time, not dreaming; but no person of self-respect, in these unpsychical days, could admit more than a dream. Perhaps this remark also applies to Walpole's 'he dreamed.' The species of the bird is left in the vague.

Moving further from the event, to 1828, we find a book styled 'Past Feelings Renovated,' a reply to Dr. Hibbert's 'Philosophy of Apparitions.' The anonymous author is 'struck with the total inadequacy of Dr. Hibbert's theory.' Among his stories he quotes Wraxall's 'Memoirs.' In 1783, Wraxall dined at Pitt Place, and visited 'the bedroom where the casement window at which Lord Lyttelton asserted the DOVE appeared to flutter* was pointed out to me.' Now the

Pitt Place document puts the vision 'in Hill Street, Berkeley Square.' So does Lord Westcote. Even a bird cannot be in two places at once, and the 'Pitt Place Anonymous' does seem to know what he is talking about. Of course Lord Lyttelton MAY have been at Pitt Place on November 24, and had his dream there. He MAY have run up to Hill Street on the 25th and delivered his speech, and MAY have returned to Pitt Place on the Friday or Saturday.** But we have no evidence for this view; and the Pitt Place document places the vision in Hill Street. Wraxall adds that he has frequently seen a painting of bird, ghost, and Lord Lyttelton, which was executed by that nobleman's stepmother in 1780. It was done 'after the description given to her by the valet de chambre who attended him, to whom his master related all the circumstances.'

* It was a ROBIN in 1779.

** Coulton says Friday; the Anonymous says Saturday, with Lord Westcote.

Our author of 1828 next produces the narrative by Lord Lyttelton's widow, Mrs. Peach, who was so soon deserted. In 1828 she is 'now alive, and resident in the south-west part of Warwickshire.' According to Lady Lyttelton (who, of course, was not present), Lord Lyttelton had gone to bed, whether in Hill Street or Pitt Place we are not told. His candle was extinguished, when he heard 'a noise resembling the fluttering of a bird at his chamber window. Looking in the direction of the sound, he saw the figure of an unhappy female, whom he had seduced and deserted, and who, when deserted, had put a violent end to her own existence, standing in the aperture of the window from which the fluttering sound had proceeded. The form approached the foot of the bed: the room was preternaturally light; the objects in the chamber were distinctly visible. The figure pointed to a clock, and announced that Lord Lyttelton would expire AT THAT VERY HOUR (twelve o'clock) in the third day after the visitation.'

We greatly prefer, as a good old-fashioned ghost story, this version of Lady Lyttelton's. There is no real bird, only a fluttering sound, as in the case of the Cock Lane Ghost, and many other examples. The room is 'preternaturally light,' as in Greek and Norse belief it should have been, and as it is in the best modern ghost stories. Moreover, we have the raison d'etre of the ghost: she had been a victim of the Chief Justice in Eyre. The touch about the clock is in good taste. We did not know all that before.

But, alas! our author of 1828, after quoting the Pitt Place Anonymous, proceeds to tell, citing no named authority, that the ghost was that of Mrs. Amphlett, mother of the two Misses Amphlett, and of a third sister, in no way less distinguished than these by his lordship. Now a ghost cannot be the ghost of two different people. Moreover, Mrs. Amphlett lived (it is said) for years after. However, Mrs. Amphlett has the preference if she 'died of grief at the precise time when the female vision appeared to his lordship,' which makes it odd that her daughters should then have been revelling at Pitt Place under the chaperonage of Mrs. Flood. We are also informed (on no authority) that Lord Lyttelton 'acknowledged' the ghost to have been that of the injured mother of the three Misses Amphlett.

Let not the weary reader imagine that the catena of evidence ends here! His lordship's own ghost did a separate stroke of business, though only in the commonplace character of a deathbed wraith, or 'veridical hallucination.'

Lord Lyttelton had a friend, we learn from 'Past Feelings Renovated' (1828), a friend named Miles Peter Andrews. 'One night after Mr. Andrews had left Pitt Place and gone to Dartford,' where he owned powder-mills, his bed-curtains were pulled open and Lord Lyttelton appeared before him in his robe de chambre and nightcap. Mr. Andrews reproached him for coming to Dartford Mills in such a guise, at such a time of night, and, 'turning to the other side of the bed, rang the bell, when Lord Lyttelton had disappeared.' The house and garden were searched in vain; and about four in the afternoon a friend arrived at Dartford with tidings of his lordship's death.

Here the reader with true common sense remarks that this second ghost, Lord Lyttelton's own, does not appear in evidence till 1828, fifty years after date, and then in an anonymous book, on no authority. We have permitted to the reader this opportunity of exercising his acuteness, while laying a little trap for him. It is not in 1828 that Mr. Andrews's story first appears. We first find it in December 1779 - that is, in the month following the alleged event. Mr. Andrews's experience, and the vision of Lord Lyttelton, are both printed in 'The Scots Magazine,' December 1779, p. 650. The account is headed 'A Dream,' and yet the author avers that Lord Lyttelton was wide awake! This illustrates beautifully the fact on which we insist, that 'dream' is eighteenth-century English for ghost, vision, hallucination, or what you will.

'Lord Lyttelton,' says the contemporary ' Scots

Magazine,' 'started up from a midnight sleep on perceiving a bird fluttering near the bed-curtains, which vanished suddenly when a female spirit in white raiment presented herself and prophesied Lord Lyttelton's death in three days. His death is attributed to convulsions while undressing.

The 'dream' of Mr. Andrews (according to 'The Scots Magazine' of December 1779)* occurred at Dartford in Kent, on the night of November 27. It represented Lord Lyttelton drawing his bed-curtains, and saying, 'It is all over,' or some such words.

*The magazine appeared at the end of December.

This Mr. Andrews had been a drysalter. He made a large fortune, owned the powder-mills at Dartford, sat in Parliament, wrote plays which had some success, and was thought a good fellow in raffish society. Indeed, the society was not always raffish. In 'Notes and Queries' (December 26, 1874) H. S. says that his mother, daughter of Sir George Prescott, often met Mr. Andrews at their house, Theobalds Park, Herts. He was extremely agreeable, and, if pressed, would tell his little anecdote of November 27, 1779.

This proof that the Andrews tale is contemporary has led us away from the description of the final scene, given in 'Past Feelings Renovated,' by the person who brought the news to Mr. Andrews. His version includes a trick played with the watches and clocks. All were set on half an hour; the valet secretly made the change in Lord Lyttelton's own timepiece. His lordship thus went to bed, as he thought, at 11.30, really at eleven o'clock, as in the Pitt Place document. At about twelve o'clock, midnight, the valet rushed in among the guests, who were discussing the odd circumstances, and said that his master was at the point of death. Lord Lyttelton had kept looking at his watch, and at a quarter past twelve (by his chronometer and his valet's) he remarked, 'This mysterious lady is not a true prophetess, I find.' The real hour was then a quarter to twelve. At about half-past twelve, by HIS watch, twelve by the real time, he asked for his physic. The valet went into the dressing-room to prepare it (to fetch a spoon by other versions), when he heard his master 'breathing very hard.' 'I ran to him, and found him in the agonies of death.'

There is something rather plausible in this narrative, corresponding, as it does, with the Pitt Place document, in which the valet, finding his master in a fit, leaves him and seeks assistance, instead of lowering his head that he might breathe more easily. Like the other, this tale makes suicide a most improbable explanation of Lord Lyttelton's death. The affair of the watches is dramatic, but not improbable in itself. A correspondent of 'The Gentleman's Magazine' (in 1815) only cites 'a London paper' as his authority. The writer of 'Past Feelings Renovated' (1828) adds that Mr. Andrews could never again be induced to sleep at Pitt Place, but, when visiting there, always lay at the Spread Eagle, in Epsom.

Let us now tabulate our results.

At Pitt Place, Epsom,
or Hill Street, Berkeley Square,
On November 24,
Lord Lyttelton
Dreamed of,
or saw,

A young woman and a robin.
A bird which became a woman.
A dove and a woman.
Mrs. Amphlett (without a dove or robin).
Some one else unknown.

In one variant, a clock and a preternatural light are thrown in, with a sermon which it were superfluous to quote. In another we have the derangement of clocks and watches. Lord Lyttelton's stepmother believed in the dove. Lady Lyttelton did without a dove, but admitted a fluttering sound.

For causes of death we have - heart disease (a newspaper), breaking of a blood-vessel (Mason), suicide (Coulton), and 'a suffocating fit' (Pitt Place document). The balance is in favour of a suffocating fit, and is against suicide. On the whole, if we follow the Pitt Place Anonymous (writing some time after the event, for he calls Mr. Fortescue 'Lord Fortescue'), we may conclude that Lord Lyttelton had been ill for some time. The making of his will suggests a natural apprehension on his part, rather than a purpose of suicide. There was a lively impression of coming death on his mind, but how it was made - whether by a dream, an hallucination, or what not - there is no good evidence to show.

There is every reason to believe, on the Pitt Place evidence, combined with the making of his will, that Lord Lyttelton had really, for some time, suffered from alarming attacks of breathlessness, due to what cause physicians may conjecture. Any one of these fits, probably, might cause death, if the obvious precaution of freeing the head and throat from encumbrances were neglected; and the Pitt Place document asserts that the frightened valet DID neglect it. Again, that persons under the strong conviction of approaching death will actually die is proved by many examples. Even Dr. Hibbert says that 'no reasonable doubt can be placed on the authenticity of the narrative' of Miss Lee's death, 'as it was drawn up by the Bishop of Gloucester' (Dr. William Nicholson) 'from the recital of the young lady's father,' Sir Charles Lee. Every one knows the tale. In a preternatural light, in a midnight chamber, Miss Lee saw a woman, who proclaimed herself Miss Lee's dead mother, 'and that by twelve o'clock of the day she should be with her.' So Miss Lee died in her chair next day, on the stroke of noon, and Dr. Hibbert rather heartlessly calls this 'a fortunate circumstance.'

The Rev. Mr. Fison, in 'Kamilaroi and Kurnai,' gives, from his own experience, similar tales of death following alleged ghostly warnings, among Fijians and Australian blacks. Lord Lyttelton's uneasiness and apprehension are conspicuous in all versions; his dreams had long been troubled, his health had caused him anxiety, the 'warning' (whatever it may have been) clinched the matter, and he died a perfectly natural death.

Mr. Coulton, omitting Walpole's statement that he 'looked ill,' and never alluding to the Pitt Place description of his very alarming symptoms, but clinging fondly to his theory of Junius, perorates thus: 'Not Dante, or Milton, or Shakespeare himself, could have struck forth a finer conception than Junius, in the pride of rank, wealth, and dignities, raised to the Council table of the sovereign he had so foully slandered - yet sick at heart and deeply stained with every profligacy - terminating his career by deliberate self-murder, with every accompaniment of audacious charlatanry that could conceal the crime.'

It is magnificent, it is worthy of Dante, or Shakespeare himself - but the conception is Mr. Coulton's.

We do not think that we have provided what Dr. Johnson 'liked,' 'evidence for the spiritual world.' Nor have we any evidence explanatory of the precise nature of Lord Lyttelton's hallucination. The problem of the authorship of the 'Junius Letters' is a malstrom into which we decline to be drawn.

But it is fair to observe that all the discrepancies in the story of the 'warning' are not more numerous, nor more at variance with each other, than remote hearsay reports of any ordinary occurrence are apt to be. And we think it is plain that, if Lord Lyttelton WAS Junius, Mr. Coulton had no right to allege that Junius went and hanged himself, or, in any other way, was guilty of self-murder.

VI.

THE MYSTERY OF AMY ROBSART

1. HISTORICAL CONFUSIONS AS TO EVENTS BEFORE AMY'S DEATH

Let him who would weep over the tribulations of the historical inquirer attend to the tale of the Mystery of Amy Robsart!

The student must dismiss from his memory all that he recollects of Scott's 'Kenilworth.' Sir Walter's chivalrous motto was 'No scandal about Queen Elizabeth,' 'tis blazoned on his title-page. To avoid scandal, he calmly cast his narrative at a date some fifteen years after Amy Robsart's death, brought Amy alive, and represented Queen Elizabeth as ignorant of her very existence. He might, had he chosen, have proved to his readers that, as regards Amy Robsart and her death, Elizabeth was in a position almost as equivocal as was Mary Stuart in regard to the murder of Darnley. Before the murder of Darnley we do not hear one word to suggest that Mary was in love with Bothwell. For many months before the death of Amy (Lady Robert Dudley), we hear constant reports that Elizabeth has a love affair with Lord Robert, and that Amy is to be divorced or murdered. When Darnley is killed, a mock investigation acquits Bothwell, and Mary loads him with honours and rewards. When Amy dies mysteriously, a coroner's inquest, deep in the country, is held, and no records of its proceedings can be found. Its verdict is unknown. After a brief tiff, Elizabeth restores Lord Robert to favour.

After Darnley's murder, Mary's ambassador in France implores her to investigate the matter with all diligence. After Amy's death, Elizabeth's ambassador in France implores her to investigate the matter with all diligence. Neither lady listens to her loyal servant, indeed Mary could not have pursued the inquiry, however innocent she might have been. Elizabeth could! In three months after Darnley's murder, Mary married Bothwell. In two months after Amy's death Cecil told (apparently) the Spanish ambassador that Elizabeth had married Lord Robert Dudley. But this point, we shall see, is dubious.

There the parallel ceases, for, in all probability, Lord Robert was not art and part in Amy's death, and, whatever Elizabeth may have done in private, she certainly did not publicly espouse Lord Robert. A Scot as patriotic as, but less chivalrous than, Sir Walter might, however, have given us a romance of Cumnor Place in which Mary would have been avenged on 'her sister and her foe.' He abstained, but wove a tale so full of conscious anachronisms that we must dismiss it from our minds.

Amy Robsart was the only daughter of Sir John Robsart and his wife Elizabeth, nee Scot, and widow of Roger Appleyard, a man of good old Norfolk family. This Roger Appleyard, dying on June 8, 1528, left a son and heir, John, aged less than two years. His widow, Elizabeth, had the life interest in his four manors, and, as we saw, she married Sir John Robsart, and by him became the mother of Amy, who had also a brother on the paternal side, Arthur Robsart, whether legitimately born or not.* Both these brothers play a part in the sequel of the mystery. Lord Robert Dudley, son of John, Duke of Northumberland, and grandson of the Dudley who, with Empson, was so unpopular under Henry VII., was about seventeen or eighteen when he married Amy Robsart - herself perhaps a year older - on June 4, 1550. At that time his father was Earl of Warwick; the wedding is chronicled in the diary of the child king, Edward VI.**

* Mr. Walter Rye in The Murder of Amy Robsart, Norwich and London, 1885, makes Arthur a bastard. Mr. Pettigrew, in An Inquiry into the Particulars connected with the Death of Amy Robsart (London, 1859), represents Arthur as legitimate.

** Mr. Rye dates the marriage in 1550. Rye, pp. 5, 36, cf. Edward VI.'s Diary, Clarendon Society. Mr. Froude cites the date, June 4, 1549, from Burnet's Collectanea, Froude, vi. p. 422, note 2 (1898), being misled by Old Style; Edward VI. notes the close of 1549 on March 24.

Amy, as the daughter of a rich knight, was (at least if we regard her brother Arthur as a bastard) a considerable heiress. Robert Dudley was a younger son. Probably the match was a family arrangement, but Mr. Froude says 'it was a love match.' His reason for this assertion seems to rest on a misunderstanding. In 1566-67, six years after Amy's death, Cecil drew up a list of the merits and demerits of Dudley (by that time Earl of Leicester) and of the Archduke Charles, as possible husbands of Elizabeth. Among other points is noted by Cecil, 'Likelihood to Love his Wife.' As to the Archduke, Cecil takes a line through his father, who 'hath been blessed with multitude of children.' As to Leicester, Cecil writes 'Nuptiae carnales a laetitia incipiunt, et in luctu terminantur' - 'Weddings of passion begin in joy and end in grief.' This is not a reference, as Mr. Froude thought, to the marriage of Amy and Dudley, it is merely a general maxim, applicable to a marriage between Elizabeth and Leicester. The Queen, according to accounts from all quarters, had a physical passion or caprice for Leicester. The marriage, if it occurred, would be nuptiae carnales, and as such, in Cecil's view, likely to end badly, while the Queen and the Archduke (the alternative suitor) had never seen each other and could not be 'carnally' affectionate.*

* Froude, ut supra, note 3.

We do not know, in short, whether Dudley and Amy were in love with each other or not. Their marriage, Cecil says, was childless.

Concerning the married life of Dudley and Amy very little is known. When he was a prisoner in the Tower under Mary Tudor, Amy was allowed to visit him. She lost her father, Sir John, in 1553. Two undated letters of Amy's exist: one shows that she was trusted by her husband in the management of his affairs (1556-57) and that both he and she were anxious to act honourably by some poor persons to whom money was due.* The other is to a woman's tailor, and, though merely concerned with gowns and collars, is written in a style of courteous friendliness.** Both letters, in orthography and sentiment, do credit to Amy's education and character. There is certainly nothing vague or morbid or indicative of an unbalanced mind in these poor epistles.

* Pettigrew, 14, note 1.

** Jackson, Nineteenth Century, March 1882, A Longleat MS.

When Elizabeth came to the throne (1558) she at once made Dudley Master of the Horse, a Privy Councillor, and a Knight of the Garter. His office necessarily caused him to be in constant attendance on the royal person, and the Knighthood of the Garter proves that he stood in the highest degree of favour.

For whatever reason, whether from distaste for Court life, or because of the confessed jealousy with which the Queen regarded the wives of her favourites - of all men, indeed - Amy did not come to Court. About 1558-59 she lived mainly at the country house of the Hydes of Detchworth, not far from Abingdon. Dudley seems to have paid several visits to the Hydes, his connections; this is proved by entries in his household books of sums of money for card-playing there.* It is also certain that Amy at that date, down to the end of 1559, travelled about freely, to London and many other places; that she had twelve horses at her service; and that, as late as March 1560 (when resident with Dudley's comptroller, Forster, at Cumnor Place) she was buying a velvet hat and shoes. In brief, though she can have seen but little of her husband, she was obviously at liberty, lived till 1560 among honourable people, her connections, and, in things material, wanted for nothing.** Yet Amy cannot but have been miserable by 1560. The extraordinary favour in which

Elizabeth held her lord caused the lewdest stories to spread among all classes, from the circle of the Court to the tattle of country folk in Essex and Devonshire.***

* Jackson, ut supra.

** For details see Canon Jackson's 'Amy Robsart,' Nineteenth Century, vol. xi. Canon Jackson used documents in the possession of the Marquis of Bath, at Longleat.

*** Cal. Dom. Eliz. p. 157, August 13, 1560; also Hatfield Calendar.

News of this kind is certain to reach the persons concerned.

Our chief authority for the gossip about Elizabeth and Dudley is to be found in the despatches of the Spanish ambassadors to their master, Philip of Spain. The fortunes of Western Europe, perhaps of the Church herself, hung on Elizabeth's marriage and on the succession to the English throne. The ambassadors, whatever their other failings, were undoubtedly loyal to Philip and to the Church, and they were not men to be deceived by the gossip of every gobemouche. The command of money gave them good intelligence, they were fair judges of evidence, and what they told Philip was what they regarded as well worthy of his attention. They certainly were not deceiving Philip.

The evidence of the Spanish ambassadors, as men concerned to find out the truth and to tell it, is therefore of the highest importance. They are not writing mere amusing chroniques scandaleuses of the court to which they are accredited, as ambassadors have often done, and what they hear is sometimes so bad that they decline to put it on paper. They are serious and wary men of the world. Unhappily their valuable despatches, now in 'the Castilian village of Simancas,' reach English inquirers in the most mangled and garbled condition. Major Martin Hume, editor of the Spanish Calendar (1892), tells us in the Introduction to the first volume of this official publication how the land lies. Not to speak of the partial English translation (1865) of Gonzales's partial summary of the despatches (Madrid, 1832) we have the fruits of the labours of Mr. Froude. He visited Simancas, consulted the original documents, and 'had a large number of copies and extracts made.' These extracts and transcripts Mr. Froude deposited in the British Museum. These transcripts, compared with the portions translated in Mr. Froude's great book, enable us to understand the causes of certain confusions in Amy Robsart's mystery. Mr. Froude practically aimed at giving the gist, as he conceived it, of the original papers of the period, which he rendered with freedom, and in his captivating style - foreign to the perplexed prolixity of the actual writers. But, in this process, points of importance might be omitted; and, in certain cases, words from letters of other dates appear to have been inserted by Mr. Froude, to clear up the situation. The result is not always satisfactory.

Next, from 1886 onwards, the Spanish Government published five volumes of the correspondence of Philip with his ambassadors at the English Court.* These papers Major Hume was to condense and edit for our official publication, the Spanish State Papers, in the series of the Master of the Rolls. But Major Hume found the papers in the Spanish official publication in a deplorably unedited state. Copyists and compositors 'seem to have had a free hand.' Major Hume therefore compared the printed Spanish texts, where he could, with Mr. Froude's transcripts of the same documents in the Museum, and the most important letter in this dark affair, in our Spanish Calendar, follows incorrectly Mr. Froude's transcript, NOT the original document, which is not printed in 'Documentos Ineditos.'** Thus, Major Hume's translation differs from Mr. Froude's translation, which, again, differs from Mr. Gairdner's translation of the original text as published by the Baron Kervyn de Lettenhove.***

* Documentos Ineditos para la Historia de Espana. Ginesta, Madrid, 1886.

** Spanish Calendar, vol. i. p. iv. Mr. Gairdner says, 'Major Hume in preparing his first volume, he informs me, took transcripts from Simancas of all the direct English correspondence,' but for letters between England and Flanders used Mr. Froude's transcripts. Gairdner, English Historical Review, January 1898, note 1.

*** Relations Politiques des Pays-Bas et de l'Anqleterre sous le Regne de Philippe II. vol. ii. pp. 529-533. Brussels, 1883. The amateur of truth, being now fully apprised of the 'hazards' which add variety to the links of history, turns to the Spanish Calendar for the reports of the ambassadors. He reaches April 18, 1559, when de Feria says: 'Lord Robert has come so much into favour that he does whatever he likes with affairs, and it is even said that her Majesty visits him in his chamber day and night. People talk of this so freely that they go so far as to say that his wife has a malady in one of her breasts and the Queen is only waiting for her to die to marry Lord Robert.'

De Feria therefore suggests that Philip might come to terms with Lord Robert. Again, on April 29, 1559, de Feria writes (according to the Calendar): 'Sometimes she' (Elizabeth) 'appears to want to marry him' (Archduke Ferdinand) 'and speaks like a woman who will only accept a great prince, and then they say she is in love with Lord Robert, and never lets him leave her.' De Feria has reason to believe that 'she will never bear children'*

Sp. Cal. i. pp. 57, 58, 63; Doc. Ineditos, 87, 171, 180.

Mr. Froude combines these two passages in one quotation, putting the second part (of April 29) first, thus: 'They tell me that she is enamoured of my Lord Robert Dudley, and will never let him leave her side. HE OFFERS ME HIS SERVICES IN BEHALF OF THE ARCH DUKE, BUT I DOUBT WHETHER IT WILL BE WELL TO USE THEM. He is in such favour that people say she visits him in his chamber day and night. Nay, it is even reported that his wife has a cancer on her breast, and that the Queen waits only till she die to marry him.'*

* Froude, vi. p. 199. De Feria to Philip, April 28 and April 29. MS. Simancas, cf. Documentos Ineditos, pp. 87, 171, 180, ut supra.

The sentence printed in capitals cannot be found by me in either of de Feria's letters quoted by Mr. Froude, but the sense of it occurs in a letter written at another date. Mr. Froude has placed, in his quotation, first a sentence of the letter of April 29, then a sentence not in either letter (as far as the Calendar and printed Spanish

Andrew Lang

documents show), then sentences from the letter of April 18. He goes on to remark that the marriage of Amy and Dudley 'was a love match of a doubtful kind,' about which we have, as has been shown, no information whatever. Such are the pitfalls which strew the path of inquiry.

One thing is plain, a year and a half before her death Amy was regarded as a person who would be 'better dead,' and Elizabeth was said to love Dudley, on whom she showered honours and gifts.

De Feria, in the summer of 1559, was succeeded as ambassador by de Quadra, bishop of Aquila. Dudley and his sister, Lady Sidney (mother of Sir Philip Sidney), now seemed to favour Spanish projects, but (November 13) de Quadra writes: 'I heard from a certain person who is accustomed to give veracious news that Lord Robert has sent to poison his wife. Certainly all the Queen has done with us and with the Swede, and will do with the rest in the matter of her marriage, is only keeping Lord Robert's enemies and the country engaged with words until this wicked deed of killing his wife is consummated.' The enemies of Dudley included the Duke of Norfolk, and most of the nation. There was talk of a plot to destroy both Dudley and the Queen. 'The Duke and the rest of them cannot put up with Lord Robert's being king.'* Further, and later, on January 16, 1560 (Amy being now probably at Cumnor), de Quadra writes to de Feria that Baron Preyner, a German diplomatist, will tell him what he knows of the poison for the wife of Milort Robert (Dudley), 'an important story and necessary to be known.'** Thus between November 1559 and January 1560, the talk is that Amy shall be poisoned, and this tale runs round the Courts of Europe.

* Sp. Cal. i. pp. 112-114.

** Relations Politiques, Lettenhove, ii. p. 187.

Mr. Froude gives, what the Calendar does not, a letter of de Quadra to de Feria and the Bishop of Arras (January 15, 1560). 'In Lord Robert it is easy to recognise the king that is to be. . . There is not a man who does not cry out on him and her with indignation.'* 'She will marry none but the favoured Robert.'** On March 7, 1560, de Quadra tells de Feria: 'Not a man in this country but cries out that this fellow' (Dudley) 'is ruining the country with his vanity.'*** 'Is ruining the country AND THE QUEEN,' is in the original Spanish.

* Froude, vi. p. 311.

** Relations Politiques, ii. 87, 183, 184.

*** Sp. Cal. i. p. 133. Major Hume translates the text of Mr. Froude's transcript in the British Museum. It is a mere fragment; in 1883 the whole despatch was printed by Baron Kervyn de Lettenhove.

On March 28 (Calendar), on March 27 (Froude) de Quadra wrote to Philip - (Calendar) -,'I have understood Lord Robert told somebody, who has not kept silence, that if he live another year he will be in a very different position from now. He is laying in a good stock of arms, and is assuming every day a more masterful part in affairs. They say that he thinks of divorcing his wife.'* So the Calendar. Mr. Froude condenses his Spanish author THUS:** 'Lord Robert says that if he lives a year he will be in another position from that which he at present holds. Every day he presumes more and more, and it is now said that he means to divorce his wife.' From the evidence of the Spanish ambassadors, it is clear that an insurance office would only have accepted Amy Robsart's life, however excellent her health, at a very high premium. Her situation was much like that of Darnley in the winter of 1566-67, when 'every one in Scotland who had the smallest judgment' knew that 'he could not long continue,' that his doom was dight.

* Sp. Cal. i, p. 141.

** Froude, vi. p. 340.

Meanwhile, through the winter, spring, and early summer of 1560, diplomatists and politicians were more concerned about the war of the Congregation against Mary of Guise in Scotland, with the English alliance with the Scottish Protestant rebels, with the siege of Leith, and with Cecil's negotiations resulting in the treaty of Edinburgh, than even with Elizabeth's marriage, and her dalliance with Dudley.

All this time, Amy was living at Cumnor Place, about three miles from Oxford. Precisely at what date she took up her abode there is not certain, probably about the time when de Quadra heard that Lord Robert had sent to poison his wife, the November of 1559. Others say in March 1560. The house was rented from a Dr. Owen by Anthony Forster. This gentleman was of an old and good family, well known since the time of Edward I.; his wife also, Ann Williams, daughter of Reginald Williams of Burghfield, Berks, was a lady of excellent social position. Forster himself had estates in several counties, and obtained many grants of land after Amy's death. He died in 1572, leaving a very equitable distribution of his properties; Cumnor he bought from Dr. Owen soon after the death of Amy. In his bequests he did not forget the Master, Fellows, and Scholars of Balliol.* There is nothing suspicious about Forster, who was treasurer or comptroller of Leicester's household expenses: in writing, Leicester signs himself 'your loving Master.' At Cumnor Place also lived Mrs. Owen, wife of Dr. Owen, the owner of the house, and physician to the Queen. There was, too, a Mrs. Oddingsell, of respectable family, one of the Hydes of Denchworth. That any or all of these persons should be concerned in abetting or shielding a murder seems in the highest degree improbable. Cumnor Place was in no respect like Kirk o' Field, as regards the character of its inhabitants. It was, however, a lonely house, and, on the day of Amy's death, her own servants (apparently by her own desire) were absent. And Amy, like Darnley, was found dead on a Sunday night, no man to this day knowing the actual cause of death in either case.

* Pettigrew, pp. 19-22.

Here it may be well to consider the version of the tragedy as printed, twenty-four years after the event, by the deadly enemies of Lord Robert, now Earl of Leicester. This is the version which, many years later, aided by local tradition, was used in Ashmole's account in his 'History and Antiquities of Berkshire,' while Sir Walter employed Ashmole's account as the basis of his romance. We find the PRINTED copy of the book usually known as 'Leicester's Commonwealth' dated 1584, but probably it had been earlier circulated in manuscript copies, of which several exist.* It purports to be a letter written by a M.A. of Cambridge to a friend in London, containing 'some talk passed of late' about Leicester. Doubtless it DOES represent the talk against Leicester that had been passing, at home and abroad, ever since 1560. Such talk, after twenty years, could not be accurate. The point of the writer is that Leicester is lucky in the deaths of inconvenient people. Thus, when he was 'in full hope to marry' the Queen 'he did but send his wife aside, to the house of his servant, Forster of Cumnor, by Oxford, where shortly after she had the chance to fall from a pair of stairs, and so to break her neck, but yet without hurting of her hood, that stood upon her head.' Except for the hood, of which we know nothing, all this is correct. In the next sentence we read: 'But Sir Richard Verney, who, by commandment, remained with her that day alone, with one man only, and had sent away perforce all her servants from her, to a market two miles off, he, I say, with his man, can tell how she died.' The man was privily killed in prison, where he lay for another offence, because he 'offered to publish' the fact; and Verney, about the same time, died in London, after raving about devils 'to a gentleman of worship of mine acquaintance.' 'The wife also of Bald Buttler, kinsman to my Lord, gave out the whole fact a little before her death.'

* Pettigrew, pp. 9, 10.

Verney, and the man, are never mentioned in contemporary papers: two Mrs. Buttelars were mourners at Amy's funeral. Verney is obscure: Canon Jackson argues that he was of the Warwickshire Verneys; Mr. Rye holds that he was of the Bucks and Herts Verneys, connections of the Dudleys. But, finding a Richard Verney made sheriff of Warwick and Leicester in 1562, Mr. Rye absurdly says: 'The former county being that in which the murder was committed,' he 'was placed in the position to suppress any unpleasant rumours.'* Amy died, of course, in Berkshire, not in Warwickshire. A Richard Verney, not the Warwickshire Sir Richard, according to Mr. Rye, on July 30, 1572, became Marshal of the Marshalsea, 'when John Appleyard, Amy's half-brother, was turned out.' This Verney died before November 15, 1575.

* Rye, p. 55.

Of Appleyard we shall hear plenty: Leicester had favoured him (he was Leicester's brother-in-law), and he turned against his patron on the matter of Amy's death. Probably the Richard Verney who died in 1575 was the Verney aimed at in 'Leicester's Commonwealth.' He was a kind of retainer of Dudley, otherwise he would not have been selected by the author of the libel. But we know nothing to prove that he was at Cumnor on September 8, 1560.

The most remarkable point in the libel avers that Leicester's first idea was to poison Amy. This had been asserted by de Quadra as early as November 1559. The libel avers that the conspirators, 'seeing the good lady sad and heavy,' asked Dr. Bayly, of Oxford, for a potion, which they 'would fetch from Oxford upon his prescription, meaning to have added also somewhat of their own for her comfort.' Bayly was a Fellow of New College; in 1558 was one of the proctors; in 1561 was Queen's Professor of Physic, and was a highly reputable man.* He died in 1592. Thus Bayly, if he chose, could have contradicted the printed libel of 1584, which avers that he refused to prescribe for Amy, 'misdoubting (as he after reported) lest if they poisoned her under the name of his potion, he might after have been hanged for a cover of their sin.'

* Pettigrew, p. 17, citing Wood's Ath. Ox. i. P. 586 (Bliss).

Nothing was more natural and innocent than that Bayly should be asked to prescribe, if Amy was ill. Nothing could be more audacious than to print this tale about him, while he lived to contradict it. But it seems far from improbable that Bayly did, for the reasons given, refuse to prescribe for Amy, seeing (as the libel says) 'the small need which the good lady had of physic.'

FOR THIS VERY REFUSAL BY BAYLY WOULD ACCOUNT FOR THE INFORMATION GIVEN BY CECIL TO DE QUADRA ON THE DAY OF AMY'S DEATH. AND IT IS NOT EASY TO EXPLAIN THE SOURCE OF CECIL'S INFORMATION IN ANY OTHER WAY.

We now reach the crucial point at which historical blunders and confusions have been most maddeningly prevalent. Mr. Pettigrew, writing in 1859, had no knowledge of Cecil's corroboration of the story of the libel - Amy in no need of physic, and the intention to poison her. Mr. Froude, however, published in his History a somewhat erroneous version of de Quadra's letter about Cecil's revelations, and Mr. Rye (1885) accused Dudley on the basis of Mr. Froude's version.*

* Froude, vi. pp. 417-421.

Mr. Froude, then, presents a letter from de Quadra of September 11, 1560, to the Duchess of Parma, governing the Netherlands from Brussels, 'this being the nearest point from which he could receive instructions. The despatches were then forwarded to Philip.' He dates de Quadra's letter at the top, 'London,

September 11.' The real date is, at the foot of the last page, 'Windsor, September 11.' Omitting the first portion of the letter, except the first sentence (which says that fresh and important events have occurred since the writer's last letter), Mr. Froude makes de Quadra write: 'On the third of THIS month' (September 1560) 'the Queen spoke to me about her marriage with the Arch Duke. She said she had made up her mind to marry and that the Arch Duke was to be the man. She has just now told me drily that she does not intend to marry, and that it cannot be.'

When, we ask, is 'just now'?

Mr. Froude goes on: 'After my conversation with the Queen, I met the Secretary, Cecil, whom I knew to be in disgrace. Lord Robert, I was aware, was endeavouring to deprive him of his place.' Briefly, Cecil said to de Quadra that he thought of retiring, that ruin was coming on the Queen 'through her intimacy with Lord Robert. The Lord Robert had made himself master of the business of the State and of the person of the Queen, to the extreme injury of the realm, with the intention of marrying her, and she herself was shutting herself up in the palace to the peril of her health and life.' Cecil begged de Quadra to remonstrate with the Queen. After speaking of her finances, Cecil went on, in Mr. Froude's version: 'Last of all he said they were thinking of destroying Lord Robert's wife. THEY HAD GIVEN OUT THAT SHE WAS ILL; BUT SHE WAS NOT ILL AT ALL; SHE WAS VERY WELL, AND WAS TAKING CARE NOT TO BE POISONED . . . .' [The capitals are mine.]

This is the very state of things reported in 'Leicester's Commonwealth.' Cecil may easily have known the circumstances, if, as stated in that libel, Bayly had been consulted, had found Amy 'in no need of physic,' and had refused to prescribe. Bayly would blab, and Cecil had spies everywhere to carry the report: the extent and precision of his secret service are well known. Cecil added some pious remarks God would not permit the crime. Mr. Froude goes on: 'The day after this conversation, the Queen on her return from hunting told me that Lord Robert's wife was dead or nearly so, and begged me to say nothing about it.' After some political speculations, the letter, in Froude, ends, 'Since this was written the death of Lord Robert's wife has been given out publicly. The Queen said in Italian "Que si ha rotto il collo" ["that she has broken her neck"]. It appears that she fell down a staircase.'

Mr. Froude, after disposing of the ideas that de Quadra lied, or that Cecil spoke 'in mere practice or diplomatic trickery,' remarks: 'Certain it is that on September 8, at the time, or within a day of the time, when Cecil told the Spanish ambassador that there was a plot to kill her, Anne Dudley [Anne or Amy] was found dead at the foot of a staircase.' This must be true, for the Queen told de Quadra, PRIVATELY, 'on the day after' Cecil unbosomed himself. The fatal news, we know, reached Windsor on September 9, we do not know at what hour. The Queen told de Quadra probably on September 9. If the news arrived late (and Dudley's first letter on the subject is 'IN THE EVENING' of September 9), Elizabeth may have told de Quadra on the morning of September 10.

The inferences were drawn (by myself and others) that Elizabeth had told de Quadra, on September 3, 'the third of THIS month' (as Mr. Froude, by a slip of the pen, translates 'a tres del passado'), that she would marry the Arch Duke; that Cecil spoke to de Quadra on the same day, and that 'the day after this conversation' (September 4) the Queen told de Quadra that Amy 'was dead or nearly so.' The presumption would be that the Queen spoke of Amy's death FOUR DAYS BEFORE IT OCCURRED, and a very awkward position, in that case, would be the Queen's. Guilty foreknowledge would be attributed to her. This is like the real situation if Dr. Ernst Bekker is right.* Dr. Bekker, knowing from the portion of de Quadra's letter omitted by Mr. Froude, that he reached the Court at Windsor on September 6, 1560, supposes that he had interviews with Elizabeth and Cecil on that day, and that Elizabeth, prematurely, announced to him Amy's death, next day, on September 7. But Mr. Gairdner has proved that this scheme of dates is highly improbable.

* Elizabeth and Leicester, Giesener Studien auf dem Gebiet der Geschichte, v p.48. Giesen, 1890.

In the 'English Historical Review,'* Mr. Gairdner, examining the question, used Mr. Froude's transcripts in the British Museum, and made some slight corrections in his translation, but omitted to note the crucial error of the 'third of THIS month ' for 'the third of LAST month.' This was in 1886. Mr. Gairdner's arguments as to dates were unconvincing, in this his first article. But in 1892 the letter of de Quadra was retranslated from Mr. Froude's transcript, in the Spanish Calendar (i. pp. 174-176). The translation was again erroneous, 'THE QUEEN HAD PROMISED ME AN ANSWER ABOUT THE SPANISH MARRIAGE BY THE THIRD INSTANT' (September 3), 'but now she coolly tells me she cannot make up her mind, and will not marry.' This is all unlike Mr. Froude's 'On the third of this month the Queen spoke to me about her marriage WITH THE ARCH DUKE. SHE SAID THAT SHE HAD MADE UP HER MIND TO MARRY AND THAT THE ARCH DUKE WAS TO BE THE MAN.' There is, in fact, in Mr. Froude's copy of the original Spanish, not a word about the Arch Duke, nor is there in Baron Lettenhove's text. The remark has crept in from an earlier letter of de Quadra, of August 4, 1560.** But neither is there anything about 'promising an answer by the third instant,' as in the Calendar; and there is nothing at all about 'the third instant,' or (as in Mr. Froude) 'the third of this month.'

* No. 2, April 1886, pp. 235-259.

** Spanish Calendar, i. pp. 171-174.

The Queen's character has thus suffered, and the whole controversy has been embroiled. In 1883, three years before the appearance of Mr. Gairdner's article of 1886, nine years before the Calendar appeared, the correct version of de Quadra's letter of September 11, 1560, had been published by Baron Kervyn de Lettenhove in his 'Relations Politiques des Pays-Bas et de l'Angleterre sous le Regne de Philippe II' (vol. ii. pp. 529, 533). In 1897, Mr. Gairdner's attention was called to the state of affairs by the article, already cited, of Dr. Ernst Bekker. Mr. Gairdner then translated the Belgian printed copy of de Quadra's letter, with comments.*

* English Historical Review, January 1898, pp. 83-90.

Matters now became clear. Mr. Froude's transcript and translation had omitted all the first long paragraph of the letter, which proved that de Quadra went to Windsor, to the Court, on September 6. Next, the passage about 'the third of THIS month' really runs 'I showed her much dissatisfaction about her marriage, in [on?] which on the third of LAST month [August] she had told me she was already resolved and that she assuredly meant to marry. Now she has coolly told me that she cannot make up her mind, and that she does not intend to marry.' (Mr. Gairdner's translation, 1898.) So the blot on the Queen's scutcheon as to her foreknowledge and too previous announcement of Amy's death disappears. But how did Mr. Gairdner, in 1886, using Mr. Froude's transcript of the original Spanish, fail to see that it contained no Arch Duke, and no 'third of the month'? Mr. Froude's transcript of the original Spanish, but not his translation thereof, was correct.*

* As to Verney, Appleyard, and Foster (see pages commencing: - 'Here it may be well to consider'), Cecil, in April 1566, names Foster and Appleyard, but not Verney, among the 'particular friends' whom Leicester, if he marries the Queen, 'will study to enhanss to welth, to Offices, and Lands.' Bartlett, Cumnor Place, p. 73, London 1850.

2. AMY'S DEATH AND WHAT FOLLOWED

So far the case against Dudley, or servants of Dudley, has looked very black. There are the scandals, too dark for ambassadors to write, but mouthed aloud among the common people, about Dudley and the Queen. There is de Quadra's talk of a purpose to poison Amy, in November-January, 1559-1560. There is the explicit statement of Cecil, as to the intended poisoning (probably derived from Dr. Bayly), and as to Dudley's 'possession of the Queen's person,' the result of his own observation. There is the coincidence of Amy's violent death with Cecil's words to de Quadra (September 8 or 9, 1560).

But here the case takes a new turn. Documents appear, letters from and to Dudley at the time of the event, which are totally inconsistent with guilt on his part. These documents (in the Pepys MSS. at Cambridge) are COPIES of letters between Dudley and Thomas Blount, a gentleman of good family, whom he addresses as 'Cousin.' Blount, long after, in May 1567, was examined on the affair before the Privy Council, and Mr. Froude very plausibly suggests that Blount produced the copies in the course of the inquiry. But why COPIES? We can only say that the originals may also have been shown, and the copies made for the convenience of the members of the Council. It is really incredible that the letters were forged, after date, to prove Dudley's innocence.

In the usual blundering way, Mr. Pettigrew dates one letter of Dudley's 'September 27.' If that date were right, it would suggest that TWO coroner's inquests were held, one after Amy's burial (on September 22), but Mr. Gairdner says that the real date of the letter is September 12.* So the date is given by Bartlett, in his 'History of Cumnor Place,' and by Adlard (1870), following Bartlett, and Craik (1848).

* English Historical Review, No. 2, p. 243, note.

The first letter, from Dudley, at Windsor 'this 9th day of September in the evening,' proves that Blount, early on September 9, the day after Amy's death, went from

Leicester, at Windsor, towards Berkshire. He had not long gone when Bowes (a retainer of Leicester, of Forster, or of Amy) brought to Dudley the fatal news. 'By him I do understand that my wife is dead and, as he saith, by a fall from a pair of stairs. Little other understanding can I have from him.' Throughout the correspondence Leicester does not utter one word of sorrow for Amy, as, had the letters been written for exhibition, he would almost certainly have done. The fear of his own danger and disgrace alone inspires him, and he takes every measure to secure a full, free, and minute examination. 'Have no respect to any living person.' A coroner's jury is to be called, the body is to be examined; Appleyard and others of Amy's kin have already been sent for to go to Cumnor.

From Cumnor, Blount replied on September 11. He only knew that 'my lady is dead, and, as it seemeth, with a fall, but yet how, or which way, I cannot learn.' Not even at Cumnor could Blount discover the manner of the accident. On the night of the ninth he had lain at Abingdon, the landlord of the inn could tell him no more than Dudley already knew. Amy's servants had been at 'the fair' at Abingdon: she herself was said to have insisted on their going thither very early in the day; among them Bowes went, as he told Blount, who met him on the road, as he rode to see Dudley. He said that Amy 'was very angry' with any who stayed, and with Mrs. Oddingsell, who refused to go. Pinto (probably Amy's maid), 'who doth love her dearly,' confirmed Bowes. She believed the death to be 'a very accident.' She had heard Amy 'divers times pray to God to deliver her from desperation,' but entirely disbelieved in suicide, which no one would attempt, perhaps, by falling down two flights of stairs.

Before Blount arrived at Cumnor on September 10, the coroner's jury had been chosen, sensible men, but some of them hostile to Forster. By September 12 (NOT 27) Dudley had retired from Court and was at Kew, but had received Blount's letter. He bade Blount tell the jury to inquire faithfully and find an honest verdict. On the thirteenth Blount again wrote from Cumnor, meaning to join Dudley next day: 'I I have ALMOST NOTHING that can make me so much [as?] to think that any man can be the doer of it. . . the circumstances and the many things which I can learn doth persuade me that only misfortune hath done it and nothing else.' There is another letter by Dudley from Windsor, without date. He has had a reassuring letter from Smythe, foreman of the jury. He wishes them to examine 'as long as they lawfully may,' and that a fresh jury should try the case again. He wishes Sir Richard Blount to help. Appleyard and Arthur Robsart have been present. He means to have no more dealings with the jury; his only 'dealings' seem to have been his repeated requests that they would be diligent and honest. 'I am right glad they be all strangers to me.'*

* Pettigrew, pp. 28-32.

These letters are wholly inconsistent with guilt, in the faintest degree, on the side of Dudley. But people were not satisfied. There is a letter to Cecil, of September 17, from Lever, a minister at Coventry, saying that the country was full of mutterings and dangerous suspicions, and that there must be earnest searching and trying of the truth.*

* Burghley Papers, Haynes, 362.

Suspicion was inevitable, but what could a jury do,

more than, according to Blount, the jury had done? Yet there is dense obscurity as to the finding of the jury. We have seen that Appleyard, Amy's half-brother, was at Cumnor during the inquest. Yet, in 1567, he did not know, or pretended not to know, what the verdict had been. 'Leicester's Commonwealth' says 'she was found murdered (as all men said) by the crowner's inquest,' as if the verdict was not published, but was a mere matter of rumour - 'as all men said.' Appleyard's behaviour need not detain us long, as he was such a shuffling knave that his statements, on either side, were just what he found expedient in varying circumstances. Dudley, after Amy's death, obtained for him various profitable billets; in 1564 he was made keeper of the Marshalsea, had a commission under the Great Seal to seize concealed prizes at sea without legal proceedings, had the Portership of Berwick, and the Sheriffship of Norfolk and Suffolk, while Leicester stood guarantor of a debt of his for 400 pounds. These facts he admitted before the Privy Council in 1567.* But Leicester might naturally do what he could for his dead wife's brother: we cannot argue that the jobs done for Appleyard were hush-money, enormous as these jobs were. Yet in this light Appleyard chose to consider them. He seems to have thought that Leicester did not treat him well enough, and wanted to get rid of him in Ireland or France, and he began, about 1566-67, to blab of what he could say an' he would. He 'let fall words of anger, and said that for Dudley's sake he had covered the murder of his sister.'

* Rye, pp. 60-62. Hatfield MSS., Calendar, i. 345-352, May 1567.

Mr. Froude has here misconceived the situation, as Mr. Gairdner shows. Mr. Froude's words are 'being examined by Cecil, he admitted the investigation at Cumnor had after all been inadequately conducted.'* In fact, Appleyard admitted that he had SAID this, and much more, in private talk among his associates. Before the Council he subsequently withdrew what he admitted having said in private talk It does not signify what he said, or what he withdrew, but Mr. Froude unluckily did not observe a document which proved that Appleyard finally ate his words, and he concludes that 'although Dudley was innocent of a direct association with the crime, the unhappy lady was sacrificed to his ambition. Dudley himself. . . used private means, notwithstanding his affectation of sincerity, to prevent the search from being pressed inconveniently far' - that is, 'if Appleyard spoke the truth.' But Appleyard denied that he had spoken the truth, a fact overlooked by Mr. Froude.**

* Froude, vi. p. 430.

** Ibid. vi. pp 430, 431.

The truth stood thus: in 1566-67 there was, or had been, some idea that Leicester might, after all, marry the Queen. Appleyard told Thomas Blount that he was being offered large sums by great persons to reopen the Cumnor affair. Blount was examined by the Council, and gave to Leicester a written account of what he told them. One Huggon, Appleyard's 'brother,' had informed Leicester that courtiers were practising on Appleyard, 'to search the manner of his sister's death.' Leicester sent Blount to examine Appleyard as to who the courtiers were. Appleyard was evasive, but at last told Blount a long tale of mysterious attempts to seduce him into stirring up the old story. He promised to meet Leicester, but did not: his brother, Huggon, named Norfolk, Sussex, and others as the 'practisers.' Later, by Leicester's command, Blount brought Appleyard to him at Greenwich. What speeches passed Blount did not know, but Leicester was very angry, and bade Appleyard begone, 'with great words of defiance.' It is clear that, with or without grounds, Appleyard was trying to blackmail Leicester.

Before the Council (May 1567) Appleyard confessed that he had said to people that he had often moved the Earl to let him pursue the murderers of Amy, 'showing certain circumstances which led him to think surely that she was murdered.' He had said that Leicester, on the other hand, cited the verdict of the jury, but he himself declared that the jury, in fact, 'had not as yet given up their verdict.' After these confessions Appleyard lay in the Fleet prison, destitute, and scarce able to buy a meal. On May 30, 1567, he wrote an abject letter to the Council. He had been offered every opportunity of accusing those whom he suspected, and he asked for 'a copy of the verdict presented by the jury, whereby I may see what the jury have found,' after which he would take counsel's advice. He got a copy of the verdict (?) (would that we had the copy!) and, naturally, as he was starving, professed himself amply satisfied by 'proofs testified under the oaths of fifteen persons,' that Amy's death was accidental. 'I have not money left to find me two meals.' In such a posture, Appleyard would, of course, say anything to get himself out of prison. Two days later he confessed that for three years he had been, in fact, trying to blackmail Leicester on several counts, Amy's murder and two political charges.*

* See the full reports, Gairdner, English Historical Review, April 1886, 249-259, and Hatfield Calendar

Andrew Lang

for the date May 1567.

The man was a rogue, however we take him, and the sole tangible fact is that a report of the evidence given at the inquest did exist, and that the verdict may have been 'Accidental Death.' We do not know but that an open verdict was given. Appleyard professes to have been convinced by the evidence, not by the verdict.

When 'Leicester's Apology' appeared (1584-85) Sir Philip Sidney, Leicester's nephew, wrote a reply. It was easy for him to answer the libeller's 'she was found murdered (as all men suppose) by the crowner's inquest' - by producing the actual verdict of the jury. He did not; he merely vapoured, and challenged the libeller to the duel.* Appleyard's statement among his intimates, that no verdict had yet been given, seems to point to an open verdict.

* Sidney's reply is given in Adlard's Amye Robsart and the Earl of Leicester. London, 1870.

The subject is alluded to by Elizabeth herself, who puts the final touch of darkness on the mystery. Just as Archbishop Beaton, Mary's ambassador in Paris, vainly adjured her to pursue the inquiry into Darnley's murder, being urged by the talk in France, so Throgmorton, Elizabeth's ambassador to the French Court, was heartbroken by what he heard. Clearly no satisfactory verdict ever reached him. He finally sent Jones, his secretary, with a verbal message to Elizabeth. Jones boldly put the question of the Cumnor affair. She said that 'the matter had been tried in the country, AND FOUND TO THE CONTRARY OF THAT WAS REPORTED.'

What 'was reported'? Clearly that Leicester and retainers of his had been the murderers of Amy. For the Queen went on, 'Lord Robert was in the Court, AND NONE OF HIS AT THE ATTEMPT AT HIS WIFE'S HOUSE.' So Verney was not there. So Jones wrote to Throgmorton on November 30, 1560.* We shall return to Throgmorton.

* Hardwicke Papers, i. 165.

If Jones correctly reported Elizabeth's words, there had been an 'attempt at' Cumnor Place, of which we hear nothing from any other source. How black is the obscurity through which Blount, at Cumnor, two days after Amy's death, could discern - nothing! 'A fall, yet how, or which way, I cannot learn.' By September 17, nine days after the death, Lever, at Coventry, an easy day's ride from Cumnor, knew nothing (as we saw) of a verdict, or, at least, of a satisfactory verdict. It is true that the Earl of Huntingdon, at Leicester, only heard of Amy's death on September 17, nine days after date.* Given 'an attempt,' Amy might perhaps break her neck down a spiral staircase, when running away in terror. A cord stretched across the top step would have done all that was needed.

* Nineteenth Century, vol. ii. p. 431. Huntingdon to Leicester, Longleat MSS. I repose on Canon Jackson's date of the manuscript letter.

We next find confusion worse confounded, by our previous deliverer from error, Baron Kervyn Lettenhove! What happened at Court immediately after Amy's death? The Baron says: 'A fragment of a despatch of de la Quadra, of the same period, reports Dudley to have said that his marriage had been celebrated in presence of his brother, and of two of the Queen's ladies.' For this, according to the Baron, Mr. Froude cites a letter of the Bishop of Aquila (de Quadra) of September 11.* Mr. Froude does nothing of the sort! He does cite 'an abstract of de Quadra's letters, MS. Simancas,' without any date at all 'The design of Cecil and of those heretics to convey the kingdom to the Earl of Huntingdon is most certain, for at last Cecil has yielded to Lord Robert, who, he says, has married the Queen in presence of his brother and two ladies of her bedchamber.' So Mr. Gairdner translates from Mr. Froude's transcript, and he gives the date (November 20) which Mr. Froude does not give. Major Hume translates, 'who, THEY say, was married.'** O History! According to Baron Kervyn de Lettenhove, DUDLEY says he has married the Queen; according to Mr. Gairdner, CECIL says so; according to Major Hume, 'they' say so!***

* Relations Politiques des Pays-Bas, etc., xlii., note 4.

** Span. Cal. i. p. 178.

*** The Spanish of this perplexing sentence is given by Froude, vi. p. 433, note 1. 'Cecil se ha rendido a Milord Roberto el qual dice que se hay casado con la Reyna. . . .'

The point is of crucial importance to Mrs. Gallup and the believers in the cipher wherein Bacon maintains that he is the legal son of a wedding between Dudley and the Queen. Was there such a marriage or even betrothal? Froude cautiously says that this was averted 'SEEMINGLY on Lord Robert's authority;' the Baron says that Lord Robert makes the assertion; Mr. Gairdner says that Cecil is the authority, and Major

Hume declares that it is a mere on-dit - 'who, they say.' It is heart-breaking.*

* For Mr. Gairdner, English Historical Review, No. 2, p. 246.

To deepen the darkness and distress, the official, printed, Spanish Documentos Ineditos do not give this abstract of November 20 at all. Major Hume translates it in full, from Mr. Froude's transcript.

Again, Mr. Froude inserts his undated quotation, really of November 20, before he comes to tell of Amy Robsart's funeral (September 22, 1560), and the Baron, as we saw, implies that Mr. Froude dates it September 11, the day on which the Queen publicly announced Amy's death.

We now have an undated letter, endorsed by Cecil 'Sept. 1560,' wherein Dudley, not at Court, and in tribulation, implores Cecil's advice and aid. 'I am sorry so sudden a chance should breed me so great a change.' He may have written from Kew, where Elizabeth had given him a house, and where he was on September 12 (not 27). On October 13 (Froude), or 14 ('Documentos Ineditos,' 88, p. 310), or 15 (Spanish Calendar, i. p. 176) - for dates are strange things - de Quadra wrote a letter of which there is only an abstract at Simancas. This abstract we quote: 'The contents of the letter of Bishop Quadra to his Majesty written on the 15th' (though headed the 14th) 'of October, and received on the 16th of November, 1560. It relates the way in which the wife of Lord Robert came to her death, the respect (reverencia) paid him immediately by the members of the Council and others, and the dissimulation of the Queen. That he had heard that they were engaged in an affair of great importance for the confirmation of their heresies, and wished to make the Earl of Huntingdon king, should the Queen die without children, and that Cecil had told him that the heritage was his as a descendant of the House of York. . . . That Cecil had told him that the Queen was resolved not to marry Lord Robert, as he had learned from herself; it seemed that the Arch Duke might be proposed.' In mid-October, then, Elizabeth was apparently disinclined to wed the so recently widowed Lord Robert, though, shortly after Amy's death, the Privy Council began to court Dudley as future king.

Mr. Froude writes - still before he comes to September 22 - 'the Bishop of Aquila reported that there were anxious meetings of the Council, the courtiers paid a partial homage to Dudley.'* This appears to be a refraction from the abstract of the letter of October 13 or 14: 'he relates the manner in which the wife of Lord Robert came to her death, the respect (reverencia) paid to him immediately by members of the Council and others.'

* Froude, vi. p. 432.

Next we come, in Mr. Froude, to Amy's funeral (September 22), and to Elizabeth's resolve not to marry Leicester (October 13, 14, 15?), and to Throgmorton's interference in October-November. Throgmorton's wails over the Queen's danger and dishonour were addressed to Cecil and the Marquis of Northampton, from Poissy, on October 10, when he also condoled with Dudley on the death of his wife! 'Thanks him for his present of a nag!'* On the same date, October 10, Harry Killigrew, from London, wrote to answer Throgmorton's inquiries about Amy's death. Certainly

Throgmorton had heard of Amy's death before October 10: he might have heard by September 16. What he heard comforted him not. By October 10 he should have had news of a satisfactory verdict. But Killigrew merely said 'she brake her neck. . . only by the hand of God, to my knowledge.'** On October 17, Killigrew writes to Throgmorton 'rumours. . . have been very rife, BUT THE QUEEN SAYS SHE WILL MAKE THEM FALSE. . . . Leaves to his judgment what he will not write. Has therefore sent by Jones and Summers' (verbally) 'what account he wished him to make of my Lord R.' (Dudley).

* For. Cal. Eliz., 1560, pp. 347-349.

** Ibid., 1560, p. 350.

Then (October 28) Throgmorton tells Cecil plainly that, till he knows what Cecil thinks, he sees no reason to advise the Queen in the matter 'of marrying Dudley.' Begs him 'TO SIGNIFY PLAINLY WHAT HAS BEEN DONE,' and implores him, 'in the bowels of Christ '. . . 'to hinder that matter.'* He writes 'with tears and sighs,' and - he declines to return Cecil's letters on the subject. 'They be as safe in my hands as in your own, and more safe in mine than in any messenger's.'

* For. Cal. Eliz., 1560, p. 376.

On October 29, Throgmorton sets forth his troubles to Chamberlain. 'Chamberlain as a wise man can conceive how much it imports the Queen's honour and her realm to have the same' (reports as to Amy's death) 'ceased.' 'He is withal brought to be weary of his life.'*

* For. Cal. Eliz., 1560, p. 376.

On November 7, Throgmorton writes to the Marquis of Northampton and to Lord Pembroke about 'the bruits lately risen from England. . .set so full with great horror,' and never disproved, despite Throgmorton's prayers for satisfaction.

Finally Throgmorton, as we saw, had the boldness to send his secretary, Jones, direct to Elizabeth. All the comfort he got from her was her statement that neither Dudley nor his retainers were at the attempt at Cumnor Place. Francis I. died in France, people had something fresh to talk about, and the Cumnor scandal dropped out of notice. Throgmorton, however, persevered till, in January 1561, Cecil plainly told him to cease to meddle. Throgmorton endorsed the letter 'A warning not to be too busy about the matters between the Queen and Lord Robert.'*

* For. Cal. Eliz., 1560, p. 498.

It is not necessary, perhaps, to pursue further the attempts of Dudley to marry the Queen. On January 22 he sent to de Quadra his brother-in-law, Sir Henry, father of Sir Philip Sidney, offering to help to restore the Church if Philip II. would back the marriage. Sidney professed to believe, after full inquiry, that Amy died by accident. But he admitted 'that no one believed it;' that 'the preachers harped on it in a manner prejudicial to the honour and service of the Queen, which had caused her to move for the remedy of the disorders of this kingdom in religion,' and so on.* De Quadra and the preachers had no belief in Amy's death by accident. Nobody had, except Dudley's relations. A year after Amy's death, on September 13, 1561, de Quadra wrote: 'The Earl of Arundel and others are drawing up copies of the testimony given in the inquiry respecting the death of Lord Robert's wife. Robert is now doing his best to repair matters' (as to a quarrel with Arundel, it seems), 'as it appears that more is being discovered in that matter than he wished.'** People were not so easily satisfied with the evidence as was the imprisoned and starving Appleyard.

* Documentos Ineditos, 88, p. 314; Span. Cal., i. p. 179; Froude, vi. p. 453. The translations vary: I give my own. The Spanish has misprints.

** Span. Cal., i. p. 213; Documentos Ineditos, 88, p. 367.

So the mystery stands. The letters of Blount and Dudley (September 9-12, 1560) entirely clear Dudley's character, and can only be got rid of on the wild theory that they were composed, later, to that very end. But the precise nature of the Cumnor jury's verdict is unknown, and Elizabeth's words about 'the attempt at her house' prove that something concealed from us did occur. It might be a mere half-sportive attempt by rustics to enter a house known to be, at the moment, untenanted by the servants, and may have caused to Amy an alarm, so that, rushing downstairs in terror, she fell and broke her neck. The coincidence of her death with the words of Cecil would thus be purely fortuitous, and coincidences as extraordinary have occurred. Or a partisan of Dudley's, finding poison difficult or impossible, may have, in his zeal, murdered Amy, under the disguise of an accident. The theory of suicide would be plausible, if it were conceivable that a person would commit suicide by throwing herself downstairs.

We can have no certainty, but, at least, we show how

Elizabeth came to be erroneously accused of reporting Amy's death before it occurred.*

* For a wild Italian legend of Amy's murder, written in 1577, see the Hatfield Calendar, ii. 165-170.

VII.

THE VOICES OF JEANNE D'ARC

Some of our old English historians write of Jeanne d'Arc, the Pucelle, as 'the Puzel.' The author of the 'First Part of Henry VI.,' whether he was Shakespeare or not, has a pun on the word:

'Pucelle or puzzel, dolphin or dogfish,'

the word 'Puzzel' carrying an unsavoury sense. (Act I. Scene 4.) A puzzle, in the usual meaning of the word, the Maid was to the dramatist. I shall not enter into the dispute as to whether Shakespeare was the author, or part author, of this perplexed drama. But certainly the role of the Pucelle is either by two different hands, or the one author was 'in two minds' about the heroine. Now she appears as la ribaulde of Glasdale's taunt, which made her weep, as the 'bold strumpet' of Talbot's insult in the play. The author adopts or even exaggerates the falsehoods of Anglo-Burgundian legend. The personal purity of Jeanne was not denied by her judges. On the other hand the dramatist makes his 'bold strumpet' a paladin of courage and a perfect patriot, reconciling Burgundy to the national cause by a moving speech on 'the great pity that was in France.' How could a ribaulde, a leaguer-lass, a witch, a sacrificer of blood to devils, display the valour, the absolute self-sacrifice, the eloquent and tender love of native land attributed to the Pucelle of the play? Are there two authors, and is Shakespeare one of them, with his understanding of the human heart? Or is there one puzzled author producing an impossible and contradictory character?

The dramatist has a curious knowledge of minute points in Jeanne's career: he knows and mocks at the sword with five crosses which she found, apparently by clairvoyance, at Fierbois, but his history is distorted and dislocated almost beyond recognition. Jeanne proclaims herself to the Dauphin as the daughter of a shepherd, and as a pure maid. Later she disclaims both her father and her maidenhood. She avers that she was first inspired by a vision of the Virgin (which she never did in fact), and she is haunted by 'fiends,' who represent her St. Michael, St. Catherine, and St. Margaret. After the relief of Orleans the Dauphin exclaims:

'No longer on Saint Denis will we cry,
But Joan la Pucelle shall be France's saint,'

a prophecy which may yet be accomplished. Already accomplished is d'Alencon's promise:

'We'll set thy statue in some holy place.'

To the Duke of Burgundy, the Pucelle of the play speaks as the Maid might have spoken:

'Look on thy country, look on fertile France,
And see the cities and the towns defaced
By wasting ruin of the cruel foe!
As looks the mother on her lowly babe,

When death doth close his tender dying eyes,
See, see, the pining malady of France;
Behold the wounds, the most unnatural wounds,
Which thou thyself hast given her woful breast!
O turn thy edged sword another way;
Strike those that hurt, and hurt not those that help!
One drop of blood drawn from thy country's bosom
Should grieve thee more than streams of foreign
gore;
Return thee, therefore, with a flood of tears,
And wash away thy country's stained spots.'

Patriotism could find no better words, and how can the
dramatist represent the speaker as a 'strumpet' inspired
by 'fiends'? To her fiends when they desert her, the
Pucelle of the play cries:

'Cannot my body, nor blood sacrifice,
Entreat you to your wonted furtherance?
Then take my soul; my body, soul, and all,
Before that England give the French the foil.'

She is willing to give body and soul for France, and
this, in the eyes of the dramatist, appears to be her
crime. For a French girl to bear a French heart is to
stamp her as the tool of devils. It is an odd theology,
and not in the spirit of Shakespeare. Indeed the
Pucelle, while disowning her father and her maidenhood, again speaks to the English as Jeanne might have
spoken:

'I never had to do with wicked spirits:
But you, that are polluted with your lusts,
Stained with the guiltless blood of innocents,
Corrupt and tainted with a thousand vices,
Because you want the grace that others have,

You judge it straight a thing impossible
To compass wonders but by help of devils.
No, misconceiv'd! Joan of Arc hath been
A virgin from her tender infancy,
Chaste and immaculate in very thought;
Whose maiden blood, thus rigorously effus'd,
Will cry for vengeance at the gates of heaven.'

The vengeance was not long delayed. 'The French and
my countrymen,' writes Patrick Abercromby, 'drove
the English from province to province, and from town
to town' of France, while on England fell the Wars of
the Roses. But how can the dramatist make the dealer
with fiends speak as the Maid, in effect, did speak at
her trial? He adds the most ribald of insults; the
Pucelle exclaiming:

'It was Alencon that enjoyed my love!'

The author of the play thus speaks with two voices: in
one Jeanne acts and talks as she might have done (had
she been given to oratory); in the other she is the
termagant of Anglo-Burgundian legend or myth.

Much of this perplexity still haunts the histories of the
Maid. Her courage, purity, patriotism, and clear-
sighted military and political common-sense; the
marvellous wisdom of her replies to her judges - as of
her own St. Catherine before the fifty philosophers of
her legend - are universally acknowledged. This girl of
seventeen, in fact, alone of the French folk, understood
the political and military situation. To restore the
confidence of France it was necessary that the Dauphin
should penetrate the English lines to Rheims, and there
be crowned. She broke the lines, she led him to
Rheims, and crowned him. England was besieging his

last hold in the north and centre, Orleans, on a military policy of pure 'bluff.' The city was at no time really invested. The besieging force, as English official documents prove, was utterly inadequate to its task, except so far as prestige and confidence gave power. Jeanne simply destroyed and reversed the prestige, and, after a brilliant campaign on the Loire, opened the way to Rheims. The next step was to take Paris, and Paris she certainly would have taken, but the long delays of politicians enabled Beaufort to secure peace with Scotland, under James I., and to throw into Paris the English troops collected for a crusade against the Hussites.* The Maid, unsupported, if not actually betrayed, failed and was wounded before Paris, and prestige returned for a while to the English party. She won minor victories, was taken at Compiegne (May 1430), and a year later crowned her career by martyrdom. But she had turned the tide, and within the six years of her prophecy Paris returned to the national cause. The English lost, in losing Paris, 'a greater gage than Orleans.'

* The Scottish immobility was secured in May-June 1429, the months of the Maid's Loire campaign. Exchequer Rolls, iv. ciii. 466. Bain, Calendar, iv. 212, Foedera, x. 428,1704-1717.

So much is universally acknowledged, but how did the Maid accomplish her marvels? Brave as she certainly was, wise as she certainly was, beautiful as she is said to have been, she would neither have risked her unparalleled adventure, nor been followed, but for her strange visions and 'voices.' She left her village and began her mission, as she said, in contradiction to the strong common-sense of her normal character. She resisted for long the advice that came to her in the apparent shape of audible external voices and external visions of saint and angel. By a statement of actual facts which she could not possibly have learned in any normal way, she overcame, it is said, the resistance of the Governor of Vaucouleurs, and obtained an escort to convey her to the King at Chinon.[*] She conquered the doubts of the Dauphin by a similar display of supernormal knowledge. She satisfied, at Poictiers, the divines of the national party after a prolonged examination, of which the record, 'The Book of Poictiers,' has disappeared. In these ways she inspired the confidence which, in the real feebleness of the invading army, was all that was needed to ensure the relief of Orleans, while, as Dunois attested, she shook the confidence which was the strength of England. About these facts the historical evidence is as good as for any other events of the war.

* Refer to paragraph commencing "The 'Journal du Siege d'Orleans'" infra.

The essence, then, of the marvels wrought by Jeanne d'Arc lay in what she called her 'Voices,' the mysterious monitions, to her audible, and associated with visions of the heavenly speakers. Brave, pure, wise, and probably beautiful as she was, the King of France would not have trusted a peasant lass, and men disheartened by frequent disaster would not have followed her, but for her voices.

The science or theology of the age had three possible ways of explaining these experiences:

1. The Maid actually was inspired by Michael, Margaret, and Catherine. From them she learned secrets of the future, of words unspoken save in the

King's private prayer, and of events distant in space, like the defeat of the French and Scots at Rouvray, which she announced, on the day of the occurrence, to Baudricourt, hundreds of leagues away, at Vaucouleurs.

2. The monitions came from 'fiends.' This was the view of the prosecutors in general at her trial, and of the author of 'Henry VI., Part I.'

3. One of her judges, Beaupere, was a man of some courage and consistency. He maintained, at the trial of Rouen, and at the trial of Rehabilitation (1452-1456), that the voices were mere illusions of a girl who fasted much. In her fasts she would construe natural sounds, as of church bells, or perhaps of the wind among woods, into audible words, as Red Indian seers do to this day.

This third solution must and does neglect, or explain by chance occurrence, or deny, the coincidences between facts not normally knowable, and the monitions of the Voices, accepted as genuine, though inexplicable, by M. Quicherat, the great palaeographer and historian of Jeanne.* He by no means held a brief for the Church; Father Ayroles continually quarrels with Quicherat, as a Freethinker. He certainly was a free thinker in the sense that he was the first historian who did not accept the theory of direct inspiration by saints (still less by fiends), and yet took liberty to admit that the Maid possessed knowledge not normally acquired. Other 'freethinking' sympathisers with the heroine have shuffled, have skated adroitly past and round the facts, as Father Ayroles amusingly demonstrates in his many passages of arms with Michelet, Simeon Luce, Henri Martin, Fabre, and his other opponents. M. Quicherat merely says that, if we are not to accept the marvels as genuine, we must abandon the whole of the rest of the evidence as to Jeanne d'Arc, and there he leaves the matter.

* Quicherat's five volumes of documents, the Procés, is now accessible, as far as records of the two trials go, in the English version edited by Mr. Douglas Murray.

Can we not carry the question further? Has the psychological research of the last half-century added nothing to our means of dealing with the problem? Negatively, at least, something is gained. Science no longer avers, with M. Lelut in his book on the Daemon of Socrates, that every one who has experience of hallucinations, of impressions of the senses not produced by objective causes, is mad. It is admitted that sane and healthy persons may have hallucinations of lights, of voices, of visual appearances. The researches of Mr. Galton, of M. Richet, of Brierre du Boismont, of Mr. Gurney, and an army of other psychologists, have secured this position.

Maniacs have hallucinations, especially of voices, but all who have hallucinations are not maniacs. Jeanne d'Arc, so subject to 'airy tongues,' was beyond all doubt a girl of extraordinary physical strength and endurance, of the highest natural lucidity and common-sense, and of health which neither wounds, nor fatigue, nor cruel treatment, could seriously impair. Wounded again and again, she continued to animate the troops by her voice, and was in arms undaunted next day. Her leap of sixty feet from the battlements of Beaurevoir stunned but did not long incapacitate her. Hunger, bonds, and the protracted weariness of months of cross-examination produced an illness but left her intellect as keen, her courage as unabated, her humour as vivacious, her memory as minutely accurate as ever. There never was a more sane and healthy human being. We never hear that, in the moments of her strange experiences, she was 'entranced,' or even dissociated from the actual occurrences of the hour. She heard her voices, though not distinctly, in the uproar of the brawling court which tried her at Rouen; she saw her visions in the imminent deadly breach, when she rallied her men to victory. In this alertness she is a contrast to a modern seeress, subject, like her, to monitions of an hallucinatory kind, but subject during intervals of somnambulisme. To her case, which has been carefully, humorously, and sceptically studied, we shall return.

Meantime let us take voices and visions on the lowest, most prevalent, and least startling level. A large proportion of people, including the writer, are familiar with the momentary visions beheld with shut eyes between waking and sleeping (illusions hypna-gogiques). The waking self is alert enough to contemplate these processions of figures and faces, these landscapes too, which (in my own case) it is incapable of purposefully calling up.

Thus, in a form of experience which is almost as common as ordinary dreaming, we see that the semi-somnolent self possesses a faculty not always given to the waking self. Compared with my own waking self, for instance, my half-asleep self is almost a personality of genius. He can create visions that the waking self can remember, but cannot originate, and cannot trace to any memory of waking impressions. These apparently trivial things thus point to the existence of almost wholly submerged potentialities in a mind so everyday, commonplace, and, so to speak, superficial as mine. This fact suggests that people who own such minds, the vast majority of mankind, ought not to make themselves the measure of the potentialities of minds of a rarer class, say that of Jeanne d'Arc. The secret of natures like hers cannot be discovered, so long as scientific men incapable even of ordinary 'visualising' (as Mr. Galton found) make themselves the canon or measure of human nature.

Let us, for the sake of argument, suppose that some sane persons are capable of hallucinatory impressions akin to but less transient than illusions hypnagogiques, when, as far as they or others can perceive, they are wide awake. Of such sane persons Goethe and Herschel were examples. In this way we can most easily envisage, or make thinkable by ourselves, the nature of the experiences of Jeanne d'Arc and other seers.

In the other state of semi-somnolence, while still alert enough to watch and reason on the phenomena, we occasionally, though less commonly, hear what may be called 'inner voices.' That is to say, we do not suppose that any one from without is speaking to us, but we hear, as it were, a voice within us making some remark, usually disjointed enough, and not suggested by any traceable train of thought of which we are conscious at the time. This experience partly enables us to understand the cases of sane persons who, when to all appearance wide awake, occasionally hear voices which appear to be objective and caused by actual vibrations of the atmosphere. I am acquainted with at least four persons, all of them healthy, and normal enough, who have had such experiences. In all four cases, the apparent voice (though the listeners have no superstitious belief on the subject) has communicated intelligence which proved to be correct. But in only one instance, I think, was the information thus communicated beyond the reach of conjecture, based perhaps on some observation unconsciously made or so little attended to when made that it could not be recalled by the ordinary memory.

We are to suppose, then, that in such cases the person concerned being to all appearance fully awake, his or her mind has presented a thought, not as a thought, but in the shape of words that seemed to be externally audible. One hearer, in fact, at the moment wondered that the apparent speaker indicated by the voice and words should be shouting so loud in an hotel. The apparent speaker was actually not in the hotel, but at a considerable distance, well out of earshot, and, though in a nervous crisis, was not shouting at all. We know that, between sleeping and waking, our minds can present to us a thought in the apparent form of articulate words, internally audible. The hearers, when fully awake, of words that seem to be externally audible, probably do but carry the semi-vigilant experience to a higher degree, as do the beholders of visual hallucinations, when wide awake. In this way, at least, we can most nearly attain to understanding their experiences. To a relatively small proportion of people, in wakeful existence, experiences occur with distinct-ness, which to a large proportion of persons occur but indistinctly,

'On the margin grey
'Twixt the soul's night and day.'

Let us put it, then, that Jeanne d'Arc's was an advanced case of the mental and bodily constitution exemplified by the relatively small proportion of people, the sane seers of visual hallucinations and hearers of unreal voices. Her thoughts - let us say the thoughts of the deepest region of her being - presented themselves in visual forms, taking the shapes of favourite saints - familiar to her in works of sacred art - attended by an hallucinatory brightness of light ('a photism'), and apparently uttering words of advice which was in conflict with Jeanne's great natural shrewdness and strong sense of duty to her parents. 'She MUST go into France,' and for two or three years she pleaded her ignorance and incompetence. She declined to go. She COULD resist her voices. In prison at Beaurevoir, they forbade her to leap from the tower. But her natural impatience and hopefulness prevailed, and she leaped. 'I would rather trust my soul to God than my body to the English.' This she confessed to as sinful, though not, she hoped, of the nature of deadly sin. Her inmost and her superficial nature were in conflict.

It is now desirable to give, as briefly as possible, Jeanne's own account of the nature of her experiences, as recorded in the book of her trial at Rouen, with other secondhand accounts, offered on oath, at her trial of Rehabilitation, by witnesses to whom she had spoken on the subject. She was always reticent on the theme.

The period when Jeanne supposed herself to see her first visions was physiologically critical. She was either between thirteen and fourteen, or between twelve and thirteen. M. Simeon Luce, in his 'Jeanne d'Arc a Domremy,' held that she was of the more advanced age, and his date (1425) fitted in with some public events, which, in his opinion, were probably the occasions of the experiences. Pere Ayroles prefers the earlier period (1424) when the aforesaid public events had not yet occurred. After examining the evidence on both sides, I am disposed to think, or rather I am certain, that Pere Ayroles is in the right. In either case Jeanne was at a critical age, when, as I understand, female children are occasionally subject to illusions. Speaking then as a non-scientific student, I submit that on the side of ordinary causes for the visions and voices we have:

1. The period in Jeanne's life when they began.

2. Her habits of fasting and prayer.

3. Her intense patriotic enthusiasm, which may, for all that we know, have been her mood before the voices announced to her the mission.

Let us then examine the evidence as to the origin and nature of the alleged phenomena.

I shall begin with the letter of the Senechal de Berry, Perceval de Boulainvilliers, to the Duke of Milan.* The date is June 21st, 1429, six weeks after the relief of Orleans. After a few such tales as that the cocks crowed when Jeanne was born, and that her flock was lucky, he dates her first vision peractis aetatis suae duodecim annis, 'after she was twelve.' Briefly, the tale is that, in a rustic race for flowers, one of the other children cried, 'Joanna, video te volantem juxta terrain,' 'Joan, I see you flying near the ground.' This is the one solitary hint of 'levitation' (so common in hagiology and witchcraft) which occurs in the career of the Maid. This kind of story is so persistent that I knew it must have been told in connection with the Irvingite movement in Scotland. And it was! There is, perhaps, just one trace that flying was believed to be an accomplishment of Jeanne's. When Frere Richard came to her at Troyes, he made, she says, the sign of the cross.** She answered, 'Approchez hardiment, je ne m'envouleray pas.' Now the contemporary St. Colette was not infrequently 'levitated'!

* Proces, v. 115.

** Proces, i. 100.

To return to the Voices. After her race, Jeanne was quasi rapta et a sensibus alienata ('dissociated'), then juxta eam affuit juvenis quidam, a youth stood by her who bade her 'go home, for her mother needed her.'

'Thinking that it was her brother or a neighbour' (apparently she only heard the voice, and did not see the speaker), she hurried home, and found that she had not been sent for. Next, as she was on the point of returning to her friends, 'a very bright cloud appeared to her, and out of the cloud came a voice,' bidding her take up her mission. She was merely puzzled, but the experiences were often renewed. This letter, being contemporary, represents current belief, based either on Jeanne's own statements before the clergy at Poictiers (April 1429) or on the gossip of Domremy. It should be observed that till Jeanne told her own tale at Rouen (1431) we hear not one word about saints or angels. She merely spoke of 'my voices,' 'my counsel,' 'my Master.' If she was more explcit at Poictiers, her confessions did not find their way into surviving letters and journals, not even into the journal of the hostile Bourgeois de Paris. We may glance at examples.

The 'Journal du Siege d'Orleans' is in parts a late

document, in parts 'evidently copied from a journal kept in presence of the actual events.'* The 'Journal,' in February 1429, vaguely says that, 'about this time' our Lord used to appear to a maid, as she was guarding her flock, or 'cousant et filant.' A St. Victor MS. has courant et saillant (running and jumping), which curiously agrees with Boulainvilliers. The 'Journal,' after telling of the Battle of the Herrings (February 12th, 1429), in which the Scots and French were cut up in an attack on an English convoy, declares that Jeanne 'knew of it by grace divine,' and that her vue a distance induced Baudricourt to send her to the Dauphin.** This was attested by Baudricourt's letters.***

* Quicherat. In Proces, iv. 95.

** Proces, iv. 125.

*** Proces, iv. 125.

All this may have been written as late as 1468, but a vague reference to an apparition of our Lord rather suggests contemporary hearsay, before Jeanne came to Orleans. Jeanne never claimed any such visions of our Lord. The story of the clairvoyance as to the Battle of the Herrings is also given in the 'Chronique de la Pucelle.'* M. Quicherat thinks that the passage is amplified from the 'Journal du Siege.' On the other hand, M. Vallet (de Viriville) attributes with assurance the 'Chronique de la Pucelle' to Cousinot de Montreuil, who was the Dauphin's secretary at Poictiers, when the Maid was examined there in April 1429.** If Cousinot was the author, he certainly did not write his chronicle till long after date. However, he avers that the story of clairvoyance was current in the spring of 1429. The dates exactly harmonise; that is to say, between the day

Andrew Lang

of the battle, February 12th, and the setting forth of the Maid from Vaucouleurs, there is just time for the bad news from Rouvray to arrive, confirming her statement, and for a day or two of preparation. But perhaps, after the arrival of the bad news, Baudricourt may have sent Jeanne to the King in a kind of despair. Things could not be worse. If she could do no good, she could do no harm.

* Proces, iv. 206.

** Histoire de Charles VII., ii. 62.

The documents, whether contemporary or written later by contemporaries, contain none of the references to visions of St. Margaret, St. Catherine, and St. Michael, which we find in Jeanne's own replies at Rouen. For this omission it is not easy to account, even if we suppose that, except when giving evidence on oath, the Maid was extremely reticent. That she was reticent, we shall prove from evidence of d'Aulon and Dunois. Turning to the Maid's own evidence in court (1431) we must remember that she was most averse to speaking at all, that she often asked leave to wait for advice and permission from her voices before replying, that on one point she constantly declared that, if compelled to speak, she would not speak the truth. This point was the King's secret. There is absolutely contemporary evidence, from Alain Chartier, that, before she was accepted, she told Charles SOMETHING which filled him with surprise, joy, and belief.* The secret was connected with Charles's doubts of his own legitimacy, and Jeanne at her trial was driven to obscure the truth in a mist of allegory, as, indeed, she confessed. Jeanne's extreme reluctance to adopt even this loyal and laudable evasion is the measure of her truthfulness in general. Still, she did say some words which, as they stand, it is difficult to believe, to explain, or to account for. From any other prisoner, so unjustly menaced with a doom so dreadful, from Mary Stuart, for example, at Fotheringay, we do not expect the whole truth and nothing but the truth. The Maid is a witness of another kind, and where we cannot understand her, we must say, like herself, passez outre!

* Proces, v. 131. Letter of July 1429. See supra, 'The False Pucelle.'

When she was 'about thirteen,' this is her own account, she had a voice from God, to aid her in governing herself. 'And the first time she was in great fear. And it came, that voice, about noonday, in summer, in her father's garden' (where other girls of old France hear the birds sing, 'Marry, maidens, marry!') 'and Jeanne had NOT fasted on the day before.* She heard the voice from the right side, towards the church, and seldom heard it without seeing a bright light. The light was not in front, but at the side whence the voice came. If she were in a wood' (as distinguished from the noise of the crowded and tumultuous court) 'she could well hear the voices coming to her.' Asked what sign for her soul's health the voice gave, she said it bade her behave well, and go to church, and used to tell her to go into France on her mission. (I do not know why the advice about going to church is generally said to have been given FIRST.) Jeanne kept objecting that she was a poor girl who could not ride, or lead in war. She resisted the voice with all her energy. She asserted that she knew the Dauphin, on their first meeting, by aid of her voices.** She declared that the Dauphin himself 'multas habuit revelationes et apparitiones pulchras.' In its literal sense, there is no evidence for this, but rather the reverse. She may mean 'revelations' through herself, or may refer to some circumstance unknown. 'Those of my party saw and knew that voice,' she said, but later would only accept them as witnesses if they were allowed to come and see her.***

* The reading is NEC not ET, as in Quicherat, Proces, i. 52, compare i. 216.

** Proces, i. 56.

*** Proces, i. 57.

This is the most puzzling point in Jeanne's confession. She had no motive for telling an untruth, unless she hoped that these remarks would establish the objectivity of her visions. Of course, one of her strange experiences may have occurred in the presence of Charles and his court, and she may have believed that they shared in it. The point is one which French writers appear to avoid as a rule.

She said that she heard the voice daily in prison, 'and stood in sore need of it.' The voice bade her remain at St. Denis (after the repulse from Paris in September 1429), but she was not allowed to remain.

On the next day (the third of the trial) she told Beaupere that she was fasting since yesterday afternoon. Beaupere, as we saw, conceived that her experiences were mere subjective hallucinations, caused by fasting, by the sound of church-bells, and so on. As to the noise of bells, Coleridge writes that their music fell on his ears, 'MOST LIKE ARTICULATE SOUNDS OF THINGS TO COME.' Beaupere's sober common-sense did not avail to help the Maid, but at the Rehabilitation (1456) he still maintained his old opinion. 'Yesterday she had heard the voices in the morning, at vespers, and at the late ringing for Ave Maria, and she heard them much more frequently than she mentioned.' 'Yesterday she had been asleep when the voice aroused her. She sat up and clasped her hands, and the voice bade her answer boldly. Other words she half heard before she was quite awake, but failed to understand.'*

* Proces, i. 62.

She denied that the voices ever contradicted themselves. On this occasion, as not having received leave from her voices, she refused to say anything as to her visions.

At the next meeting she admitted having heard the voices in court, but in court she could not distinguish the words, owing to the tumult. She had now, however, leave to speak more fully. The voices were those of St. Catherine and St. Margaret. Later she was asked if St. Margaret 'spoke English.' Apparently the querist thought that the English Margaret, wife of Malcolm of Scotland, was intended. They were crowned with fair crowns, as she had said at Poictiers two years before. She now appealed to the record of her examination there, but it was not in court, nor was it used in the trial of Rehabilitation. It has never been recovered. A witness who had examined her at Poictiers threw no light (twenty years later) on the saints and voices. Seven years ago (that is, when she was twelve) she first saw the saints. On the attire of the saints she had not leave to speak. They were preceded by St. Michael 'with the angels of heaven.' 'I saw them as clearly as I see you, and I used to weep when they departed, and would fain that they should have taken me with them.'

As to the famous sword at Fierbois, she averred that she had been in the church there, on her way to Chinon, that the voices later bade her use a sword which was hidden under earth - she thinks behind, but possibly in front of the altar - at Fierbois. A man unknown to her was sent from Tours to fetch the sword, which after search was found, and she wore it.

Asked whether she had prophesied her wound by an arrow at Orleans, and her recovery, she said 'Yes.'

This prediction is singular in that it was recorded before the event. The record was copied into the registre of Brabant, from a letter written on April 22nd, 1429, by a Flemish diplomatist, De Rotselaer, then at Lyons.* De Rotselaer had the prophecy from an officer of the court of the Dauphin. The prediction was thus noted on April 22nd; the event, the arrow-wound in the shoulder, occurred on May 7th. On the fifth day of the trial Jeanne announced that, before seven years were gone, the English 'shall lose a dearer gage than Orleans; this I know by revelation, and am wroth that it is to be so long deferred.' Mr. Myers observes that 'the prediction of a great victory over the English within seven years was not fulfilled in any exact way.' The words of the Maid are 'Angli demittent majus vadium quam fecerunt coram Aurelianis,' and, as prophecies go, their loss of Paris (1436) corresponds very well to the Maid's announcement. She went on, indeed, to say that the English 'will have greater loss than ever they had, through a great French victory,' but this reads like a gloss on her original prediction. 'She knew it as well as that we were there.'** 'You shall not have the exact year, but well I wish it might be before the St. John;'

however, she had already expressed her sorrow that this was NOT to be. Asked, on March 1st, whether her liberation was promised, she said, 'Ask me in three months, and I will tell you.' In three months exactly, her stainless soul was free.

* Proces, iv. 425.

** Proces, i. 84.

On the appearance, garb, and so on of her saints, she declined to answer questions.

She had once disobeyed her voices, when they forbade her to leap from the tower of Beaurevoir. She leaped, but they forgave her, and told her that Compiegne (where she was captured on May 23rd, 1430) would be relieved 'before Martinmas.' It was relieved on October 26th, after a siege of five months. On March 10th an effort was made to prove that her voices had lied to her, and that she had lied about her voices. The enemy maintained that on May 23rd, 1430, she announced a promised victory to the people of Compiegne, vowing that St. Margaret and St. Catherine had revealed it to her. Two hostile priests of Compiegne were at Rouen, and may have carried this tale, which is reported by two Burgundian chroniclers, but NOT by Monstrelet, who was with the besieging army.* In court she said n'eust autre commandement de yssir: she had no command from her voices to make her fatal sally. She was not asked whether she had pretended to have received such an order. She told the touching story of how, at Melun, in April 1430, the voices had warned her that she would be taken prisoner before mid-summer; how she had prayed for death, or for tidings as to the day and hour. But no tidings were given to her, and her old belief, often expressed, that she 'should last but one year or little more,' was confirmed. The Duc d'Alencon had heard her say this several times; for the prophecy at Melun we have only her own word.

* I have examined the evidence in Macmillan's Magazine for May 1894, and, to myself, it seems inadequate.

She was now led into the allegory intended to veil the King's secret, the allegory about the Angel (herself) and the Crown (the coronation at Rheims). This allegory was fatal, but does not bear on her real belief about her experiences. She averred, returning to genuine confessions, that her voices often came spontaneously; if they did not, she summoned them by a simple prayer to God. She had seen the angelic figures moving, invisible save to her, among men. The voices HAD promised her the release of Charles d'Orleans, but time had failed her. This was as near a confession of failure as she ever made, till the day of her burning, if she really made one then.* But here, as always, she had predicted that she would do this or that if she were sans empeschement. She had no revelation bidding her attack Paris when she did, and after the day at Melun she submitted to the advice of the other captains. As to her release, she was only bidden 'to bear all cheerfully; be not vexed with thy martyrdom, thence shalt thou come at last into the kingdom of Paradise.'

* As to her 'abjuration' and alleged doubts, see L'Abjuration du Cimetiere Saint-Ouen, by Abbe Ph. H. Dunard; Poussielgue, Paris, 1901.

To us, this is explicit enough, but the poor child explained to her judges that by martire she understood the pains of prison, and she referred it to her Lord, whether there were more to bear. In this passage the original French exists, as well as the Latin translation. The French is better.

'Ne te chaille de ton martire, tu t'en vendras enfin en royaulme de Paradis.'

'Non cures de martyrio tuo: tu venies finaliter in regnum paradisi.'

The word hinc is omitted in the bad Latin. Unluckily we have only a fragment of the original French, as taken down in court. The Latin version, by Courcelles, one of the prosecutors, is in places inaccurate, in others is actually garbled to the disadvantage of the Maid.

This passage, with some others, may perhaps be regarded as indicating that the contents of the communications received by Jeanne were not always intelligible to her.

That her saints could be, and were, touched physically by her, she admitted.* Here I am inclined to think that she had touched with her ring (as the custom was) a RELIC of St. Catherine at Fierbois. Such relics, brought from the monastery of Sinai, lay at Fierbois, and we know that women loved to rub their rings on the ring of Jeanne, in spite of her laughing remonstrances. But apart from this conjecture, she regarded her saints as tangible by her. She had embraced both St. Margaret and St. Catherine.**

* Proces, i. 185.

** Proces, i. 186.

For the rest, Jeanne recanted her so-called recantation, averring that she was unaware of the contents or full significance of the document, which certainly is not the very brief writing to which she set her mark Her voices recalled her to her duty, for them she went to the stake, and if there was a moment of wavering on the day of her doom, her belief in the objective reality of the phenomena remained firm, and she recovered her faith in the agony of her death.

Of EXTERNAL evidence as to her accounts of these experiences, the best is probably that of d'Aulon, the maitre d'Hotel of the Maid, and her companion through her career. He and she were reposing in the same room at Orleans, her hostess being in the chamber (May 1429), and d'Aulon had just fallen asleep, when the Maid awoke him with a cry. Her voices bade her go against the English, but in what direction she knew not. In fact, the French leaders had begun, without her knowledge, an attack on St. Loup, whither she galloped and took the fort.* It is, of course, conceivable that the din of onset, which presently became audible, had vaguely reached the senses of the sleeping Maid. Her page confirms d'Aulon's testimony.

* Proces, iii. 212.

D'Aulon states that when the Maid had any martial adventure in prospect, she told him that her 'counsel' had given her this or that advice. He questioned her as to the nature of this 'counsel.' She said 'she had three councillors, of whom one was always with her, a second went and came to her, and the third was he with whom the others deliberated.' D'Aulon 'was not worthy to see this counsel.' From the moment when he heard this, d'Aulon asked no more questions. Dunois also gave some evidence as to the 'counsel.' At Loches, when Jeanne was urging the journey to Rheims, Harcourt asked her, before the King, what the nature (modus) of the council was; HOW it communicated with her. She replied that when she was met with incredulity, she went apart and prayed to God. Then she heard a voice say, Fille De, va, va, va, je serai a ton aide, va! 'And when she heard that voice she was right glad, and would fain be ever in that state.' 'As she spoke thus, ipsa miro modo exsultabat, levando suos oculos ad coelum.'* (She seemed wondrous glad, raising her eyes to heaven.) Finally, that Jeanne maintained her belief to the moment of her death, we learn from the priest, Martin Ladvenu, who was with her to the last.** There is no sign anywhere that at the moment of an 'experience' the Maid's aspect seemed that of one 'dissociated,' or uncanny, or abnormal, in the eyes of those who were in her company.

* Proces, iii. 12.

** Proces, iii. 170.

These depositions were given twenty years later (1452-56), and, of course, allowance must be made for weakness of memory and desire to glorify the Maid. But there is really nothing of a suspicious character about them. In fact, the 'growth of legend' was very slight, and is mainly confined to the events of the martyrdom, the White Dove, the name of Christ blazoned in flame, and so forth.* It should also have been mentioned that at the taking of St. Pierre de Moustier (November 1429) Jeanne, when deserted by her forces, declared to d'Aulon that she was 'not alone, but surrounded by fifty thousand of her own.' The men therefore rallied and stormed the place.

This is the sum of the external evidence as to the phenomena.

* For German fables see Lefevre-Pontalis, Les Sources Allemandes, Paris, 1903. They are scanty, and, in some cases, are distortions of real events.

As to the contents of the communications to Jeanne, they were certainly sane, judicious, and heroic. M. Quicherat (Apercus Nouveaux, p. 61) distinguishes three classes of abnormally conveyed knowledge, all on unimpeachable evidence.

(1.) THOUGHT-READING, as in the case of the King's secret; she repeated to him the words of a prayer which he had made mentally in his oratory.

(2.) CLAIRVOYANCE, as exhibited in the affair of the sword of Fierbois.

(3.) PRESCIENCE, as in the prophecy of her arrow-wound at Orleans. According to her confessor, Pasquerel, she repeated the prophecy and indicated the spot in which she would be wounded (under the right shoulder) on the night of May 6. But this is later evidence given in the trial of Rehabilitation. Neither Pasquerel nor any other of the Maid's party was heard at the trial of 1431.

To these we might add the view, from Vaucouleurs, a hundred leagues away, of the defeat at Rouvray; the prophecy that she 'would last but a year or little more;' the prophecy, at Melun, of her capture; the prophecy of the relief of Compiegne; and the strange affair of the bon conduit at the battle of Pathay.* For several of these predictions we have only the Maid's word, but to be plain, we can scarcely have more unimpeachable testimony.

* Proces, iv. 371, 372. Here the authority is Monstrelet, a Burgundian.

Here the compiler leaves his task: the inferences may be drawn by experts. The old theory of imposture, the Voltairean theory of a 'poor idiot,' the vague charge of 'hysteria,' are untenable. The honesty and the genius of Jeanne are no longer denied. If hysteria be named, it is plain that we must argue that, because hysteria is accompanied by visionary symptoms, all visions are proofs of hysteria. Michelet holds by hallucinations which were unconsciously externalised by the mind of Jeanne. That mind must have been a very peculiar intellect, and the modus is precisely the difficulty. Henri Martin believes in some kind of manifestation revealed to the individual mind by the Absolute: perhaps this word is here equivalent to 'the subliminal self' of Mr. Myers. Many Catholics, as yet unauthorised, I conceive, by the Church, accept the theory of Jeanne herself; her saints were true saints from Paradise. On the other hand it is manifest that visions of a bright light and 'auditions' of voices are common enough phenomena in madness, and in the experiences of very uninspired sane men and women. From the sensations of these people Jeanne's phenomena are only differentiated by their number, by their persistence through seven years of an almost abnormally healthy life, by their importance, orderliness, and veracity, as well as by their heroic character.

Mr. Myers has justly compared the case of Jeanne with that of Socrates. A much humbler parallel, curiously close in one respect, may be cited from M. Janet's article, 'Les Actes Inconscients dans le Somnambulisme' ('Revue Philosophique,' March 1888).

The case is that of Madame B., a peasant woman near Cherbourg. She has her common work-a-day personality, called, for convenience, 'Leonie.' There is also her hypnotic personality, 'Leontine.' Now Leontine (that is, Madame B. in a somnambulistic state) was one day hysterical and troublesome. Suddenly she exclaimed in terror that she heard A VOICE ON THE LEFT, crying, 'Enough, be quiet, you are a nuisance.' She hunted in vain for the speaker, who, of course, was inaudible to M. Janet, though he was present. This sagacious speaker (a faculty of Madame B.'s own nature) is 'brought out' by repeated passes, and when this moral and sensible phase of her character is thus evoked, Madame B. is 'Leonore.' Madame B. now sometimes assumes an expression of beatitude, smiling and looking upwards. As Dunois said of Jeanne when she was recalling her visions, 'miro modo exsultabat, levando suos oculos ad coelum.' This ecstasy Madame B. (as Leonie) dimly remembers, averring that 'she has been dazzled BY A LIGHT ON THE LEFT SIDE.' Here apparently we have the best aspect of poor Madame B. revealing itself in a mixture of hysterics and hypnotism, and associating itself with an audible sagacious voice and a dazzling light on the left, both hallucinatory.

The coincidence (not observed by M. Janet) with Jeanne's earliest experience is most curious. Audivit vocem a dextero latere. . . .claritas est ab eodem latere in quo vox auditur, sed ibi communiter est magna claritas. (She heard a voice from the right. There is usually a bright light on the same side as the voice.) Like Madame B., Jeanne was at first alarmed by these sensations.

The parallel, so far, is perfectly complete (except that 'Leonore' merely talks common sense, while Jeanne's voices gave information not normally acquired). But in Jeanne's case I have found no hint of temporary unconsciousness or 'dissociation.' When strung up to the most intense mental eagerness in court, she still heard her voices, though, because of the tumult of the assembly, she heard them indistinctly. Thus her experiences are not associated with insanity, partial unconsciousness, or any physical disturbance (as in some tales of second sight), while the sagacity of the communications and their veracity distinguish them from the hallucinations of mad people. As far as the affair of Rouvray, the prophecy of the instant death of an insolent soldier at Chinon (evidence of Pasquerel, her confessor), and such things go, we have, of course, many alleged parallels in the predictions of Mr. Peden and other seers of the Covenant. But Mr. Peden's political predictions are still unfulfilled, whereas concerning the 'dear gage' which the English should lose in France within seven years, Jeanne may be called successful.

On the whole, if we explain Jeanne's experiences as the expressions of her higher self (as Leonore is Madame B.'s higher self), we are compelled to ask what is the nature of that self?

Another parallel, on a low level, to what may be called the mechanism of Jeanne's voices and visions is found in Professor Flournoy's patient, 'Helene Smith.'* Miss

'Smith,' a hardworking shopwoman in Geneva, had, as a child, been dull but dreamy. At about twelve years of age she began to see, and hear, a visionary being named Leopold, who, in life, had been Cagliostro. His appearance was probably suggested by an illustration in the Joseph Balsamo of Alexandre Dumas. The saints of Jeanne, in the same way, may have been suggested by works of sacred art in statues and church windows. To Miss Smith, Leopold played the part of Jeanne's saints. He appeared and warned her not to take such or such a street when walking, not to try to lift a parcel which seemed light, but was very heavy, and in other ways displayed knowledge not present to her ordinary workaday self.

* See Flournoy, Des Indes a la Planete Mars. Alcan, Paris, 1900.

There was no real Leopold, and Jeanne's St. Catherine cannot be shown to have ever been a real historical personage.** These figures, in fact, are more or less akin to the 'invisible playmates' familiar to many children.** They are not objective personalities, but part of the mechanism of a certain class of mind. The mind may be that of a person devoid of genius, like Miss Smith, or of a genius like Goethe, Shelley, or Jeanne d'Arc, or Socrates with his 'Daemon,' and its warnings. In the case of Jeanne d'Arc, as of Socrates, the mind communicated knowledge not in the conscious everyday intelligence of the Athenian or of la Pucelle. This information, in Jeanne's case, was presented in the shape of hallucinations of eye and ear. It was sane, wise, noble, veracious, and concerned not with trifles, but with great affairs. We are not encouraged to suppose that saints or angels made themselves audible and visible. But, by the mechanism of such appearances to the senses, that which was divine in the Maid - in all of us, if we follow St. Paul - that 'in which we live and move and have our being,' made itself intelligible to her ordinary consciousness, her workaday self, and led her to the fulfilment of a task which seemed impossible to men.

* See the Life and Martyrdom of St. Katherine of Alexandria. (Roxburghe Club, 1884, Introduction by Mr. Charles Hardwick). Also the writer's translation of the chapel record of the 'Miracles of Madame St. Catherine of Fierbois,' in the Introduction. (London, Nutt.)

** See the writer's preface to Miss Corbet's Animal Land for a singular example in our own time.

VIII.

THE MYSTERY OF JAMES DE LA CLOCHE

'P'raps he was my father - though on this subjict I can't speak suttinly, for my ma wrapped up my buth in a mistry. I may be illygitmit, I may have been changed at nuss.'

In these strange words does Mr. Thackeray's Jeames de la Pluche anticipate the historical mystery of James de la Cloche. HIS 'buth' is 'wrapped up in a mistry,' HIS 'ma' is a theme of doubtful speculation; his father (to all appearance) was Charles II. We know not whether James de la Cloche - rejecting the gaudy lure of three crowns - lived and died a saintly Jesuit; or whether, on the other hand, he married beneath him, was thrown into gaol, was sentenced to a public whipping, was pardoned and released, and died at the age of twenty-three, full of swaggering and impenitent impudence. Was there but one James de la Cloche, a scion of the noblest of European royal lines? Did he, after professions of a holy vocation, suddenly assume the most secular of characters, jilting Poverty and Obedience for an earthly bride? Or was the person who appears to have acted in this unworthy manner a mere impostor, who had stolen James's money and jewels and royal name? If so, what became of the genuine and saintly James de la Cloche? He is never heard of any more, whether because he assumed an ecclesiastical alias, or because he was effectually silenced by the person who took his character, name, money, and parentage.

There are two factions in the dispute about de la Cloche. The former (including the late Lord Acton and Father Boero) believe that James adhered to his sacred vocation, while the second James was a rank impostor. The other party holds that the frivolous and secular James was merely the original James, who suddenly abandoned his vocation, and burst on the world as a gay cavalier, and claimant of the rank of Prince of Wales, or, at least, of the revenues and perquisites of that position.

The first act in the drama was discovered by Father Boero, who printed the documents as to James de la Cloche in his 'History of the Conversion to the Catholic Church of Charles II., King of England,' in the sixth and seventh volumes, fifth series, of La Civilta Cattolica (Rome, 1863). (The essays can be procured in a separate brochure.) Father Boero says not a word about the second and secular James, calling himself 'Giacopo Stuardo.' But the learned father had communicated the papers about de la Cloche to Lord Acton, who wrote an article on the subject, 'The Secret History of Charles II.,' in 'The Home and Foreign Review,' July 1862. Lord Acton now added the story of the second James, or of the second avatar of the first James, from State Papers in our Record Office. The documents as to de la Cloche are among the MSS. of the Society of Jesus at Rome.

The purpose of Father Boero was not to elucidate a romance in royal life, but to prove that Charles II. had, for many years, been sincerely inclined to the Catholic creed, though thwarted by his often expressed disinclination to 'go on his travels again.' In point of fact, the religion of Charles II. might probably be stated in a celebrated figure of Pascal's. Let it be granted that reason can discover nothing as to the existence of any ground for religion. Let it be granted that we cannot know whether there is a God or not. Yet either there is, or there is not. It is even betting, heads or tails, croix ou pile. This being so, it is wiser to bet that there is a God. It is safer. If you lose, you are just where you were, except for the pleasures which you desert. If you win, you win everything! What you stake is finite, a little pleasure; if you win, you win infinite bliss.

So far Charles was prepared theoretically to go but he would not abandon his diversions. A God there is, but 'He's a good fellow, and 'twill all be well.' God would never punish a man, he told Burnet, for taking 'a little irregular pleasure.' Further, Charles saw that, if bet he must, the safest religion to back was that of Catholicism. Thereby he could - it was even betting - actually ensure his salvation. But if he put on his money publicly, if he professed Catholicism, he certainly lost his kingdoms. Consequently he tried to be a crypto-Catholic, but he was not permitted to practise one creed and profess another. THAT the Pope would not stand. So it was on his death-bed that he made his desperate plunge, and went, it must be said, bravely, on the darkling voyage.

Not to dwell on Charles's earlier dalliances with Rome, in November 1665, his kinsman, Ludovick Stewart, Sieur d'Aubigny, of the Scoto-French Lennox Stewarts, was made a cardinal, and then died. Charles had now no man whom he could implicitly trust in his efforts to become formally, but secretly, a Catholic. And now James de la Cloche comes on the scene. Father Boero publishes, from the Jesuit archives, a strange paper, purporting to be written and signed by the King's hand, and sealed with his private seal, that diamond seal, whereof the impression brought such joy to the soul of the disgraced Archbishop Sharp. Father Boero attests the authenticity of seal and handwriting. In this paper, Charles acknowledges his paternity of James Stuart, 'who, by our command, has hitherto lived in France and other countries under a feigned name.' He has come to London, and is to bear the name of 'de la Cloche du Bourg de Jarsey.' De la Cloche is not to produce this document, 'written in his own language' (French), till after the King's death. (It is important to note that James de la Cloche seems to have spoken no language except French.) The paper is dated 'Whitehall, September 27, 1665,' when, as Lord Acton observes, the Court, during the Plague, was NOT at Whitehall.*

* Civ. Catt. Series V., vol. vi. 710. Home and Foreign Review, vol. i. 156.

Lord Acton conjectured that the name 'de la Cloche' was taken from that of a Protestant minister in Jersey (circ. 1646). This is the more probable, as Charles later invented a false history of his son, who was to be described as the son of 'a rich preacher, deceased.' The surname, de la Cloche, had really been that of a preacher in Jersey, and survives in Jersey.

After 1665, James de la Cloche was pursuing his studies in Holland, being at this time a Protestant. Conceivably he had been brought up in a French

Huguenot family, like that of the de Rohan. On February 7, 1667, Charles wrote a new document. In this he grants to de la Cloche 500 pounds a year, while he lives in London and adheres to 'the religion of his father and the Anglican service book.' But, in that very year (July 29, 1667), de la Cloche went to Hamburg, and was there received into the Catholic Church, forfeiting his pension.

Christina of Sweden was then residing in Hamburg. De la Cloche apprised her of his real position - a son of the King of England - and must have shown her in proof Charles's two letters of 1665 and 1667. If so - and how else could he prove his birth? - he broke faith with Charles, but, apparently, he did not mean to use Charles's letters as proof of his origin when applying, as he did, for admission to the novitiate of the Jesuits at Rome. He obtained from Christina a statement, in Latin, that Charles had acknowledged him, privately, to her, as his son. This note of Christina's, de la Cloche was to show to his director at Rome.

It does not appear that Charles had ever told Christina a word about the matter. These pious monarchs were far from being veracious. However, Christina's document would save the young man much trouble, on the point of his illegitimacy, when, on April 11, 1668, he entered St. Andrea al Quirinale as a Jesuit novice. He came in poverty. His wardrobe was of the scantiest. He had two shirts, a chamois leather chest protector, three collars, and three pairs of sleeves. He described himself as 'Jacques de la Cloche, of Jersey, British subject,' and falsely, or ignorantly, stated his age as twenty-four. Really he was twenty-two.* Why he told Christina his secret, why he let her say that Charles had told her, we do not know. It may be that the General of the Jesuits, Oliva, did not yet know who de la Cloche really was. Meanwhile, his religious vocation led him to forfeit 500 pounds yearly, and expectations, and to disobey his father and king.

* Civ. Catt., ut supra, 712, 713, and notes.

The good King took all very easily. On August 3, 1668, he wrote a longa et verbosa epistola, from Whitehall, to the General of the Jesuits. His face was now set towards the secret treaty of Dover and conversion. The conversion of his son, therefore, seemed truly providential. Charles had discussed it with his own mother and his wife. To Oliva he wrote in French, explaining that his Latin was 'poor,' and that, if he wrote English, an interpreter would be needed, but that no Englishman was to 'put his nose' into this affair. He had long prayed God to give him a safe and secret chance of conversion, but he could not use, without exciting suspicion, the priests then in England. On the other hand, his son would do: the young cavalier then at Rome, named de la Cloche de Jersey. This lad was the pledge of an early love for 'a young lady of a family among the most distinguished in our kingdoms.' He was a child of the King's 'earliest youth,' that is, during his residence in Jersey, March-June 1646, when Charles was sixteen. In a few years, the King hoped to recognise him publicly. With him alone could Charles practise secretly the mysteries of the Church. To such edifying ends had God turned an offence against His laws, an amourette. De la Cloche, of course, was as yet not a priest, and could not administer sacraments, an idea which occurred to Charles himself.

The Queen of Sweden, Charles added, was prudent,

but, being a woman, she probably could not keep a secret. Charles wants his son to come home, and asks the Jesuit to put off Christina with any lie he pleases, if she asks questions. In short, he regards the General of the Jesuits as a person ready to tell any convenient falsehood, and lets this opinion appear with perfect naivete! He will ask the Pope to hurry de la Cloche into priest's orders, or, if that is not easy, he will have the thing done in Paris, by means of Louis XIV., or his own sister, Henrietta (Madame). Or the Queen and Queen Mother can have it done in London, as they 'have bishops at their will.' The King has no desire to interrupt his son's vocation as a Jesuit. In London the young man must avoid Jesuit society, and other occasions of suspicion. He ends with a promise of subscriptions to Jesuit objects.*

* Civ. Catt. Series V., vii. 269-274.

By the same courier, the King wrote to 'Our most honoured son, the Prince Stuart, dwelling with the R.P. Jesuits under the name of Signor de la Cloche.' James may be easy about money. He must be careful of his health, which is delicate, and not voyage at an unhealthy season. The Queens are anxious to see him. He should avoid asceticism. He may yet be recognised, and take precedence of his younger and less nobly born brother, the Duke of Monmouth. The King expresses his affection for a son of excellent character, and distinguished by the solidity of his studies and acquirements. If toleration is gained, de la Cloche has some chance of the English throne, supposing Charles and the Duke of York to die without issue male. Parliament will be unable to oppose this arrangement, unless Catholics are excluded from the succession.

This has a crazy sound. The Crown would have been in no lack of legitimate heirs, failing offspring male of the King and the Duke of York.

If de la Cloche, however, persists in his vocation, so be it. The King may get for him a cardinal's hat. The King assures his son of his affection, not only as the child of his extreme youth, but for the virtues of his character. De la Cloche must travel as a simple gentleman.*

* Ut supra, 275, 278.

On August 29, Charles again wrote to Oliva. He had heard that the Queen of Sweden was going to Rome. De la Cloche must not meet her, she might let out the secret: he must come home at once. If Charles is known to be a Catholic, there will be tumults, and he will lose his life. Another letter, undated, asks that the novice, contrary to rule, may travel alone, with no Jesuit chaperon, and by sea, direct from Genoa. Consulting physicians, the King has learned that sea sickness is never fatal, rather salutary. His travelling name should be Henri de Rohan, as if he were of that Calvinistic house, friends of the King. The story must be circulated that de la Cloche is the son of a rich preacher, deceased, and that he has gone to visit his mother, who is likely to be converted. He must leave his religious costume with the Jesuits at Genoa, and pick it up there on his return. He must not land at the port of London, but at some other harbour, and thence drive to town.*

* Ut supra, 283-287.

On October 14, d'Oliva, from Leghorn, wrote to Charles that 'the French gentleman' was on the seas.

On November 18, Charles wrote to d'Oliva that his son was returning to Rome as his secret ambassador, and, by the King's orders, was to come back to London, bearing answers to questions which he will put verbally. In France he leaves a Jesuit whom he is to pick up as he again makes for England *

* Father Florent Dumas, in a rather florid essay on 'The Saintly Son of Charles II,' supposes that, after all, he had a Jesuit chaperon during his expedition to England (Jesuit Etudes de Rel., Hist. et Lit., Paris, 1864-1865).

The questions to which de la Cloche is to bring answers doubtless concerned the wish of Charles to be a Catholic secretly, and other arrangements which he is known to have suggested on another occasion.

After this letter of November 18, 1668, WE NEVER HEAR A WORD ABOUT JAMES DE LA CLOCHE.* No later letters from the King to d'Oliva are found, the name of James de la Cloche does not occur again in the Records of the Society of Jesus.

* Ut supra, 418-420.

Father Boero argues that James would return to London, under a third name, unknown. But it would be risky for one who had appeared in England under one name in 1665, and under another (Rohan) in 1668, to turn up under a third in 1669. To take aliases, often three or four, was, however, the custom of the English Jesuits, and de la Cloche may have chosen his fourth. Thus we could not trace him, in records, unless Charles wrote again to d'Oliva about his son. No such letter exists. In his letter of November 18, Charles promises, in a year, a subscription to the Jesuit building fund - this at his son's request. I know not if the money was ever paid. He also asks Oliva to give James 800 doppie for expenses, to be repaid in six months.

James did not leave the Society of Jesus, argues Father Boero, for, had he left, he would have carried away the papers in which Charles acknowledges him and promises a pension of 500 pounds yearly. But that document would be useless to James, whether he remained a Jesuit or not, for the condition of the pension (1667) was that he should be a Protestant of the Anglican sect, and live in London. However, Charles's letter of 1668 was in another tune, and James certainly left THAT with the Jesuits in Rome; at least, they possess it now. But suppose that James fled secretly from the Jesuits, then he probably had no chance of recovering his papers. He was not likely to run away, however, for, Charles says, he 'did not like London,' or the secular life, and he appears to have returned to Rome at the end of 1668, with every intention of fulfilling his mission and pursuing his vocation. His return mission to England over, he probably would finish his Jesuit training at a college in France or Flanders, say St. Omer's, where Titus Oates for a while abode. No James de la Cloche is known there or elsewhere, but he might easily adopt a new alias, and Charles would have no need to write to Oliva about him. It may be that James was the priest at St. Omer's, whom, in 1670, Charles had arranged to send, but did not send, to Clement IX.* He may also be the priest secretly brought from abroad to Charles during the Popish Plot (1678-1681).**

* Mignet, Neg. rel. Succ. d'Espagne, iii. 232.

** Welwood, Memoirs, 146.

These are suggestions of Lord Acton, who thinks that de la Cloche may also have been the author of two papers, in French, on religion, left by Charles, in his own hand, at his death.* These are conjectures. If we accept them, de la Cloche was a truly self-denying young semi-Prince, preferring an austere life to the delights and honours which attended his younger brother, the Duke of Monmouth. But, just when de la Cloche should have been returning from Rome to London, at the end of 1668 or beginning of 1669, a person calling himself James Stuart, son of Charles II., by an amour, at Jersey, in 1646, with a 'Lady Mary Henrietta Stuart,' appeared in some magnificence at Naples. This James Stuart either was, or affected to be, James de la Cloche. Whoever he was, the King's carefully guarded secret was out, was public property.

*Home and Foreign Review, i. 165.

Our information as to this James Stuart, or Giacopo Stuardo, son of the King of England - the cavalier who appears exactly when the Jesuit novice, James de la Cloche, son of the King of England, vanishes - is derived from two sources. First there are Roman newsletters, forwarded to England by Kent, the English agent at Rome, with his own despatches in English. It does not appear to me that Kent had, as a rule, any intimate purveyor of intelligence at Naples. He seems, in his own letters to Williamson,* merely to follow and comment on the Italian newsletters which he forwards and the gossip of 'the Nation,' that is, the English in Rome. The newsletters, of course, might be under the censorship of Rome and Naples. Such is one of our sources.**

* See 'The Valet's Master,' for other references to Williamson.

** State Papers, Italian, 1669, Bundle 10, Record Office.

Lord Acton, in 1862, and other writers, have relied solely on this first set of testimonies. But the late Mr. Maziere Brady has apparently ignored or been unacquainted with these materials, and he cites a printed book not quoted by Lord Acton.* This work is the third volume of the 'Lettere' of Vincenzo Armanni of Gubbio, who wrote much about the conversion of England, and had himself been in that country. The work quoted was printed (privately?) by Giuseppe Piccini, at Macerata, in 1674, and, so far, I have been unable to see an example. The British Museum Library has no copy, and the 'Lettere' are unknown to Brunet. We have thus to take a secondhand version of Armanni's account. He says that his informant was one of two confessors, employed successively by Prince James Stuart, at Naples, in January-August 1669. Now, Kent sent to England an English translation of the Italian will of James Stuart. A will is also given, of course in Italian, by Vincenzo Armanni; a copy of this is in the Record Office.

* Maziere Brady, Anglo-Roman Papers, pp. 93-121 (Gardner Paisley, 1890).

It appears from this will that James Stuart, for reasons of his own, actually did enjoy the services of two successive confessors, at Naples, in 1669. The earlier of these two was Armanni's informant. His account of James Stuart differs from that of Kent and the Italian newsletters, which we repeat, alone are cited by Lord

Acton (1862); while Mr. Brady (1890), citing Armanni, knows nothing of the newsletters and Kent, and conceives himself to be the first writer in English on the subject.

Turning to our first source, the newsletters of Rome, and the letters of Kent, the dates in each case prove that Kent, with variations, follows the newsletters. The gazzetta of March 23, 1669, is the source of Kent's despatch of March 30. On the gazzette of April 6, 13, and 20, he makes no comment, but his letter of June 16 varies more or less from the newsletter of June 11. His despatch of September 7 corresponds to the newsletter of the same date, but is much more copious.

Taking these authorities in order of date, we find the newsletter of Rome (March 23, 1669) averring that an unknown English gentleman has been 'for some months' at Naples, that is, since January at least, and has fallen in love with the daughter of a poor innkeeper, or host (locandiere). He is a Catholic and has married the girl. The newly made father-in-law has been spending freely the money given to him by the bridegroom. Armanni, as summarised by Mr. Brady, states the matter of the money thus: 'The Prince was anxious to make it appear that his intended father-in-law was not altogether a pauper, and accordingly he gave a sum of money to Signor Francesco Corona to serve as a dowry for Teresa. Signor Corona could not deny himself the pleasure of exhibiting this money before his friends, and he indiscreetly boasted before his neighbours concerning his rich son-in-law.'

From Armanni's version, derived from the confessor of James Stuart, it appears that nothing was said as to James's royal birth till after his arrest, when he informed the Viceroy of Naples in self-defence.

To return to the newsletter of March 23, it represents that the Viceroy heard of the unwonted expenditure of money by Corona, and seized the English son-in-law on suspicion. In his possession the Viceroy found about 200 doppie, many jewels, and some papers in which he was addressed as Altezza (Highness). The word doppie is used by Charles (in Boero's Italian translation) for the 800 coins which he asks Oliva to give to de la Cloche for travelling expenses. Were James Stuart's 200 doppie the remains of the 800? Lord Acton exaggerates when he writes vaguely that Stuart possessed 'heaps of pistoles.' Two hundred doppie (about 150 or 160 pounds) are not 'heaps.' To return to the newsletter, the idea being current that the young man was a natural son of the King of England, he was provisionally confined in the castle of St. Elmo. On April 6, he is reported to be shut up in the castle of Gaeta. On the 20th, we hear that fifty scudi monthly have been assigned to the prisoner for his support. The Viceroy has written (to England) to ask what is to be done with him.

On June 11, it is reported that, after being removed to the Vicaria, a prison for vulgar malefactors, the captive has been released. He is NOT the son of the King of England.

Kent's letter of March 30 follows the newsletter of March 23. He adds that the unknown Englishman 'seems' to have 'vaunted to bee the King of England's sonne BORNE AT GERSEY,' a fact never expressly stated about de la Cloche. It is not clear that James Stuart vaunted his birth before his arrest made it necessary for him to give an account of himself. Kent also says that the unknown sent for the English consul, Mr. Browne, 'to assist his delivery out of the castle. But it seems he could not speake a word of English nor give any account of the birth he pretended to.' On Kent's showing, he had no documentary proofs of his royal birth. French was de la Cloche's language, if this unknown was he, and if Kent is right, he had not with him the two documents and the letter of Charles II. and the certificate of the Queen of Sweden. 'This is all the light I can picke out of the Nation, or others, of his extravagant story, which whether will end in Prince or cheate I shall endeavour to inform you hereafter.'

Kent's next letter (June 16) follows, with variations, the newsletter of June 11: -

Kent to J. Williamson

June 16, 1669.

The Gentleman who WOULD HAVE BEENE HIS MAT'YS BASTARD at Naples, vpon the receipt of his Ma'ties Letters to that Vice King was immediately taken out of the Castle of Gaetta brought to Naples and Cast into the Grand Prison called the Vicaria, where being thrust amongst the most Vile and infamous Rascalls, the Vice King intended to have Caused him to bee whipt about the Citty, but meanes was made by his wife's kindred (Who was Likewise taken with this pretended Prince) to the Vice-Queene, who, in compassion to her and her kindred, prevailed with Don Pedro to deliver him from that Shame [and from gaol, it seems], and soe ends the Story of this fourb WHO SPEAKS NOE LANGUADGE BUT FFRENCH.

The newsletter says nothing of the intended whipping,
or of the intercession of the family of the wife of the
unknown. These points may be the additions of
gossips.

In any case the unknown, with his wife, after a stay of
no long time in the Vicaria, is set at liberty. His release
might be explained on the ground that Charles
disavowed and cast him off, which he might safely do,
if the man was really de la Cloche, but had none of the
papers proving his birth, the papers which are still in
the Jesuit archives. Or he may have had the papers, and
they may have been taken from him and restored to the
Jesuit General.

So far, the betting as to whether de la Cloche and the
Naples pretender were the same man or not is at evens.
Each hypothesis is beset by difficulties. It is highly
improbable that the unworldly and enthusiastic Jesuit
novice threw up, at its very crisis, a mission which
might lead his king, his father, and the British Empire
back into the one Fold. De la Cloche, forfeiting his
chances of an earthly crown, was on the point of
gaining a heavenly one. It seems to the last degree
unlikely that he would lose this and leave the Jesuits to
whom he had devoted himself, and the quiet life of
study and religion, for the worldly life which he
disliked, and for that life on a humble capital of a few
hundred pounds, and some jewels, presents, perhaps
from the two Queens, his grandmother and stepmother.
De la Cloche knew that Charles, if the novice clung to
religion, had promised to procure for him, if he desired
it, a cardinal's hat; while if, with Charles's approval, he
left religion, he might be a prince, perhaps a king. He
had thus every imaginable motive for behaving with
decorum - in religion or out of it. Yet, if he is the

Naples pretender, he suddenly left the Jesuits without Charles's knowledge and approval, but by a freakish escapade, like 'The Start' of Charles himself as a lad, when he ran away from Argyll and the Covenanters. And he did this before he ever saw Teresa Corona. He reminds one of the Huguenot pastor in London, whom an acquaintance met on the Turf. 'I not preacher now, I gay dog,' explained the holy man.

All this is, undeniably, of a high improbability. But on the other side, de la Cloche was freakish and unsettled. He had but lately (1667) asked for and accepted a pension to be paid while he remained an Anglican, then he was suddenly received into the Roman Church, and started off, probably on foot, with his tiny 'swag' of three shirts and three collars, to walk to Rome and become a Jesuit. He may have deserted the Jesuits as suddenly and recklessly as he had joined them. It is not impossible. He may have received the 800 pounds for travelling expenses from Oliva; not much of it was left by March 1669 - only about 150 pounds. On the theory that the man at Naples was an impostor, it is odd that he should only have spoken French, that he was charged with no swindles, that he made a very poor marriage in place of aiming at a rich union; that he had, somehow, learned de la Cloche's secret; and that, possessing a fatal secret, invaluable to a swindler and blackmailer, he was merely disgraced and set free. Louis XIV. would, at least, have held him a masked captive for the rest of his life. But he was liberated, and, after a brief excursion, returned to Naples, where he died, maintaining that he was a prince.

Thus, on either view, 'prince or cheat,' we are met by things almost impossible.

We now take up the Naples man's adventure as narrated by Kent. He writes:

Kent to Jo: Williamson

Rome: August 31, 1669.

That certaine fellow or what hee was, who pretended to bee his Ma'ties naturall sonn at Naples is dead and haueing made his will they write mee from thence wee shall with the next Poast know the truth of his quality.

September 7, 1669.

That certaine Person at Naples who in his Lyfe tyme would needes bee his Ma'ties naturall Sonne is dead in the same confidence and Princely humour, for haueing Left his Lady Teresa Corona, an ordinary person, 7 months gone with Child, hee made his Testament, and hath Left his most Xtian Ma'tie (whom he called Cousin) executor of it.

Hee had been absent from Naples some tyme pretending to haue made a journey into France to visit his Mother, Dona Maria Stuarta of His Ma'tie Royall Family, which neernes and greatnes of Blood was the cause, Saies hee, that his Ma'tie would never acknowledge him for his Sonn, his mother Dona Maria Stuarta was, it seemes, dead before hee came into France. In his will hee desires the present King of England Carlo 2nd to allow His Prince Hans in Kelder eighty thousand Ducketts, which is his Mother's Estate, he Leaues Likewise to his Child and Mother Teresa 291 thousand Ducketts which hee calls Legacies. Hee was buried in the Church of St. Fran'co Di Paolo out of the Porta Capuana (for hee dyed of this Religion). He left 400 pounds for a Lapide to have his name and quality engrauen vpon it for hee called himself Don Jacopo Stuarto, and this is the end of that Princely Cheate or whatever hee was.

The newsletter of September 7 merely mentions the death and the will. On this occasion Kent had private intelligence from a correspondent in Naples. Copies of the will, in English and in Italian, were forwarded to England, where both copies remain.

'This will,' Lord Acton remarked, 'is fatal to the case for the Prince.' If not fatal, it is a great obstacle to the cause of the Naples man. He claims as his mother, Donna Maria Stewart, 'of the family of the Barons of San Marzo.' If Marzo means 'March,' the Earl of March was a title in the Lennox family. The only Mary Stewart in that family known to Douglas's 'Peerage' was younger than James de la Cloche, and died, the wife of the Earl of Arran, in 1667, at the age of eighteen. She may have had some outlying cousin Mary, but nothing is known of such a possible mother of de la Cloche. Again, the testator begs Charles II. to give his unborn child 'the ordinary principality either of Wales or Monmouth, or other province customary to be given to the natural sons of the Crown;' to the value of 100,000 scudi!

Could de la Cloche be so ignorant as to suppose that a royal bastard might be created Prince of Wales? He certainly knew, from Charles's letter, that his younger brother was already Duke of Monmouth. His legacies are of princely munificence, but - he is to be buried at the expense of his father-in-law.

By way of security for his legacies, the testator 'assigns and gives his lands, called the Marquisate of Juvignis, worth 300,000 scudi.'

Mr. Brady writes: 'Juvignis is probably a mistake for Aubigny, the dukedom which belonged to the Dukes of Richmond and Lennox by the older creation.' But a dukedom is not a marquisate, nor could de la Cloche hold Aubigny, of which the last holder was Ludovick Stewart, who died, a cardinal, in November 1665. The lands then reverted to the French Crown. Moreover, there are two places called Juvigny, or Juvignis, in north-eastern France (Orne and Manche). Conceivably one or other of these belonged to the house of Rohan, and James Stuart's posthumous son, one of whose names is 'Roano,' claimed a title from Juvigny or Juvignis, among other absurd pretensions. 'Henri de Rohan' was only the travelling name of de la Cloche in 1668, though it is conceivable that he was brought up by the de Rohan family, friendly to Charles II.

The whole will is incompatible with all that de la Cloche must have known. Being in Italian it cannot have been intelligible to him, and may conceivably be the work of an ignorant Neapolitan attorney, while de la Cloche, as a dying man, may have signed without understanding much of what he signed. The folly of the Corona family may thus (it is a mere suggestion) be responsible for this absurd testament. Armanni, however, represents the man as sane, and very devout, till his death.

A posthumous child, a son, was born and lived a scrambling life, now 'recognised' abroad, now in prison and poverty, till we lose him about 1750.*

Andrew Lang

* A. F. Steuart, Engl. Hist. Review, July 1903, 'The Neapolitan Stuarts.' Maziere Brady, ut supra.

Among his sham titles are Dux Roani and 'de Roano,' clearly referring, as Mr. Steuart notices, to de la Cloche's travelling name of Henri de Rohan. The Neapolitan pretender, therefore, knew the secret of that incognito, and so of de la Cloche's mission to England in 1668. That, possessing this secret, he was set free, is a most unaccountable circumstance. Charles had written to Oliva that his life hung on absolute secrecy, yet the owner of the secret is left at liberty.

Our first sources leave us in these perplexities. They are not disentangled by the 'Lettere' of Vincenzo Armanni (1674). I have been unable, as has been said, to see this book. In the summary by Mr. Brady we read that (1668-1669) Prince James Stuart, with a French Knight of the Order of St. John of Jerusalem, came to Naples for his health. This must have been in December 1668 or January 1669; by March 1669 the pretender had been 'for some months' in Naples. The Frenchman went by way of Malta to England, recommending Prince James to a confessor at Naples, who was a parish priest. This priest was Armanni's informant. He advised the Prince to lodge with Corona, and here James proposed to Teresa. She at first held aloof, and the priest discountenanced the affair. The Prince ceased to be devout, but later chose another confessor. Both priests knew, in confession, the secret of his birth: the Prince says so in his will, and leaves them great legacies. So far Armanni's version is corroborated.

Mr. Brady goes on, citing Armanni: 'At last he chose another spiritual director, to whom he revealed not only his passion for Teresa Corona, but also the secret of his birth, showing to him the letters written by the Queen of Sweden and the Father General of the Jesuits.' Was the latter document Oliva's note from Leghorn of October 14, 1668? That did not contain a word about de la Cloche's birth: he is merely styled 'the French gentleman.' Again, the letter of the Queen of Sweden is now in the Jesuit archives; how could it be in the possession of the pretender at Naples? Was it taken from him in prison, and returned to Oliva?

The new confessor approved of the wedding which was certainly celebrated on February 19, 1669. Old Corona now began to show his money: his new son-in-law was suspected of being a false coiner, and was arrested by the Viceroy. 'The certificates and papers attesting the parentage of James Stuart were then produced. . . 'How could this be - they were in the hands of the Jesuits at Rome. Had de la Cloche brought them to Naples, the Corona family would have clung to them, but they are in the Gesu at Rome to this day. The rest is much as we know it, save, what is important, that the Prince, from prison, 'wrote to the General of the Jesuits, beseeching him to interpose his good offices with the Viceroy, and to obtain permission for him to go to England via Leghorn' (as in 1688) 'and Marseilles.'

Armanni knew nothing, or says nothing, of de la Cloche's having been in the Jesuit novitiate. His informant, the priest, must have known that, but under seal of confession, so he would not tell Armanni. He did tell him that James Stuart wrote to the Jesuit general, asking his help in procuring leave to go to England. The General knew de la Cloche's hand, and would not be taken in by the impostor's. This point is in favour of the identity of James Stuart with de la Cloche. The Viceroy had, however, already written to London, and waited for a reply. 'Immediately on arrival of the answer from London, the Prince was set at liberty and left Naples. It may be supposed he went to England. After a few months he returned to Naples with an assignment of 50,000 scudi,' and died of fever.

Nothing is said by Armanni of the imprisonment among the low scum of the Vicaria: nothing of the intended whipping, nothing of the visit by James Stuart to France. The 50,000 scudi have a mythical ring. Why should James, if he had 50,000 scudi, be buried at the expense of his father-in-law, who also has to pay 50 ducats to the notary for drawing the will of this 'prince or cheate'? Probably the parish priest and ex-confessor of the prince was misinformed on some points. The Corona family would make out the best case they could for their royal kinsman.

Was the man of Naples 'prince or cheate'? Was he de la Cloche, or, as Lord Acton suggests, a servant who had robbed de la Cloche of money and papers?

Every hypothesis (we shall recapitulate them) which we can try as a key fails to fit the lock. Say that de la Cloche had confided his secret to a friend among the Jesuit novices; say that this young man either robbed de la Cloche, or, having money and jewels of his own, fled from the S. Andrea training college, and, when arrested, assumed the name and pretended to the rank of de la Cloche. This is not inconceivable, but it is odd that he had no language but French, and that, possessing secrets of capital importance, he was released from prison, and allowed to depart where he would, and return to Naples when he chose.

Say that a French servant of de la Cloche robbed and perhaps even murdered him. In that case he certainly would not have been released from prison. The man at Naples was regarded as a gentleman, but that is not so important in an age when the low scoundrel, Bedloe, could pass in Spain and elsewhere for an English peer.

But again, if the Naples man is a swindler, as already remarked, he behaves unlike one. A swindler would have tried to entrap a woman of property into a marriage - he might have seduced, but would not have married, the penniless Teresa Corona, giving what money he had to her father. When arrested, the man had not in money more than 160 pounds. His maintenance, while in prison, was paid for by the Viceroy. No detaining charges, from other victims, appear to have been lodged against him. His will ordains that the document shall be destroyed by his confessor, if the secret of his birth therein contained is divulged before his death. The secret perhaps was only known - before his arrest - to his confessors; it came out when he was arrested by the Viceroy as a coiner of false money. Like de la Cloche, he was pious, though not much turns on that. If Armanni's information is correct, if, when taken, the man wrote to the General of the Jesuits - who knew de la Cloche's handwriting - we can scarcely escape the inference that he was de la Cloche.

On the other hand is the monstrous will. Unworldly as de la Cloche may have been, he can hardly have fancied that Wales was the appanage of a bastard of the Crown; and he certainly knew that 'the province of Monmouth' already gave a title to his younger brother, the duke, born in 1649. Yet the testator claims Wales or Monmouth for his unborn child. Again, de la Cloche may not have known who his mother was. But not only can no Mary, or Mary Henrietta, of the Lennox family be found, except the impossible Lady Mary who was younger than de la Cloche; but we observe no trace of the presence of any d'Aubigny, or even of any Stewart, male or female, at the court of the Prince of Wales in Jersey, in 1646.*

* See Hoskins, Charles II. in the Channel islands (Bentley, London, 1854).

The names of the suite are given by Dr. Hoskins from the journal (MS.) of Chevalier, a Jersey man, and from the Osborne papers. No Stewart or Stuart occurs, but, in a crowd of some 3,000 refugees, there MAY have been a young lady of the name. Lady Fanshaw, who was in Jersey, is silent. The will is absurd throughout, but whether it is all of the dying pretender's composition, whether it may not be a thing concocted by an agent of the Corona family, is another question.

It is a mere conjecture, suggested by more than one inquirer, as by Mr. Steuart, that the words 'Signora D. Maria Stuardo della famiglia delli Baroni di S. Marzo,' refer to the Lennox family, which would naturally be spoken of as Lennox, or as d'Aubigny. About the marquisate of Juvigny (which cannot mean the dukedom of d'Aubigny) we have said enough. In short, the whole will is absurd, and it is all but inconceivable that the real de la Cloche could have been so ignorant as to compose it.

So the matter stands; one of two hypotheses must be correct - the Naples man was de la Cloche or he was not - yet either hypothesis is almost impossible.*

* I was at first inclined to suppose that the de la Cloche papers in the Gesu - the letters of Charles II. and the note of the Queen of Sweden - were forgeries, part of an impostor's apparatus, seized at Naples and sent to Oliva for inspection. But the letters - handwriting and royal seal apart - show too much knowledge of Charles's secret policy to have been feigned. We are not told that the certificates of de la Cloche's birth were taken from James Stuart in prison, and, even if he possessed them, as Armanni says he did, he may have stolen them, and they may have been restored by the Viceroy of Naples, as we said, to the Jesuits. As to whether Charles II. paid his promised subscription to the Jesuit building fund, Father Boero says: 'We possess a royal letter, proving that it was abundant' (Boero, Istoria etc., p. 56, note 1), but he does not print the letter; and Mr. Brady speaks now of extant documents proving the donation, and now of 'a traditional belief that Charles was a benefactor of the Jesuit College.'

It may be added that, on December 27, 1668, Charles wrote to his sister, Henrietta, Duchess of Orleans: 'I assure you that nobody does, nor shall, know anything of it here' (of his intended conversion and secret dealings with France) 'but my selfe, and that one person more, till it be fitte to be publique. . .' 'That one person more' is not elsewhere referred to in Charles's known letters to his sister, unless he be 'he that came last, and delivered me your letter of the 9th December; he has given me a full account of what he was charged with, and I am very well pleased with what he tells me' (Whitehall, December 14, 1668).

This mysterious person, the one sharer of the King's secret, may be de la Cloche, if he could have left

England by November 18, visited Rome, and returned to Paris by December 9. If so, de la Cloche may have fulfilled his mission. Did he return to Italy, and appear in Naples in January or February 1669? (See Madame, by Julia Cartwright, pp. 274, 275, London, 1894.)

IX.

THE TRUTH ABOUT 'FISHER'S GHOST'

Everybody has heard about 'Fisher's Ghost.' It is one of the stock 'yarns' of the world, and reappears now and again in magazines, books like 'The Night Side of Nature,' newspapers, and general conversation. As usually told, the story runs thus: One Fisher, an Australian settler of unknown date, dwelling not far from Sydney, disappeared. His overseer, like himself an ex-convict, gave out that Fisher had returned to England, leaving him as plenipotentiary. One evening a neighbour (one Farley), returning from market, saw Fisher sitting on the fence of his paddock, walked up to speak to him, and marked him leave the fence and retreat into the field, where he was lost to sight. The neighbour reported Fisher's return, and, as Fisher could nowhere be found, made a deposition before magistrates. A native tracker was taken to the fence where the pseudo Fisher sat, discovered 'white man's blood' on it, detected 'white man's fat' on the scum of a pool hard by, and, finally, found 'white man's body' buried in a brake. The overseer was tried, condemned, and hanged after confession.

Such is the yarn: occasionally the ghost of Fisher is said to have been viewed several times on the fence.

Now, if the yarn were true, it would be no proof of a ghost. The person sitting on the fence might be mistaken for Fisher by a confusion of identity, or might be a mere subjective hallucination of a sort recognised even by official science as not uncommon. On the other hand, that such an illusion should perch exactly on the rail where 'white man's blood' was later found, would be a very remarkable coincidence. Finally, the story of the appearance might be explained as an excuse for laying information against the overseer, already suspected on other grounds. But while this motive might act among a Celtic population, naturally credulous of ghosts, and honourably averse to assisting the law (as in Glenclunie in 1749), it is not a probable motive in an English Crown colony, as Sydney then was. Nor did the seer inform against anybody.

The tale is told in 'Tegg's Monthly Magazine' (Sydney, March 1836); in 'Household Words' for 1853; in Mr. John Lang's book, 'Botany Bay' (about 1840), where the yarn is much dressed up; and in Mr. Montgomery Martin's 'History of the British Colonies,' vol. iv. (1835). Nowhere is a date given, but Mr. Martin says that the events occurred while he was in the colony. His most intimate surviving friend has often heard him tell the tale, and discuss it with a legal official, who is said to have been present at the trial of the overseer.* Other living witnesses have heard the story from a gentleman who attended the trial. Mr. Martin's narrative given as a lowest date, the occurrences were before 1835. Moreover, the yarn of the ghost was in circulation before that year, and was accepted by a serious writer on a serious subject. But we have still no date for the murder.

* So the friend informs me in a letter of November 1896.

That date shall now be given. Frederick Fisher was murdered by George Worrall, his overseer, at Campbelltown on June 16 (or 17), 1826. After that date, as Fisher was missing, Worrall told various tales to account for his absence. The trial of Worrall is reported in the 'Sydney Gazette' of February 5, 1827. Not one word is printed about Fisher's ghost; but the reader will observe that there is a lacuna in the evidence exactly where the ghost, if ghost there were, should have come in. The search for Fisher's body starts, it will be seen, from a spot on Fisher's paddock-fence, and the witness gives no reason why that spot was inspected, or rather no account of how, or by whom, sprinkled blood was detected on the rail. Nobody saw the murder committed. Chief-Justice Forbes said, in summing up (on February 2, 1827), that the evidence was purely circumstantial. We are therefore so far left wholly in the dark as to why the police began their investigations at a rail in a fence.

At the trial Mr. D. Cooper deposed to having been owed 80 pounds by Fisher. After Fisher's disappearance Cooper frequently spoke to Worrall about this debt, which Worrall offered to pay if Cooper would give up to him certain papers (title-deeds) of Fisher's in his possession. Worrall even wrote, from Banbury Curran, certifying Cooper of Fisher's departure from the colony, which, he said, he was authorised to announce. Cooper replied that he would wait for his 80 pounds if Fisher were still in the country. Worrall exhibited uneasiness, but promised to show a written commission to act for Fisher. This document he never produced, but was most anxious to get back Fisher's papers and to pay the 80 pounds. This arrangement was refused by Cooper.

James Coddington deposed that on July 8, 1826, when Fisher had been missing for three weeks, Worrall tried to sell him a colt, which Coddington believed to be Fisher's. Worrall averred that Fisher had left the country. A few days later Worrall showed Coddington Fisher's receipt for the price paid to him by Worrall for the horse. 'Witness, from having seen Fisher write, had considerable doubt as to the genuineness of the receipt.'

James Hamilton swore that in August 1826 he bluntly told Worrall that foul play was suspected; he 'turned pale, and endeavoured to force a smile.' He merely said that Fisher 'was on salt water,' but could not or would not name his ship. A receipt to Worrall from Fisher was sworn to by Lewis Solomon as a forgery.

Samuel Hopkins, who lived under Fisher's roof, last saw Fisher on June 17, 1826 (June 16 may be meant), in the evening. Some other people, including one Lawrence, were in the house, they left shortly after Fisher went out that evening, and later remarked on the strangeness of his not returning. Nathaniel Cole gave evidence to the same effect. Fisher, in short, strolled out on June 17 (16?), 1826, and was seen no more in the body.

Robert Burke, of Campbelltown, constable, deposed to having apprehended Worrall. We may now give in full the evidence as to the search for Fisher's body on October 20, 1826.

Here let us first remark that Fisher's body was not

easily found. A reward for its discovery was offered by Government on September 27, 1826, when Fisher had been dead for three months, and this may have stimulated all that was immortal of Fisher to perch on his own paddock-rail, and so draw attention to the position of his body. But on this point we have no information, and we proceed to real evidence. From this it appears that though a reward was offered on September 27, the local magistrates (to whom the ghost-seer went, in the yarn) did not bid their constable make SPECIAL researches till October 20, apparently after the seer told his tale.

'George Leonard, a constable at Campbelltown, stated that by order of the bench of the magistrates he commenced a search for the body of the deceased on the 20th of October last: witness WENT TO A PLACE WHERE SOME BLOOD WAS SAID TO HAVE BEEN DISCOVERED, and saw traces of it on several rails of a fence at the corner of the deceased's paddock adjoining the fence of Mr. Bradbury, and about fifty rods from prisoner's house: witness proceeded to search with an iron rod over the ground, when two black natives came up and joined in the search till they came to a creek where one of them saw something on the water: a man named Gilbert, a black native, went into the water, and scumming some of the top with a leaf, which he afterwards tasted, called out that "there was the fat of a white man" [of which he was clearly an amateur]: they then proceeded to another creek about forty or fifty yards farther up, STILL LED BY THE NATIVES, when one of them struck the rod into some marshy ground and called out that "there was something there:" a spade was immediately found, and the place dug, when the first thing that presented itself was the left hand of a man lying on his side, which witness, from a long acquaintance with him, immediately declared to be the hand of Frederick Fisher: the body was decayed a little, particularly the under-jaw: witness immediately informed Mr. William Howe and the Rev. Mr. Reddall, and obtained a warrant to apprehend the parties who were supposed to be concerned in the murder; the coroner was sent for, and, the body being taken out of the earth the next morning, several fractures were found in the head: an inquest was held, and a verdict of wilful murder against some person or persons unknown was returned: witness particularly examined the fence: there appeared to have been a fire made under the lower rail, as if to burn out the mark: the blood seemed as if it were sprinkled over the rails. . . .

'The declaration of the prisoner' (Worrall) 'was put in and read: it stated that, on the evening of the 17th of June, a man named Lawrence got some money from the deceased, and together with four others went to a neighbouring public-house to drink: that after some time they returned, and the prisoner being then outside the house, and not seen by the others, he saw two of them enter, whilst the other two, one of whom was Lawrence, remained at the door: the prisoner then went down to the bottom of the yard, and after a little time heard a scuffle, and saw Lawrence and the others drag something along the yard, which they struck several times. The prisoner then came forward, and called out to know who it was. One of them replied, "It is a dog." The prisoner coming up said, "It is Fisher, and you have prevented him from crying out any more." They said they had murdered him in order to possess themselves of what money he had, and bound the prisoner by a solemn pledge not to reveal it.

'For the prisoner Nathaniel Boom deposed: he knew deceased, and intended to institute a prosecution against him for forgery when he disappeared.

'Chief-justice summed up: observed it was a case entirely of circumstances. The jury were first to consider if identity of body with Fisher was satisfactorily established. If not: no case. If so: they would then consider testimony as affecting prisoner. Impossible, though wholly circumstantial, for evidence to be stronger. He offered no opinion, but left case to jury.

'The jury returned a verdict of guilty. Sentence of death passed.'

'February 6, 1827. Sydney Gazette.

'George Worrall, convicted on Friday last of murder of F. Fisher, yesterday suffered the last penalty of the law. Till about 5 o'clock on the morning of his execution, he persisted in asserting his innocence, when he was induced to confess to a gentleman who had sat up with him during the night, that he alone had perpetrated the murder, but positively affirmed it was not his intention at the time to do so.'

We need not follow Worrall's attempts to explain away the crime as an accident. He admitted that 'he had intended to hang Lawrence and Cole.'

It is a curious case. WHY WAS NOBODY INTERROGATED ABOUT THE DISCOVERY, ON THE RAIL, OF BLOOD THREE MONTHS OLD, if not four months? What was the apparent date of the fire under the rail? How did the ghost-story get into circulation, and reach Mr. Montgomery Martin (1835)?

To suggest a solution of these problems, we have a precisely analogous case in England.

On October 25, 1828, one William Edden, a market-gardener, did not come home at night. His wife rushed into the neighbouring village, announcing that she had seen her husband's ghost; that he had a hammer, or some such instrument, in his hand; that she knew he had been hammered to death on the road by a man whose name she gave, one Tyler. Her husband was found on the road, between Aylesbury and Thame, killed by blows of a blunt instrument, and the wife in vain repeatedly invited the man, Joseph Tyler, to come and see the corpse. Probably she believed that it would bleed in his presence, in accordance with the old superstition. All this the poor woman stated on oath at an inquiry before the magistrates, reported in the Buckinghamshire county paper of August 29, 1829.

Here is her evidence, given at Aylesbury Petty Sessions, August 22, before Lord Nugent, Sir J. D. King, R. Brown, Esq., and others:

'"After my husband's corpse was brought home, I sent to Tyler, for some reasons I had, to come and see the corpse. I sent for him five or six times. I had some particular reason for sending for him which I never did divulge. . . . I will tell my reasons if you gentlemen ask me, in the face of Tyler, even if my life should be in danger for it. When I was ironing a shirt, on the Saturday night my husband was murdered, something came over me - something rushed over me - and I thought my husband came by me. I looked up, and I thought I heard the voice of my husband come from near my mahogany table, as I turned from my ironing. I ran out and said, 'Oh dear God! my husband is murdered, and his ribs are broken.' I told this to several of my neighbours. Mrs. Chester was the first to whom I told it. I mentioned it also at the Saracen's Head."

'Sir J. D. King. - "Have you any objection to say why you thought your husband had been murdered?"

"'No! I thought I saw my husband's apparition and the man that had done it, and that man was Tyler, and that was the reason I sent for him. . . . When my neighbours asked me what was the matter when I ran out, I told them that I had seen my husband's apparition. . . .When I mentioned it to Mrs. Chester, I said: 'My husband is murdered, and his ribs are broken; I have seen him by the mahogany table.' I did not tell her who did it. . . . I was always frightened, since my husband had been stopped on the road." (The deceased Edden had once before been waylaid, but was then too powerful for his assailants.) "In consequence of what I saw, I went in search of my husband, until I was taken so ill I could go no further."

'Lord Nugent. - "What made you think your husband's ribs were broken?"

"'He held up his hand like this" (holds up her arm), "and I saw a hammer, or something like a hammer, and it came into my mind that his ribs were broken."

'Sewell stated that the murder was accomplished by means of a hammer. The examination was continued on August 31 and September 13; and finally both prisoners were discharged for want of sufficient evidence. Sewell declared that he had only been a looker-on, and his accusations against Tyler were so full of prevarications that they were not held sufficient to incriminate him. The inquiry was again resumed on February 11, 1830, and Sewell, Tyler, and a man named Gardner were committed for trial.

'The trial (see "Buckingham Gazette," March 13, 1830) took place before Mr. Baron Vaughan and a grand jury at the Buckingham Lent Assizes, March 5, 1830; BUT IN THE REPORT OF MRS. EDDEN'S EVIDENCE NO MENTION IS MADE OF THE VISION.

'Sewell and Tyler were found guilty, and were executed, protesting their innocence, on March 8, 1830.

'Miss Browne, writing to us [Mr. Gurney] from Farnham Castle, in January 1884, gives an account of the vision which substantially accords with that here recorded, adding: -

'"The wife persisted in her account of the vision; consequently the accused was taken up, and, with some circumstantial evidence in addition to the woman's story, committed for trial by two magistrates - my father, Colonel Robert Browne, and the Rev. Charles Ackfield.

'"The murderer was convicted at the assizes, and hanged at Aylesbury.

'"It may be added that Colonel Browne was remarkably free from superstition, and was a thorough disbeliever in 'ghost stories.'"*

* From Phantasms of the Living, Gurney and Myers, vol. ii. p. 586.

Now, in the report of the trial at assizes in 1830 there is not one word about the 'ghost,' though he is conspicuous in the hearing at petty sessions. The parallel to Fisher's case is thus complete. And the reason for omitting the ghost in a trial is obvious. The murderers of Sergeant Davies of Guise's, slain in the autumn of 1749 in Glenclunie, were acquitted by an Edinburgh jury in 1753 in face of overpowering evidence of their guilt, partly because two Highland witnesses deposed to having seen the ghost of the sergeant, partly because the jury were Jacobites. The prisoners' counsel, as one of them told Sir Walter Scott, knew that their clients were guilty. A witness had seen them in the act. But the advocate (Lockhart, a Jacobite) made such fun out of the ghost that an Edinburgh jury, disbelieving in the spectre, and not loving the House of Hanover, very logically disregarded also the crushing evidence for a crime which was actually described in court by an eye-witness.

Thus, to secure a view of the original form of the yarn of Fisher's Ghost, what we need is what we are not likely to get - namely, a copy of the depositions made before the bench of magistrates at Campbelltown in October 1826.

For my own part, I think it highly probable that the story of Fisher's Ghost was told before the magistrates, as in the Buckinghamshire case, and was suppressed in the trial at Sydney.

Worrall's condemnation is said to have excited popular discontent, as condemnations on purely circumstantial evidence usually do. That dissatisfaction would be increased if a ghost were publicly implicated in the matter, just as in the case of Davies's murder in 1749. We see how discreetly the wraith or ghost was kept out of the Buckinghamshire case at the trial, and we see why, in Worrall's affair, no questions were asked as to the discovery of sprinkled blood, not proved by analysis to be human, on the rail where Fisher's ghost was said to perch.

I had concluded my inquiry here, when I received a letter in which Mr. Rusden kindly referred me to his 'History of Australia' (vol. ii. pp. 44, 45). Mr. Rusden there gives a summary of the story, in agreement with that taken from the Sydney newspaper. He has 'corrected current rumours by comparison with the words of a trustworthy informant, a medical man, who lived long in the neighbourhood, and attended Farley [the man who saw Fisher's ghost] on his death-bed. He often conversed with Farley on the subject of the vision which scared him. . . . These facts are compiled from the notes of Chief-Justice Forbes, who presided at the trial, with the exception of the references to the apparition, which, although it led to the discovery of Fisher's body, could not be alluded to in a court of justice, or be adduced as evidence.'* There is no justice for ghosts.

* Thanks to the kindness of the Countess of Jersey, and the obliging researches of the Chief Justice of New South Wales, I have received a transcript of the judge's notes. They are correctly analysed by Mr. Rusden.

An Australian correspondent adds another example. Long after Fisher's case, this gentleman was himself present at a trial in Maitland, New South Wales. A servant-girl had dreamed that a missing man told her who had killed him, and where his body was concealed. She, being terrified, wanted to leave the house, but her mistress made her impart the story to the chief constable, a man known to my informant, who also knew, and names, the judge who tried the case. The constable excavated at the spot pointed out in the dream, unearthed the body, and arrested the criminal, who was found guilty, confessed, and was hanged. Not a word was allowed to be said in court about the dream. All the chief constable was permitted to say was, that 'from information received' he went to Hayes's farm, and so forth.

Here, then, are two parallels to Fisher's ghost, and very hard on psychical science it is that ghostly evidence should be deliberately burked through the prejudices of lawyers. Mr. Suttar, in his 'Australian Stories Retold' (Bathurst, 1887), remarks that the ghost is not a late mythical accretion in Fisher's story. 'I have the authority of a gentleman who was intimately connected with the gentleman who had the charge of the police when the murder was done, that Farley's story did suggest the search for the body in the creek.' But Mr. Suttar thinks that Farley invented the tale as an excuse for laying information. That might apply, as has been said, to Highland witnesses in 1753, but hardly to an Englishman in Australia. Besides, if Farley knew the facts, and had the ghost to cover the guilt of peaching, WHY DID HE NOT PEACH? He only pointed to a fence, and, but for the ingenious black Sherlock Holmes, the body would never have been found. What Farley did was not what a man would do who, knowing the facts of the crime, and lured by a reward of 20 pounds, wished to play the informer under cover of a ghost-story.

The case for the ghost, then, stands thus, in my

opinion. Despite the silence preserved at the trial, Farley's ghost-story was really told before the discovery of Fisher's body, and led to the finding of the body. Despite Mr. Suttar's theory (of information laid under shelter of a ghost-story), Farley really had experienced an hallucination. Mr Rusden, who knew his doctor, speaks of his fright, and, according to the version of 1836, he was terrified into an illness. Now, the hallucination indicated the exact spot where Fisher was stricken down, and left traces of his blood, which no evidence shows to have been previously noticed. Was it, then, a fortuitous coincidence that Farley should be casually hallucinated exactly at the one spot - the rail in the fence - where Fisher had been knocked on the head? That is the question, and the state of the odds may be reckoned by the mathematician.

As to the Australian servant-girl's dream about the place where another murdered body lay, and the dreams which led to the discovery of the Red Barn and Assynt murders, and (May 1903) to the finding of the corpse of a drowned girl at Shanklin, all these may be mere guesses by the sleeping self, which is very clever at discovering lost objects.

X.

THE MYSTERY OF LORD BATEMAN

Ever and again, in the literary and antiquarian papers, there flickers up debate as to the Mystery of Lord Bateman. This problem in no way concerns the existing baronial house of Bateman, which, in Burke, records no predecessor before a knight and lord mayor of 1717. Our Bateman comes of lordlier and more ancient lineage. The question really concerns 'The Loving Ballad of Lord Bateman. Illustrated by George Cruikshank, London: Charles Tilt, Fleet Street. And Mustapha Syried, Constantinople. MDCCCXXXIX.'

The tiny little volume in green cloth, with a design of Lord Bateman's marriage ceremony, stamped in gold, opens with a 'Warning to the Public, concerning the Loving Ballad of Lord Bateman.' The Warning is signed George Cruikshank, who, however, adds in a postscript: 'The above is not my writing.' The ballad follows, and then comes a set of notes, mainly critical. The author of the Warning remarks: 'In some collection of old English Ballads there is an ancient ditty, which, I am told, bears some remote and distant resemblance to the following Epic Poem.'

Again, the text of the ballad, here styled 'The Famous History of Lord Bateman,' with illustrations by

Thackeray, 'plain' (the original designs were coloured), occurs in the Thirteenth Volume of the Biographical Edition of Thackeray's works. (pp. lvi-lxi).

The problems debated are: 'Who wrote the Loving Ballad of Lord Bateman, and who wrote the Notes?' The disputants have not shown much acquaintance with ballad lore in general.

First let us consider Mr. Thackeray's text of the ballad. It is closely affiliated to the text of 'The Loving Ballad of Lord Bateman,' whereof the earliest edition with Cruikshank's illustrations was published in 1839.* The edition here used is that of David Bryce and Son, Glasgow (no date).

* There are undated cheap broadside copies, not illustrated, in the British Museum.

Mr. Blanchard Jerrold, in his 'Life of Cruikshank,' tells us that the artist sang this 'old English ballad' at a dinner where Dickens and Thackeray were present. Mr. Thackeray remarked: 'I should like to print that ballad with illustrations,' but Cruikshank 'warned him off,' as he intended to do the thing himself. Dickens furnished the learned notes. This account of what occurred was given by Mr. Walter Hamilton, but Mr. Sala furnished another version. The 'authorship of the ballad,' Mr. Sala justly observed, 'is involved in mystery.' Cruikshank picked it up from the recitation of a minstrel outside a pot-house. In Mr. Sala's opinion, Mr. Thackeray 'revised and settled the words, and made them fit for publication.' Nor did he confine himself to the mere critical work; he added, in Mr. Sala's opinion, that admired passage about 'The young bride's mother, who never before was heard to speak so free,' also contributing 'The Proud Young Porter,' Jeames. Now, in fact, both the interpellation of the bride's mamma, and the person and characteristics of the proud young porter, are of unknown antiquity, and are not due to Mr. Thackeray - a scholar too conscientious to 'decorate ' an ancient text. Bishop Percy did such things, and Scott is not beyond suspicion; but Mr. Thackeray, like Joseph Ritson, preferred the authentic voice of tradition. Thus, in the text of the Biographical Edition, he does not imitate the Cockney twang, phonetically rendered in the version of Cruikshank. The second verse, for example, runs thus:

Cruikshank:

> He sail-ed east, he sail-ed vest,
> Until he came to famed Tur-key,
> Vere he vos taken and put to prisin,
> Until his life was quite wea-ry.

Thackeray:

> He sailed East, and he sailed West,
> Until he came to proud Turkey,
> Where he was taken and put to prison,
> Until his life was almost weary.

There are discrepancies in the arrangement of the verses, and a most important various reading.

Cruikshank:

> Now sevin long years is gone and past,
> And fourteen days vell known to me;
> She packed up all her gay clouthing,

And swore Lord Bateman she would go see.

To this verse, in Cruikshank's book, a note (not by Cruikshank) is added:

"'Now sevin long years is gone and past,
And fourteen days well known to me.

In this may be recognised, though in a minor degree, the same gifted hand that portrayed the Mussulman, the pirate, the father, and the bigot, in two words ("This Turk").

"'The time is gone, the historian knows it, and that is enough for the reader. This is the dignity of history very strikingly exemplified.'"

That note to Cruikshank's text is, like all the delightful notes, if style is evidence, not by Dickens, but by Thackeray. Yet, in his own text, with an exemplary fidelity, he reads: 'And fourteen days well known to THEE.' To whom? We are left in ignorance; and conjecture, though tempting, is unsafe. The reading of Cruikshank, 'vell known to ME' - that is, to the poet - is confirmed by the hitherto unprinted 'Lord Bedmin.' This version, collected by Miss Wyatt Edgell in 1899, as recited by a blind old woman in a workhouse, who had learned it in her youth, now lies before the present writer. He owes this invaluable document to the kindness of Miss Wyatt Edgell and Lady Rosalind Northcote. Invaluable it is, because it proves that Lord Bateman (or Bedmin) is really a volkslied, a popular and current version of the ancient ballad. 'Famed Turkey' becomes 'Torquay' in this text, probably by a misapprehension on the part of the collector or reciter. The speech of the bride's mother is here omitted, though it occurs in older texts; but, on the whole, the blind old woman's memory has proved itself excellent. In one place she gives Thackeray's reading in preference to that of Cruikshank, thus:

Cruikshank:

Ven he vent down on his bended knee.

Thackeray:

Down on his bended knees fell he.

Old Woman:

Down on his bended knee fell he.

We have now ascertained the following facts: Cruikshank and Thackeray used a text with merely verbal differences, which was popular among the least educated classes early in last century. Again, Thackeray contributed the notes and critical apparatus to Cruikshank's version. For this the internal evidence of style is overpowering: no other man wrote in the manner and with the peculiar humour of Mr. Titmarsh. In the humble opinion of the present writer these Notes ought to be appended to Mr. Thackeray's version of 'Lord Bateman.' Finally, Mr. Sala was wrong in supposing that Mr. Thackeray took liberties with the text received from oral tradition.

What was the origin of that text? Professor Child, in the second part of his 'English and Scottish Popular Ballads'* lays before us the learning about Lord Bateman, Lord Bedmin, Young Bicham, Young Brechin, Young Bekie, Young Beichan and Susie Pie (the heroine, Sophia, in Thackeray), Lord Beichan, Young Bondwell, and Markgraf Backenweil; for by all these names is Lord Bateman known. The student must carefully note that 'Thackeray's List of Broadsides,' cited, is NOT by Mr. W. M. Thackeray.

* Pt. ii. p. 454 et seq., and in various other places.

As the reader may not remember the incidents in the Thackeray, Cruikshank, and Old Woman version (which represents an ancient ballad, now not so much popularised as vulgarised), a summary may be given. Lord Bateman went wandering: 'his character, at this time, and his expedition, would seem to have borne a striking resemblance to those of Lord Byron. . . . SOME foreign country he wished to see, and that was the extent of his desire; any foreign country would answer his purpose - all foreign countries were alike to him.'- (Note, apud Cruikshank.) Arriving in Turkey (or Torquay) he was taken and fastened to a tree by his captor. He was furtively released by the daughter of 'This Turk.' 'The poet has here, by that bold license which only genius can venture upon, surmounted the extreme difficulty of introducing any particular Turk, by assuming a foregone conclusion in the reader's mind; and adverting, in a casual, careless way, to a Turk hitherto unknown as to an old acquaintance. . . . "THIS Turk he had" is a master-stroke, a truly Shakespearian touch' - (Note.) The lady, in her father's cellar ('Castle,' Old Woman's text), consoles the captive with 'the very best wine,' secretly stored, for his private enjoyment, by the cruel and hypocritical Mussulman. She confesses the state of her heart, and inquires as to Lord Bateman's real property, which is 'half Northumberland.' To what period in the complicated mediaeval history of the earldom of

Northumberland the affair belongs is uncertain.

The pair vow to be celibate for seven years, and Lord Bateman escapes. At the end of the period, Sophia sets out for Northumberland, urged, perhaps, by some telepathic admonition. For, on arriving at Lord Bateman's palace (Alnwick Castle?), she summons the proud porter, announces herself, and finds that her lover has just celebrated a marriage with another lady. In spite of the remonstrances of the bride's mamma, Lord Bateman restores that young lady to her family, observing

She is neither the better nor the worse for me.

So Thackeray and Old Woman. Cruikshank prudishly reads,

O you'll see what I'll do for you and she.

'Lord Bateman then prepared another marriage, having plenty of superfluous wealth to bestow upon the Church.' - (Note.) All the rest was bliss.

The reader may ask: How did Sophia know anything about the obscure Christian captive? WHY did she leave home exactly in time for his marriage? How came Lord Bateman to be so fickle? The Annotator replies: 'His lordship had doubtless been impelled by despair of ever recovering his lost Sophia, and a natural anxiety not to die without leaving an heir to his estate.' Finally how was the difficulty of Sophia's religion overcome?

To all these questions the Cockney version gives no replies, but the older forms of the ballad offer sufficient though varying answers, as we shall see.

Meanwhile one thing is plain from this analysis of the pot-house version of an old ballad, namely, that the story is constructed out of fragments from the great universal store of popular romance. The central ideas are two: first, the situation of a young man in the hands of a cruel captor (often a god, a giant, a witch, a fiend), but here - a Turk. The youth is loved and released (commonly through magic spells) by the daughter of the gaoler, god, giant, witch, Turk, or what not. In Greece, Jason is the Lord Bateman, Medea is the Sophia, of the tale, which was known to Homer and Hesiod, and was fully narrated by Pindar. THE OTHER YOUNG PERSON, the second bride, however, comes in differently, in the Greek. In far-off Samoa, a god is the captor.* The gaoler is a magician in Red Indian versions.**

* Turner's 'Samoa,' p. 102.

** For a list, though an imperfect one, of the Captor's Daughter story, see the Author's Custom and Myth, pp. 86-102.

As a rule, in these tales, from Finland to Japan, from Samoa to Madagascar, Greece and India, the girl accompanies her lover in his flight, delaying the pursuer by her magic. In 'Lord Bateman' another formula, almost as widely diffused, is preferred.

The old true love comes back just after her lover's wedding. He returns to her. Now, as a rule, in popular tales, the lover's fickleness is explained by a spell or by a breach of a taboo. The old true love has great difficulty in getting access to him, and in waking him from a sleep, drugged or magical.

> The bloody shirt I wrang for thee,
> The Hill o' Glass I clamb for thee,
> And wilt thou no waken and speak to me?

He wakens at last, and all is well. In a Romaic ballad the deserted girl, meeting her love on his wedding-day, merely reminds him of old kindness. He answers -

> Now he that will may scatter nuts,
> And he may wed that will,
> But she that was my old true love
> Shall be my true love still.

This incident, the strange, often magically caused oblivion of the lover, whose love returns to him, like Sophia, at, or after, his marriage, is found in popular tales of Scotland, Norway, Iceland, Germany, Italy, Greece, and the Gaelic Western Islands. It does not occur in 'Lord Bateman,' where Mr. Thackeray suggests probable reasons for Lord Bateman's fickleness. But the world-wide incidents are found in older versions of 'Lord Bateman,' from which they have been expelled by the English genius for the commonplace.

Thus, if we ask, how did Sophia at first know of Bateman's existence? The lovely and delicate daughter of the Turk, doubtless, was unaware that, in the crowded dungeons of her sire, one captive of wealth, noble birth, and personal fascination, was languishing. The Annotator explains: 'She hears from an aged and garrulous attendant, her only female adviser (for her mother died while she was yet an infant), of the sorrows and sufferings of the Christian captive.' In ancient versions of the ballad another explanation occurs. She overhears a song which he sings about his unlucky condition. This account is in Young Bekie (Scottish: mark the name, Bekie), where France is the scene and the king's daughter is the lady. The same formula of the song sung by the prisoner is usual. Not uncommon, too, is a TOKEN carried by Sophia when she pursues her lost adorer, to insure her recognition. It is half of her broken ring. Once more, why does Sophia leave home to find Bateman in the very nick of time? Thackeray's version does not tell us; but Scottish versions do. 'She longed fu' sair her love to see.' Elsewhere a supernatural being, 'The Billy Blin,' or a fairy, clad in green, gives her warning. The fickleness of the hero is caused, sometimes, by constraint, another noble 'has his marriage,' as his feudal superior, and makes him marry, but only in form.

> There is a marriage in yonder hall,
> Has lasted thirty days and three,
> The bridegroom winna bed the bride,
> For the sake o' one that's owre the sea.

In this Scottish version, by the way, occurs -

> Up spoke the young bride's mother,
> Who never was heard to speak so free,

wrongly attributed to Mr. Thackeray's own pen.

The incident of the magical oblivion which comes over the bridegroom occurs in Scandinavian versions of 'Lord Bateman' from manuscripts of the sixteenth century.* Finally, the religious difficulty in several Scottish versions is got over by the conversion and baptism of Sophia, who had professed the creed of

Islam. That all these problems in 'Lord Bateman' are left unsolved is, then, the result of decay. The modern vulgar English version of the pot-house minstrel (known as 'The Tripe Skewer,' according to the author of the Introduction to Cruikshank's version) has forgotten, has been heedless of, and has dropped the ancient universal elements of folk-tale and folk-song.

* Child, ii. 459-461.

These graces, it is true, are not too conspicuous even in the oldest and best versions of 'Lord Bateman.' Choosing at random, however, we find a Scots version open thus:

> In the lands where Lord Beichan was born,
> Among the stately steps o' stane,
> He wore the goud at his left shoulder,
> But to the Holy Land he's gane.

That is not in the tone of the ditty sung by the Tripe Skewer. Again, in his prison,

> He made na his moan to a stock,
> He made na it to a stone,
> But it was to the Queen of Heaven
> That he made his moan.

The lines are from a version of the North of Scotland, and, on the face of it, are older than the extirpation of the Catholic faith in the loyal North. The reference to Holy Land preserves a touch of the crusading age. In short, poor as they may be, the Scottish versions are those of a people not yet wholly vulgarised, not yet lost to romance. The singers have 'half remembered and half forgot' the legend of Gilbert Becket (Bekie,

Beichan), the father of St. Thomas of Canterbury. Gilbert, in the legend, went to Holy Land, was cast into a Saracen's prison, and won his daughter's heart. He escaped, but the lady followed him, like Sophia, and, like Sophia, found and wedded him; Gilbert's servant, Richard, playing the part of the proud young porter. Yet, as Professor Child justly observes, the ballad 'is not derived from the legend,' though the legend as to Gilbert Becket exists in a manuscript of about 1300. The Bateman motive is older than Gilbert Becket, and has been attached to later versions of the adventures of that hero. Gilbert Becket about 1300 was credited with a floating, popular tale of the Bateman sort, and out of his legend, thus altered, the existing ballads drew their 'Bekie' and 'Beichan,' from the name of Becket.

The process is: First, the popular tale of the return of the old true love; that tale is found in Greece, Scandinavia, Denmark, Iceland, Faroe, Spain, Germany, and so forth. Next, about 1300 Gilbert Becket is made the hero of the tale. Next, our surviving ballads retain a trace or two of the Becket form, but they are not derived from the Becket form. The fancy of the folk first evolved the situations in the story, then lent them to written literature (Becket's legend, 1300), and thirdly, received the story back from written legend with a slight, comparatively modern colouring.

In the dispute as to the origin of our ballads one school, as Mr. T. F. Henderson and Professor Courthope, regard them as debris of old literary romances, ill-remembered work of professional minstrels.* That there are ballads of this kind in England, such as the Arthurian ballads, I do not deny. But in my opinion many ballads and popular tales are in origin older than the mediaeval romances, as a rule.

As a rule the romances are based on earlier popular data, just as the 'Odyssey' is an artistic whole made up out of popular tales. The folk may receive back a literary form of its own ballad or story, but more frequently the popular ballad comes down in oral tradition side by side with its educated child, the literary romance on the same theme.

* Cf. The Queen's Marie.

Mr. Henderson has answered that the people is unpoetical. The degraded populace of the slums may be unpoetical, like the minstrel named 'Tripe Skewer,' and may deprave the ballads of its undegraded ancestry into such modern English forms as 'Lord Bateman.' But I think of the people which, in Barbour's day, had its choirs of peasant girls chanting rural snatches on Bruce's victories, or, in still earlier France, of Roland's overthrow. If THEIR songs are attributed to professional minstrels, I turn to the Greece of 1830, to the Finland of to-day, to the outermost Hebrides of to-day, to the Arapahoes of Northern America, to the Australian blacks, among all of whom the people are their own poets and make their own dirges, lullabies, chants of victory, and laments for defeat. THESE peoples are not unpoetical. In fact, when I say that the people has been its own poet I do not mean the people which goes to music halls and reads halfpenny newspapers. To the true folk we owe the legend of Lord Bateman in its ancient germs; and to the folk's degraded modern estate, crowded as men are in noisome streets and crushed by labour, we owe the Cockney depravation, the Lord Bateman of Cruikshank and Thackeray. Even that, I presume, being old, is now forgotten, except by the ancient blind woman in the workhouse. To the workhouse has come the native popular culture - the last lingering shadow of old romance. That is the moral of the ballad of Lord Bateman.

In an article by Mr. Kitton, in Literature (June 24, 1899, p. 699), this learned Dickensite says: 'The authorship of this version' (Cruikshank's) 'of an ancient ballad and of the accompanying notes has given rise to much controversy, and whether Dickens or Thackeray was responsible for them is still a matter of conjecture, although what little evidence there is seems to favour Thackeray.'

For the ballad neither Thackeray nor Dickens is responsible. The Old Woman's text settles that question: the ballad is a degraded Volkslied. As to the notes, internal evidence for once is explicit. The notes are Thackeray's. Any one who doubts has only to compare Thackeray's notes to his prize poem on 'Timbuctoo.'

The banter, in the notes, is academic banter, that of a university man, who is mocking the notes of learned editors. This humour is not the humour of Dickens, who, however, may very well have written the Introduction to Cruikshank's version. That morceau is in quite a different taste and style. I ought, in fairness, to add the following note from Mr. J. B. Keene, which may be thought to overthrow belief in Thackeray's authorship of the notes: -

Dear Sir, - Your paper in the 'Cornhill' for this month on the Mystery of Lord Bateman interested me greatly, but I must beg to differ from you as to the authorship of the Notes, and for this reason.

I have before me a copy of the first edition of the 'Loving Ballad' which was bought by my father soon after it was issued. At that time - somewhere about 1840 - there was a frequent visitor at our house, named Burnett, who had married a sister of Charles Dickens, and who gave us the story of its production.

He said, as you state, that Cruikshank had got the words from a pot-house singer, but the locality he named was Whitechapel,* where he was looking out for characters. He added that Cruikshank sung or hummed the tune to him, and he gave it the musical notation which follows the preface. He also said that Charles Dickens wrote the notes. His personal connection with the work and his relation to Dickens are, I think, fair evidence on the question.

I am, dear Sir,

Yours truly,
J. B. KEENE.

Kingsmead House, 1 Hartham Road,
Camden Road, N., Feb. 13,1900.

Mr. Keene's evidence may, perhaps, settle the question. But, if Dickens wrote the Introduction, that might be confused in Mr. Burnett's memory with the Notes, from internal evidence the work of Thackeray. If not, then in the Notes we find a new aspect of the inexhaustible humour of Dickens. It is certain, at all events, that neither Dickens nor Thackeray was the author of the 'Loving Ballad.'

P.S. - The preface to the ballad says Battle Bridge.

XI.

THE QUEEN'S MARIE

Little did my mother think
That day she cradled me
What land I was to travel in,
Or what death I should die.

Writing to Mrs. Dunlop on January 25, 1790, Burns
quoted these lines, 'in an old Scottish ballad, which,
notwithstanding its rude simplicity, speaks feelingly to
the heart.' Mr. Carlyle is said, when young, to have
written them on a pane of glass in a window, with a
diamond, adding, characteristically, 'Oh foolish Thee!'
In 1802, in the first edition of 'The Border Minstrelsy,'
Scott cited only three stanzas from the same ballad, not
including Burns's verse, but giving

Yestreen the Queen had four Maries,
The night she'll hae but three,
There was Marie Seaton, and Marie Beaton,
And Marie Carmichael and me.

In later editions Sir Walter offered a made-up copy of
the ballad, most of it from a version collected by
Charles Kirkpatrick Sharpe.

It now appeared that Mary Hamilton was the heroine,

The Valet's Tragedy   269

that she was one of Queen Marie's four Maries, and that she was hanged for murdering a child whom she bore to Darnley. Thus the character of Mary Hamilton was 'totally lost,' and Darnley certainly 'had not sufficient for two.' Darnley, to be sure, told his father that 'I never offended the Queen, my wife, in meddling with any woman in thought, let be in deed,' and, whether Darnley spoke truth or not, there was, among the Queen's Maries, no Mary Hamilton to meddle with, just as there was no Mary Carmichael.

The Maries were attendant on the Queen as children ever since she left Scotland for France. They were Mary Livingstone (mentioned as 'Lady Livinston' in one version of the ballad),* who married 'John Sempill, called the Dancer,' who, says Laing, 'acquired the lands of Beltree, in Renfrewshire.'**

* Child, vol. iii. p. 389.

** Laing's Knox, ii. 415, note 3.

When Queen Mary was a captive in England she was at odds with the Sempill pair about some jewels of hers in their custody. He was not a satisfactory character, he died before November 1581. Mary Fleming, early in 1587, married the famous William Maitland of Lethington, 'being no more fit for her than I to be a page,' says Kirkcaldy of Grange. Her life was wretched enough, through the stormy career and sad death of her lord. Mary Beaton, with whom Randolph, the English ambassador, used to flirt, married, in 1566, Ogilvy of Boyne, the first love of Lady Jane Gordon, the bride of Bothwell. Mary Seaton remained a maiden and busked the Queen's hair during her English captivity. We last hear of her from James Maitland of Lethington, in

1613, living at Rheims, very old, 'decrepid,' and poor. There is no room in the Four for Mary Hamilton, and no mention of her appears in the records of the Court.

How, then, did Mary Hamilton find her way into the old ballad about Darnley and the Queen?

To explain this puzzle, some modern writers have denied that the ballad of 'The Queen's Marie' is really old; they attribute it to the eighteenth century. The antiquary who launched this opinion was Scott's not very loyal friend, Charles Kirkpatrick Sharpe. According to him, a certain Miss Hambledon (no Christian name is given), being Maid of Honour to the Empress Catherine of Russia, had three children by an amour, and murdered all three. Peter the Great caused her to be, not hanged, but decapitated. Sharpe took his facts from 'a German almanac,' and says: 'The Russian tragedy must be the original.' The late Professor Child, from more authentic documents, dates Miss Hambledon's or Hamilton's execution on March 14, 1719. At that time, or nearly then, Charles Wogan was in Russia on a mission from the Chevalier de St. George (James III.), and through him the news might reach Scotland. Mr. Courthope, in his 'History of English Poetry,' followed Sharpe and Professor Child, and says: 'It is very remarkable that one of the very latest of the Scottish popular ballads should be one of the very best.'

The occurrence would not only be remarkable, but, as far as possibility goes in literature, would be impossible, for several reasons. One is that neither literary men nor mere garreteers and makers of street ballads appear, about 1719-1730, to have been capable of recapturing the simplicity and charm of the old ballad style, at its best, or anything near its best. There is no mistaking the literary touch in such ballads as Allan Ramsay handled, or in the imitation named 'Hardyknute ' in Allan's 'Tea Table Miscellany,' 1724. 'It was the first poem I ever learned, the last I shall ever forget,' said Scott, and, misled by boyish affection, he deemed it 'just old enough,' 'a noble imitation.'* But the imitation can deceive nobody, and while literary imitators, as far as their efforts have reached us, were impotent to deceive, the popular Muse, of 1714-1730, was not attempting deception. Ballads of the eighteenth century were sarcastic, as in those on Sheriffmuir and in Skirving's amusing ballad on Preston Pans, or were mere doggerel, or were brief songs to old tunes. They survive in print, whether in flying broadsides or in books, but, popular as is 'The Queen's Marie,' in all its many variants (Child gives no less than eighteen), we do not know a single printed example before Scott's made-up copy in the 'Border Minstrelsy.' The latest ballad really in the old popular manner known to me is that of 'Rob Roy,' namely, of Robin Oig and James More, sons of Rob Roy, and about their abduction of an heiress in 1752. This is a genuine popular poem, but in style and tone and versification it is wholly unlike 'The Queen's Marie.' I scarcely hope that any one can produce, after 1680, a single popular piece which could be mistaken for a ballad of or near Queen Mary's time.

* Lockhart, i. 114, x. 138.

The known person least unlike Mr. Courthope's late 'maker' was 'Mussel-mou'd Charlie Leslie,' 'an old Aberdeenshire minstrel, the very last, probably, of the race,' says Scott. Charlie died in 1782. He sang, and sold PRINTED ballads. 'Why cannot you sing other songs than those rebellious ones?' asked a Hanoverian Provost of Aberdeen. 'Oh ay, but - THEY WINNA BUY THEM!' said Charlie. 'Where do you buy them?' 'Why, faur I get them cheapest.' He carried his ballads in 'a large harden bag, hung over his shoulder.' Charlie had tholed prison for Prince Charles, and had seen Provost Morison drink the Prince's health in wine and proclaim him Regent at the Cross of Aberdeen. If Charlie (who lived to be a hundred and two) composed the song, 'Mussel-mou'd Charlie ' ('this sang Charlie made hissel"), then this maker could never have produced 'The Queen's Marie,' nor could any maker like him. His ballads were printed, as any successful ballad of 1719 would probably have been, in broadsides.* Against Mr. Child and Mr. Courthope, then, we argue that, after 1600, a marked decadence of the old ballad style set in--that the old style (as far as is known) died soon after Bothwell Brig (1679), in the execrable ballads of both sides, such as 'Philiphaugh,' and that it soon was not only dead as a form in practical use, but was entirely superseded by new kinds of popular poetry, of which many examples survive, and are familiar to every student. How, or why, then, should a poet, aiming at popularity, about 1719-1730, compose 'The Queen's Marie' in an obsolete manner? The old ballads were still sung, indeed; but we ask for proof that new ballads were still composed in the ancient fashion.

* See, for example, Mr. Macquoid's Jacobite Songs and Ballads, pp. 424, 510, with a picture of Charlie.

Secondly, WHY, and how tempted, would a popular poet of 1719 transfer a modern tragedy of Russia to the year 1563, or thereabouts? His public would naturally desire a ballad gazette of the mournful new tale, concerning a lass of Scottish extraction, betrayed, tortured, beheaded, at the far-off court of a Muscovite tyrant. The facts 'palpitated with actuality,' and, since Homer's day, 'men desire' (as Homer says) 'the new songs' on the new events. What was gained by going back to Queen Mary? Would a popular 'Musselmou'd Charlie' even know, by 1719, the names of the Queen's Maries? Mr. Courthope admits that 'he may have been helped by some ballad,' one of those spoken of, as we shall see, by Knox. If that ballad told the existing Marian story, what did the 'maker' add? If it did NOT, what did he borrow? No more than the names could he borrow, and no more than the name 'Hamilton' from the Russian tragedy could he add. One other thing he might be said to add, the verses in which Mary asks 'the jolly sailors' not to

'Let on to my father and mother
But that I'm coming hame.'

This passage, according to Mr. Courthope, 'was suggested partly by the fact of a Scotswoman being executed in Russia.' C. K. Sharpe also says: 'If Marie Hamilton was executed in Scotland, it is not likely' (why not?) 'that her relations resided beyond seas.' They MAY have been in France, like many another Hamilton! Mr. Child says: 'The appeal to the sailors shows that Mary Hamilton dies in a foreign land - not that of her ancestors.' Yet the ballad makes her die in or near the Canongate! Moreover, the family of the Mary Hamilton of 1719 had been settled in Russia for generations, and were reckoned of the Russian noblesse. The verses, therefore, on either theory, are probably out of place, and are perhaps an interpolation suggested to some reciter (they only occur in some of the many versions) by a passage in 'The

Twa Brithers.'*

* Child, i. 439.

We now reach the most important argument for the antiquity of 'The Queen's Marie.' Mr. Courthope has theoretically introduced as existing in, or after, 1719, 'makers' who could imitate to deception the old ballad style. Now Maidment remarks that 'this ballad was popular in Galloway, Selkirkshire, Lanarkshire, and Aberdeen, AND THE VERY STRIKING DISCREPANCIES GO FAR TO REMOVE EVERY SUSPICION OF FABRICATION.' Chambers uses (1829) against Sharpe the same argument of 'universal diffusion in Scotland.' Neither Mr. Child nor Mr. Courthope draws the obvious inferences from the extraordinary discrepancies in the eighteen variants. Such essential discrepancies surely speak of a long period of oral recitation by men or women accustomed to interpolate, alter, and add, in the true old ballad manner. Did such rhapsodists exist after 1719? Old Charlie, for one, did not sing or sell the old ballads. Again, if the ballad (as it probably would be in 1719) was PRINTED, or even if it was not, could the variations have been evolved between 1719 and 1802?

These variations are numerous, striking, and fundamental. In many variants even the name of the heroine does not tally with that of the Russian maid of honour. That most important and telling coincidence wholly disappears. In a version of Motherwell's, from Dumbartonshire, the heroine is Mary Myle. In a version known to Scott ('Minstrelsy,' 1810, iii. 89, note), the name is Mary Miles. Mr. Child also finds Mary Mild, Mary Moil, and Lady Maisry. This Maisry is daughter of the Duke of York! Now, the Duke of

York whom alone the Scottish people knew was James Stuart, later James II. Once more the heroine is daughter of the Duke of Argyll, therefore a Campbell. Or she is without patronymic, and is daughter of a lord or knight of the North, or South, or East, and one of her sisters is a barber's wife, and her father lives in England! - (Motherwell.) She, at least, might invoke 'Ye mariners, mariners, mariners!' (as in Scott's first fragment) not to carry her story. Now we ask whether, after the ringing tragedy of Miss Hamilton in Russia, in the year of grace 1719, contemporaries who heard the woeful tale could, between 1719 and 1820, call the heroine - (1) Hamilton; (2) Mild, Moil, Myle, Miles; (3) make her a daughter of the Duke of York, or of the Duke of Argyll, or of lords and of knights from all quarters of the compass, and sister-in-law to an English barber, also one of the Queen's 'serving-maids.' We at least cannot accept those numerous and glittering contradictions as corruptions which could be made soon after the Russian events, when the true old ballad style was dead.

We now produce more startling variations. The lover is not only 'the King,' 'the Prince,' Darnley, 'the highest Stuart o' a',' but he is also that old offender, 'Sweet Willie,' or he is Warrenston (Warriston?). Mary is certainly not hanged (the Russian woman was beheaded) away from her home; she dies in Edinburgh, near the Tolbooth, the Netherbow, the Canongate, and -

> O what will my three brothers say
> When they COME HAME frae sea,
> When they see three locks o' my yellow hair
> Hinging under a gallows tree?

It is impossible here to give all the variations. Mary pulls, or does not pull, or her lover pulls, the leaf of the Abbey, or 'savin,' or other tree; the Queen is 'auld,' or not 'auld;' she kicks in Mary's door and bursts the bolts, or does nothing so athletic and inconsistent with her advanced age. The heroine does, or does not, appeal vainly to her father. Her dress is of all varieties. She does, or does not, go to the Tolbooth and other places. She is, or is not, allured to Edinburgh, 'a wedding for to see.' Her infanticide is variously described, or its details are omitted, and the dead body of the child is found in various places, or not found at all. Though drowned in the sea, it is between the bolster and the wall, or under the blankets! She expects, or does not expect, to be avenged by her kin. The king is now angry, now clement - inviting Mary to dinner! Mary is hanged, or (Buchan's MS.) is not hanged, but is ransomed by Warrenston, probably Johnston of Warriston! These are a few specimens of variations in point of fact: in language the variations are practically countless. How could they arise, if the ballad is later than 1719?

We now condescend to appeal to statistics. We have examined the number of variants published by Mr. Child in his first six volumes, on ballads which have, or may have, an historical basis. Of course, the older and more popular the ballads, the more variants do we expect to discover - time and taste producing frequent changes. Well, of 'Otterburn' Mr. Child has five versions; of the 'Hunting of the Cheviot' he has two, with minor modifications indicated by letters from the 'lower case.' Of 'Gude Wallace' he has eight. Of 'Johnnie Armstrong' he has three. Of 'Kinmont Willie' he has one. Of 'The Bonnie Earl o' Moray' he has two. Of 'Johnnie Cock' he has thirteen. Of 'Sir Patrick

Spens' he has eighteen. And of 'The Queen's Marie'
(counting Burns's solitary verse and other brief
fragments) Mr. Child has eighteen versions or variants

Thus a ballad made, ex hypothesi Sharpiana, in or after
1719, has been as much altered in oral tradition as the
most popular and perhaps the oldest historical ballad of
all, 'Sir Patrick Spens,' and much more than any other
of the confessedly ancient semi-historical popular
poems. The historical event which may have suggested
'Sir Patrick Spens' is 'plausibly,' says Mr. Child, fixed
in 1281: it is the marriage of Margaret of Scotland to
Eric, King of Norway. Others suggest so late a date as
the wooing of Anne of Denmark by James VI. Nothing
is known. No wonder, then, that in time an orally
preserved ballad grows rich in variants. But that a
ballad of 1719 should, in eighty modern non-
balladising years, become as rich in extant variants,
and far more discrepant in their details, as 'Sir Patrick
Spens' is a circumstance for which we invite
explanation.

Will men say, 'The later the ballad, the more it is
altered in oral tradition'? If so, let them, by all means,
produce examples! We should, on this theory, have
about a dozen 'Battles of Philiphaugh,' and at least
fifteen 'Bothwell Brigs,' a poem, by the way, much in
the old manner, prosaically applied, and so recent that,
in art at least, it was produced after the death of the
Duke of Monmouth, slain, it avers, by the
machinations of Claverhouse! Of course we are not
asking for exact proportions, since many variants of
ballads may be lost, but merely for proof that, the later
a ballad is, the more variants of it occur. But this
contention is probably impossible, and the numerous
variations in 'The Queen's Marie' are really a proof of

long existence in oral tradition, and contradict the theory espoused by Mr. Child, who later saw the difficulty involved in his hypothesis.

This argument, though statistical, is, we think, conclusive, and the other considerations which we have produced in favour of the antiquity of 'The Queen's Marie' add their cumulative weight.

We have been, in brief, invited to suppose that, about 1719, a Scot wrote a ballad on an event in contemporary Russian Court life; that (contrary to use and wont) he threw the story back a century and a half; that he was a master of an old style, in the practice of his age utterly obsolete and not successfully imitated; that his poem became universally popular, and underwent, in eighty years, even more vicissitudes than most other ballads encounter in three or five centuries. Meanwhile it is certain that there had been real ancient ballads, contemporary with the Marian events - ballads on the very Maries two or three of whom appear in the so-called poem of 1719; while exactly the same sort of scandal as the ballad records had actually occurred at Queen Mary's Court in a lower social rank. The theory of Mr. Child is opposed to our whole knowledge of ballad literature, of its age, decadence (about 1620-1700), and decease (in the old kind) as a popular art.

To agree with Mr. Child, we must not only accept one great ballad-poet, born at least fifty years too late; we must not only admit that such a poet would throw back his facts for a century and a half; but we must also conceive that the balladising humour, with its ancient methods, was even more vivacious in Scotland for many years after 1719 than, as far as we know, it had ever been before. Yet there is no other trace known to us of the existence of the old balladising humour and of the old art in all that period. We have no such ballad about the English captain shot by the writer's pretty wife, none about the bewitched son of Lord Torphichen, none about the Old Chevalier, or Lochiel, or Prince Charlie: we have merely Shenstone's 'Jemmy Dawson' and the Glasgow bellman's rhymed history of Prince Charles. In fact, 'Jemmy Dawson' is a fair instantia contradictoria as far as a ballad by a man of letters is to the point. Such a ballad that age could indeed produce: it is not very like 'The Queen's Marie'! No, we cannot take refuge in 'Townley's Ghost' and his address to the Butcher Cumberland: -

Imbrued in bliss, imbathed in case,
Though now thou seem'st to lie,
My injured form shall gall thy peace,
And make thee wish to die!

THAT is a ballad of the eighteenth century, and it is not in the manner of 'The Queen's Marie.'

These considerations, now so obvious to a student of the art of old popular poetry, if he thinks of the matter, could not occur to Charles Kirkpatrick Sharpe. He was a great collector of ballads, but not versed in, or interested in, their 'aesthetic' - in the history and evolution of ballad-making. Mr. Child, on the other hand, was the Grimm or Kohler of popular English and Scottish poetry. Our objections to his theory could scarcely have been collected in such numbers, without the aid of his own assortment of eighteen versions or fragments, with more lectiones variae. But he has not allowed for the possible, the constantly occurring, chance of coincidence between fancy and fact; nor, perhaps, has he reflected on the changed condition of ballad poetry in the eighteenth century, on the popular love of a new song about a new event, and on the entire lack of evidence (as far as I am aware) for the existence of ballad-poets in the old manner during the reign of George I. The ballad-reading public of 1719 would have revelled in a fresh ballad of a Scottish lass, recently betrayed, tortured, and slain far away by a Russian tyrant. A fresh ballad on Queen Mary's Court, done in the early obsolete manner, would, on the other hand, have had comparatively little charm for the ballad-buying lieges in 1719. The ballad-poet had thus in 1719 no temptation to be 'archaistic,' like Mr. Rossetti, and to sing of old times. He had, on the contrary, every inducement to indite a 'rare new ballad' on the last tragic scandal, with its poignant details, as of Peter kissing the dead girl's head.

The hypothesis of Mr. Child could only be DEMONSTRATED incorrect by proving that there was no Russian scandal at all, or by producing a printed or manuscript copy of 'The Queen's Marie' older than 1719. We can do neither of these things; we can only give the reader his choice of two improbabilities - (a) that an historical event, in 1718-19, chanced to coincide with the topic of an old ballad; (b) that, contrary to all we know of the evolution of ballads and the state of taste, a new popular poem on a fresh theme was composed in a style long disused,* was offered most successfully to the public of 1719, and in not much more than half a century was more subjected to alterations and interpolations than ballads which for two or three hundred years had run the gauntlet of oral tradition.

* A learned Scots antiquary writes to me: 'The real ballad manner hardly came down to 1600. It was killed

by the Francis Roos version of the Psalms, after which the Scottish folk of the Lowlands cast everything into that mould.' I think, however, that 'Bothwell Brig' is a true survival of the ancient style, and there are other examples, as in the case of the ballad on Lady Warriston's husband murder.

As for our own explanation of the resemblance between the affair of Miss Hamilton, in 1719, and the ballad story of Mary Hamilton (alias Mild, Myle, Moil, Campbell, Miles, or Stuart, or anonymous, or Lady Maisry), we simply, with Scott, regard it as 'a very curious coincidence.' On the other theory, on Mr. Child's, it is also a curious coincidence that a waiting-woman of Mary Stuart WAS hanged (not beheaded) for child-murder, and that there WERE written, simultaneously, ballads on the Queen's Maries. Much odder coincidences than either have often, and indisputably, occurred, and it is not for want of instances, but for lack of space, that we do not give examples.

Turning, now, to a genuine historic scandal of Queen Mary's reign, we find that it might have given rise to the many varying forms of the ballad of 'The Queen's Marie.' There is, practically, no such ballad; that is, among the many variants, we cannot say which comes nearest to the 'original' lay of the frail maid and her doom. All the variants are full of historical impossibilities, due to the lapses of memory and the wandering fancy of reciters, altering and interpolating, through more than two centuries, an original of which nothing can now be known. The fancy, if not of the first ballad poet who dealt with a real tragic event, at least of his successors in many corners of Scotland, raised the actors and sufferers in a sad story, elevating a French waiting-maid to the rank of a Queen's Marie, and her lover, a French apothecary, to the place of a queen's consort, or, at lowest, of a Scottish laird.

At the time of the General Assembly which met on Christmas Day 1563, a French waiting-maid of Mary Stuart, 'ane Frenche woman that servit in the Queenis chalmer,' fell into sin 'with the Queenis awin hipoticary.' The father and mother slew the child, and were 'dampned to be hangit upoun the publict streit of Edinburgh.' No official report exists: 'the records of the Court of Justiciary at this time are defective,' says Maidment, and he conjectures that the accused may have been hanged without trial, 'redhand.' Now the Queen's apothecary must have left traces in the royal account-books. No writer on the subject has mentioned them. I myself have had the Records of Privy Council and the MS. Treasurer's Accounts examined, with their statement of the expenses of the royal household. The Rev. John Anderson was kind enough to undertake this task, though with less leisure than he could have desired. There is, unluckily, a gap of some months in 1563. In June 1560, Mr. Anderson finds mention of a 'medicinar,' 'apoticarre,' 'apotigar,' but no name is given, and the Queen was then in France. One Nicholas Wardlaw of the royal household was engaged, in 1562, to a Miss Seton of Parbroath, but it needed a special royal messenger to bring the swain to the altar. 'Ane appotigar' of 1562 is mentioned, but not named, and we hear of Robert Henderson, chirurgeon, who supplied powders and odours to embalm Huntley. There is no trace of the hanging of any 'appotigar,' or of any one of the Queen's women, 'the maidans,' spoken of collectively. So far, the search for the apothecary has been a failure. More can be learned from Randolph's letter to Cecil (December 31, 1563), here copied from the MS. in the Public Record Office. The austerity of Mary's Court, under Mr. Knox, is amusingly revealed: -

'For newes yt maye please your honour to knowe that the Lord Treasurer of Scotlande for gettinge of a woman with chylde muste vpon Sondaye nexte do open penance before the whole congregation and mr knox mayke the sermonde. Thys my Lord of murraye wylled me to wryte vnto you for a note of our greate severitie in punyshynge of offenders. THE FRENCHE POTTICARIE AND THE WOMAN HE GOTTE WITH CHYLDE WERE BOTHE HANGED THYS PRESENT FRIDAYE. Thys hathe made myche sorrowe in our Courte. Maynie evle fortunes we have had by our Frenche fowlkes, and yet I feare we love them over well.'

After recording the condemnation of the waiting-woman and her lover, Knox tells a false story about 'shame hastening the marriage' of Mary Livingstone. Dr. Robertson, in his 'Inventories of Queen Mary,' refutes this slander, which he deems as baseless as the fables against Knox's own continence. Knox adds: 'What bruit the Maries and the rest of the danseris of the Courte had, the ballads of that age did witness, quhilk we for modesteis sake omit.' Unlucky omission, unfortunate 'modestei'! From Randolph's Letters it is known that Knox, at this date, was thundering against 'danseris.' Here, then, is a tale of the Queen's French waiting-woman hanged for murder, and here is proof that there actually were ballads about the Queen's Maries. These ladies, as we know from Keith, were, from the first, in the Queen's childhood, Mary Livingstone, Mary Seatoun, Mary Beatoun, and Mary Fleming.

We have, then, a child-murder, by a woman of the Queen, we have ballads about her Maries, and, as Scott says, 'the tale has suffered great alterations, as handed down by tradition, the French waiting-woman being changed into Mary Hamilton, and the Queen's apothecary into Henry Darnley,' who, as Mr. Child shows, was not even in Scotland in 1563. But gross perversion of contemporary facts does not prove a ballad to be late or apocryphal. Mr. Child even says that accuracy in a ballad would be very 'suspicious.' Thus, for example, we know, from contemporary evidence, that the murder of the Bonny Earl Murray, in 1592, by Huntley, was at once made the topic of ballads. Of these, Aytoun and Mr. Child print two widely different in details: in the first, Huntley has married Murray's sister; in the second, Murray is the lover of the Queen of James VI. Both statements are picturesque; but the former is certainly, and the latter is probably, untrue. Again, 'King James and Brown,' in the Percy MS., is accepted as a genuine contemporary ballad of the youth of gentle King Jamie. James is herein made to say to his nobles, -

'My grandfather you have slaine,
And my own mother you hanged on a tree.'

Even if we read 'father' (against the manuscript) this is absurd. James V. was not 'slaine,' neither Darnley nor Mary was 'hanged on a tree.' Ballads are always inaccurate; they do not report events, so much as throw into verse the popular impression of events, the magnified, distorted, dramatic rumours. That a ballad-writer should promote a Queen's tirewoman into a Queen's Marie, and substitute Darnley (where HE is the lover, which is not always) for the Queen's apothecary, is a license quite in keeping with precedent. Mr. Child, obviously, would admit this. In producing a Marie who never existed, the 'maker' shows the same delicacy as Voltaire, when he brings into 'Candide' a Pope who never was born.

Finally, a fragment of a variant of the ballad among the Abbotsford MSS.* does mention an apothecary as the lover of the heroine, and, so far, is true to historical fact, whether the author was well informed, or merely, in the multitude of variations, deviated by chance into truth.

There can, on the whole, be no reasonable doubt that the ballad is on an event in Scotland of 1563, not of 1719, in Russia, and Mr. Child came to hold that this opinion was, at least, the more probable.**

* Child, vol. iv. p. 509.

** Ibid., vol. v. pp. 298, 299.

XII.

THE SHAKESPEARE-BACON IMBROGLIO*

The hypothesis that the works of Shakespeare were written by Bacon has now been before the world for more than forty years. It has been supported in hundreds of books and pamphlets, but, as a rule, it has been totally neglected by scholars. Perhaps their indifference may seem wise, for such an opinion may appear to need no confutation. 'There are foolisher fellows than the Baconians,' says a sage - 'those who argue against them.' On the other hand, ignorance has often cherished beliefs which science has been obliged reluctantly to admit. The existence of meteorites, and the phenomena of hypnotism, were familiar to the ancient world, and to modern peasants, while philosophy disdained to investigate them. In fact, it is never really prudent to overlook a widely spread opinion. If we gain nothing else by examining its grounds, at least we learn something about the psychology of its advocates. In this case we can estimate the learning, the logic, and the general intellect of people who form themselves into Baconian Societies, to prove that the poems and plays of Shakespeare were written by Bacon. Thus a light is thrown on the nature and origin of popular delusions.

* (1) 'Bacon and Shakespeare,' by William Henry

Smith (1857); (2) 'The Authorship of Shakespeare,' by Nathaniel Holmes (1875); (3) 'The Great Cryptogram,' by Ignatius Donnelly (1888); (4) 'The Promus of Formularies and Elegancies of Francis Bacon,' by Mrs. Henry Pott (1883); (5) 'William Shakespeare,' by Georg Brandes (1898); (6) 'Shakespeare,' by Sidney Lee (in the Dictionary of National Biography, 1897); (7) 'Shakespeare Dethroned' (in Pearson's Magazine, December 1897); (8) 'The Hidden Lives of Shakespeare and Bacon,' by W. G. Thorpe, F.S.A. (1897). (9) 'The Mystery of William Shakespeare,' by Judge Webb (1902).

The Baconian creed, of course, is scouted equally by special students of Bacon, special students of Shakespeare, and by almost all persons who devote themselves to sound literature. It is equally rejected by Mr. Spedding, the chief authority on Bacon; by Mr. H. H. Furness, the learned and witty American editor of the 'Variorum Shakespeare;' by Dr. Brandes, the Danish biographer and critic; by Mr. Swinburne, with his rare knowledge of Elizabethan and, indeed, of all literature; and by Mr. Sidney Lee, Shakespeare's latest biographer. Therefore, the first point which strikes us in the Baconian hypothesis is that its devotees are nobly careless of authority. We do not dream of converting them, but it may be amusing to examine the kind of logic and the sort of erudition which go to support an hypothesis not freely welcomed even in Germany.

The mother of the Baconian theory (though others had touched a guess at it) was undeniably Miss Delia Bacon, born at Tallmadge, Ohio, in 1811. Miss Bacon used to lecture on Roman history, illustrating her theme by recitations from Macaulay's 'Lays.' 'Her very heart was lacerated,' says Mr. Donnelly, 'and her womanly pride wounded, by a creature in the shape of a man - a Reverend (!) Alexander MacWhorter.' This Celtic divine was twenty-five, Miss Bacon was thirty-five; there arose a misunderstanding; but Miss Bacon had developed her Baconian theory before she knew Mr. MacWhorter. 'She became a monomaniac on the subject,' writes Mr. Wyman, and 'after the publication and non-success of her book she lost her reason WHOLLY AND ENTIRELY.' But great wits jump, and, just as Mr. Darwin and Mr. Wallace simultaneously evolved the idea of Natural Selection, so, unconscious of Miss Delia, Mr. William Henry Smith developed the Baconian verity.

From the days of Mr. William Henry Smith, in 1856, the great Baconian argument has been that Shakespeare could not conceivably have had the vast learning, classical, scientific, legal, medical, and so forth, of the author of the plays. Bacon, on the other hand, and nobody else, had this learning, and had, though he concealed them, the poetic powers of the unknown author. Therefore, prima facie, Bacon wrote the works of Shakespeare. Mr. Smith, as we said, had been partly anticipated, here, by the unlucky Miss Delia Bacon, to whose vast and wandering book Mr. Hawthorne wrote a preface. Mr. Hawthorne accused Mr. Smith of plagiarism from Miss Delia Bacon; Mr. Smith replied that, when he wrote his first essay (1856), he had never even heard the lady's name. Mr. Hawthorne expressed his regret, and withdrew his imputation. Mr. Smith is the second founder of Baconomania.

Like his followers, down to Mr. Ignatius Donnelly, and Mr. Bucke, and General Butler, and Mr. Atkinson, who writes in 'The Spiritualist,' and Mrs. Gallup, and Judge Webb, Mr. Smith rested, first, on Shakespeare's lack of education, and on the wide learning of the author of the poems and plays. Now, Ben Jonson, who knew both Shakespeare and Bacon, averred that the former had 'small Latin and less Greek,' doubtless with truth. It was necessary, therefore, to prove that the author of the plays had plenty of Latin and Greek. Here Mr. John Churton Collins suggests that Ben meant no more than that Shakespeare was not, in the strict sense, a scholar. Yet he might read Latin, Mr. Collins thinks, with ease and pleasure, and might pick out the sense of Greek books by the aid of Latin translations. To this view we return later.

Meanwhile we shall compare the assertions of the laborious Mr. Holmes, the American author of 'The Authorship of Shakespeare' (third edition, 1875), and of the ingenious Mr. Donnelly, the American author of 'The Great Cryptogram.' Both, alas! derive in part from the ignorance of Pope. Pope had said: 'Shakespeare follows the Greek authors, and particularly Dares Phrygius.' Mr. Smith cites this nonsense; so do Mr. Donnelly and Mr. Holmes. Now the so-called Dares Phrygius is not a Greek author. No Greek version of his early mediaeval romance, 'De Bello Trojano,' exists. The matter of the book found its way into Chaucer, Boccaccio, Lydgate, Guido de Colonna, and other authors accessible to one who had no Greek at all, while no Greek version of Dares was accessible to anybody.* Some recent authors, English and American, have gone on, with the credulity of 'the less than half educated,' taking a Greek Dares for granted, on the authority of Pope, whose Greek was 'small.' They have clearly never looked at a copy of Dares, never known that the story attributed to Dares was familiar, in English and French, to everybody. Mr. Holmes quotes Pope, Mr. Donnelly quotes Mr. Holmes, for this Greek Dares Phrygius. Probably Shakespeare had Latin enough to read the pseudo-Dares, but probably he did not take the trouble.

* See Brandes, William Shakespeare, ii. 198-202.

This example alone proves that men who are not scholars venture to pronounce on Shakespeare's scholarship, and that men who take absurd statements at second hand dare to constitute themselves judges of a question of evidence and of erudition.

The worthy Mr. Donnelly then quotes Mr. Holmes for Shakespeare's knowledge of the Greek drama. Turning to Mr. Holmes (who takes his motto, if you please, from Parmenides), we find that the author of 'Richard II.' borrowed from a Greek play by Euripides, called 'Hellene,' as did the author of the sonnets. There is, we need not say, no Greek play of the name of 'Hellene.' As Mr. Holmes may conceivably mean the 'Helena' of Euripides, we compare Sonnet cxxi. with 'Helena,' line 270. The parallel, the imitation of Euripides, appears to be -

By their dark thoughts my deeds must not be shown,

with -

Prooton men ouk ons adikoz eimi duskleez,

which means, 'I have lost my reputation though I have done no harm.' Shakespeare, then, could not complain of calumny without borrowing from 'Hellene,' a name which only exists in the fancy of Mr. Nathaniel Holmes. This critic assigns 'Richard II.,' act ii., scene 1, to 'Hellene' 512-514. We can find no resemblance whatever between the three Greek lines cited, from the 'Helena,' and the scene in Shakespeare. Mr. Holmes appears to have reposed on Malone, and Malone may have remarked on fugitive resemblances, such as inevitably occur by coincidence of thought. Thus the similarity of the situations of Hamlet and of Orestes in the 'Eumenides' is given by similarity of legend, Danish and Greek. Authors of genius, Greek or English, must come across analogous ideas in treating analogous topics. It does not follow that the poet of 'Hamlet' was able to read AEschylus, least of all that he could read him in Greek.

Anglicised version of the author's original Greek text.

The 'Comedy of Errors' is based on the 'Menaechmi' of Plautus. It does not follow that the author of the 'Comedy of Errors' could read the 'Menaechmi' or the 'Amphitryon,' though Shakespeare had probably Latin enough for the purpose. The 'Comedy of Errors' was acted in December 1594. A translation of the Latin play bears date 1595, but this may be an example of the common practice of post-dating a book by a month or two, and Shakespeare may have seen the English translation in the work itself, in proof, or in manuscript. In those days MSS. often circulated long before they were published, like Shakespeare's own 'sugared sonnets.' However, it is highly probable that Shakespeare was equal to reading the Latin of Plautus.

In 'Twelfth Night' occurs -

Like the Egyptian thief, at point of death, kill what I
love.

Mr. Donnelly writes: 'This is an allusion to a story
from Heliodorus's "AEthiopica." I do not know of any
English translation of it in the time of Shakespeare.'
The allusion is, we conceive, to Herodotus, ii. 121, the
story of Rhampsinitus, translated by 'B. R.' and
published in 1584. In 'Macbeth' we find -

All our yesterdays have LIGHTED fools
The way to dusty death. Out, out, BRIEF
CANDLE.

This is 'traced,' says Mr. Donnelly, 'to Catullus.' He
quotes: -

Soles occidere et redire possunt:
Nobis, cum semel occidit brevis lux,
Nox est perpetuo una dormienda.

Where is the parallel? It is got by translating Catullus
thus: -

The LIGHTS of heaven go out and return;
When once our BRIEF CANDLE goes out,
One night is to be perpetually slept.

But soles are not 'lights,' and brevis lux is not 'brief
candle.' If they were, the passages have no
resemblance. 'To be, or not to be,' is 'taken almost
verbatim from Plato.' Mr. Donnelly says that Mr.
Follett says that the Messrs. Langhorne say so. But,
where is the passage in Plato?

Such are the proofs by which men ignorant of the

classics prove that the author of the poems attributed to Shakespeare was a classical scholar. In fact, he probably had a 'practicable' knowledge of Latin, such as a person of his ability might pick up at school, and increase by casual study: points to which we return. For the rest, classical lore had filtered into contemporary literature and translations, such as North's Plutarch.

As to modern languages, Mr. Donnelly decides that Shakespeare knew Danish, because he must have read Saxo Grammaticus 'in the original tongue' - which, of course, is NOT Danish! Saxo was done out of the Latin into French. Thus Shakespeare is not exactly proved to have been a Danish scholar. There is no difficulty in supposing that 'a clayver man,' living among wits, could pick up French and Italian sufficient for his uses. But extremely stupid people are naturally amazed by even such commonplace acquirements. When the step is made from cleverness to genius, then the dull disbelieve, or cry out of a miracle. Now, as 'miracles do not happen,' a man of Shakespeare's education could not have written the plays attributed to him by his critics, companions, friends, and acquaintances. Shakespeare, ex hypothesi, was a rude unlettered fellow. Such a man, the Baconians assume, would naturally be chosen by Bacon as his mask, and put forward as the author of Bacon's pieces. Bacon would select a notorious ignoramus as a plausible author of pieces which, by the theory, are rich in knowledge of the classics, and nobody would be surprised. Nobody would say: 'Shakespeare is as ignorant as a butcher's boy, and cannot possibly be the person who translated Hamlet's soliloquy out of Plato, "Hamlet" at large out of the Danish; who imitated the "Hellene" of Euripides, and borrowed "Troilus and Cressida" from the Greek of Dares Phrygius' - which happens not to exist. Ignorance can go no further than in thesearguments. Such are the logic and learning of American amateurs, who sometimes do not even know the names of the books they talk about, or the languages in which they are written. Such learning and such logic are passed off by 'the less than half educated' on the absolutely untaught, who decline to listen to scholars.

We cannot of course furnish a complete summary of all that the Baconians have said in their myriad pages. All those pages, almost, really flow from the little volume of Mr. Smith. We are obliged to take the points which the Baconians regard as their strong cards. We have dealt with the point of classical scholarship, and shown that the American partisans of Bacon are not scholars, and have no locus standi. We shall take next in order the contention that Bacon was a poet; that his works contain parallel passages to Shakespeare, which can only be the result of common authorship; that Bacon's notes, called 'Promus,' are notes for Shakespeare's plays; that, in style, Bacon and Shakespeare are identical. Then we shall glance at Bacon's motives for writing plays by stealth, and blushing to find it fame. We shall expose the frank folly of averring that he chose as his mask a man who (some assert) could not even write; and we shall conclude by citing, once more, the irrefragable personal testimony to the genius and character of Shakespeare.

To render the Baconian theory plausible it is necessary to show that Bacon had not only the learning needed for 'the authorship of Shakespeare,' but that he gives some proof of Shakespeare's poetic qualities; that he had reasons for writing plays, and reasons for concealing his pen, and for omitting to make any claim to his own literary triumphs after Shakespeare was dead. Now, as to scholarship, the knowledge shown in the plays is not that of a scholar, does not exceed that of a man of genius equipped with what, to Ben Jonson, seemed 'small Latin and less Greek,' and with abundance of translations, and books like 'Euphues,' packed with classical lore, to help him. With the futile attempts to prove scholarship we have dealt. The legal and medical lore is in no way beyond the 'general information' which genius inevitably amasses from reading, conversation, reflection, and experience.

A writer of to-day, Mr. Kipling, is fond of showing how easily a man of his rare ability picks up the terminology of many recondite trades and professions. Again, evidence taken on oath proves that Jeanne d'Arc, a girl of seventeen, developed great military skill, especially in artillery and tactics, that she displayed political clairvoyance, and that she held her own, and more, among the subtlest and most hostile theologians. On the ordinary hypothesis, that Shakespeare was a man of genius, there is, then, nothing impossible in his knowledge, while his wildly daring anachronisms could have presented no temptation to a well-regulated scientific intellect like that of Bacon. The Baconian hypothesis rests on the incredulity with which dulness regards genius. We see the phenomenon every day when stupid people talk about people of ordinary cleverness, and 'wonder with a foolish face of praise.' As Dr. Brandes remarks, when the Archbishop of Canterbury praises Henry V. and his universal accomplishments, he says:

Which is a wonder, how his grace should glean it,

Since his addiction was to courses vain,
His companies unletter'd, rude, and shallow,
His hours fill'd up with riots, banquets, sports
AND NEVER NOTED IN HIM ANY STUDY,
Any retirement, any sequestration,
From open haunts and popularity.

Yet, as the Archbishop remarks (with doubtful orthodoxy), 'miracles are ceased.'

Shakespeare in these lines describes, as only he could describe it, the world's wonder which he himself was. Or, if Bacon wrote the lines, then Bacon, unlike his advocates, was prepared to recognise the possible existence of such a thing as genius. Incredulity on this head could only arise in an age and in peoples where mediocrity is almost universal. It is a democratic form of disbelief.

For the hypothesis, as we said, it is necessary to show that Bacon possessed poetic genius. The proof cannot possibly be found in his prose works. In the prose of Mr. Ruskin there are abundant examples of what many respectable minds regard as poetic qualities. But, if the question arose, 'Was Mr. Ruskin the author of Tennyson's poems?' the answer could be settled, for once, by internal evidence. We have only to look at Mr. Ruskin's published verses. These prove that a great writer of 'poetical prose' may be at the opposite pole from a poet. In the same way, we ask, what are Bacon's acknowledged compositions in verse? Mr. Holmes is their admirer. In 1599 Bacon wrote in a letter, 'Though I profess not to be a poet, I prepared a sonnet,' to Queen Elizabeth. He PREPARED a sonnet! 'Prepared' is good. He also translated some of the Psalms into verse, a field in which success is not to be won. Mr.

Holmes notes, in Psalm xc., a Shakespearean parallel. 'We spend our years as a tale that is told.' Bacon renders:

As a tale told, which sometimes men attend,
And sometimes not, our life steals to an end.

In 'King John,' iii. 4, we read: -

Life is as tedious as a twice-told tale
Vexing the dull ear of a drowsy man.

Now, if we must detect a connection, Bacon might have read 'King John' in the Folio, for he versified the Psalms in 1625. But it is unnecessary to suppose a reminiscence. Again, in Psalm civ. Bacon has -

The greater navies look like walking woods.

They looked like nothing of the sort; but Bacon may have remembered Birnam Wood, either from Boece or Holinshed, or from the play itself. One thing is certain: Shakespeare did not write Bacon's Psalms or compare navies to 'walking woods'! Mr. Holmes adds: 'Many of the sonnets [of Shakespeare] show the strongest internal evidence that they were addressed [by Bacon] to the Queen, as no doubt they were.' That is, Bacon wrote sonnets to Queen Elizabeth, and permitted them to pass from hand to hand, among Shakespeare's 'private friends,' as Shakespeare's (1598). That was an odd way of paying court to Queen Elizabeth. Chalmers had already conjectured that Shakespeare (not Bacon) in the sonnets was addressing the Virgin Queen, whom he recommended to marry and leave offspring - rather late in life. Shakespeare's apparent allusions to his profession -

I have gone here and there,
And made myself a motley to the view,

and

The public means which public manners breeds,

refer, no doubt, to Bacon's versatile POLITICAL
behaviour. It has hitherto been supposed that sonnet
lvii. was addressed to Shakespeare's friend, a man, not
to any woman. But Mr. Holmes shows that the Queen
is intended. Is it not obvious?

I, MY SOVEREIGN, watch the clock for you.

Bacon clearly had an assignation with Her Majesty - so
here is 'scandal about Queen Elizabeth.' Mr. Holmes
pleasingly remarks that Twickenham is 'within sight of
Her Majesty's Palace of White Hall.' She gave Bacon
the reversion of Twickenham Park, doubtless that,
from the windows of White Hall, she might watch her
swain. And Bacon wrote a masque for the Queen; he
skilfully varied his style in this piece from that which
he used under the name of Shakespeare. With a
number of other gentlemen, some named, some
unnamed, Bacon once, at an uncertain date, interested
himself in a masque at Gray's Inn, while he and his
friends 'partly devised dumb shows and additional
speeches,' in 1588.

Nothing follows as to Bacon's power of composing
Shakespeare's plays. A fragmentary masque, which
may or may not be by Bacon, is put forward as the
germ of what Bacon wrote about Elizabeth in the
'Midsummer Night's Dream.' An Indian WANDERER
from the West Indies, near the fountain of the

AMAZON, is brought to Elizabeth to be cured of blindness. Now the fairy, in the 'Midsummer Night's Dream,' says, capitalised by Mr. Holmes:

I DO WANDER EVERYWHERE.

Here then are two wanderers - and there is a river in Monmouth and a river in Macedon. Puck, also, is 'that merry WANDERER of the night.' Then 'A BOUNCING AMAZON' is mentioned in the 'Midsummer Night's Dream,' and 'the fountain of the great river of the Amazons' is alluded to in the fragment of the masque. Cupid too occurs in the play, and in the masque the wanderer is BLIND; now Cupid is blind, sometimes, but hardly when 'a certain aim he took.' The Indian, in the masque, presents Elizabeth with 'his gift AND PROPERTY TO BE EVER YOUNG,' and the herb, in the play, has a 'VIRTUOUS PROPERTY.'

For such exquisite reasons as these the masque and the 'Midsummer Night's Dream' are by one hand, and the masque is by Bacon. For some unknown cause the play is full of poetry, which is entirely absent from the masque. Mr. Holmes was a Judge; sat on the bench of American Themis - and these are his notions of proof and evidence. The parallel passages which he selects are on a level with the other parallels between Bacon and Shakespeare. One thing is certain: the writer of the masque shows no signs of being a poet, and a poet Bacon explicitly 'did not profess to be.' One piece of verse attributed to Bacon, a loose paraphrase of a Greek epigram, has won its way into 'The Golden Treasury.' Apart from that solitary composition, the verses which Bacon 'prepared' were within the powers of almost any educated Elizabethan. They are on a level with the rhymes of Mr. Ruskin. It was only when he wrote as Shakespeare that Bacon wrote as a poet.

We have spoken somewhat harshly of Mr. Holmes as a classical scholar, and as a judge of what, in literary matters, makes evidence. We hasten to add that he could be convinced of error. He had regarded a sentence of Bacon's as a veiled confession that Bacon wrote 'Richard II.,' 'which, though it grew from me, went after about in others' names.' Mr. Spedding averred that Mr. Holmes's opinion rested on a grammatical misinterpretation, and Mr. Holmes accepted the correction. But 'nothing less than a miracle' could shake Mr. Holmes's belief in the common authorship of the masque (possibly Bacon's) and the 'Midsummer Night's Dream' - so he told Mr. Spedding. To ourselves nothing short of a miracle, or the visitation of God in the shape of idiocy, could bring the conviction that the person who wrote the masque could have written the play. The reader may compare the whole passage in Mr. Holmes's work (pp. 228-238). We have already set forth some of those bases of his belief which only a miracle could shake. The weak wind that scarcely bids the aspen shiver might blow them all away.

Vast space is allotted by Baconians to 'parallel passages' in Bacon and Shakespeare. We have given a few in the case of the masque and the 'Midsummer Night's Dream.' The others are of equal weight. They are on a level with 'Punch's' proofs that Alexander Smith was a plagiarist. Thus Smith:

No CHARACTER that servant WOMAN asked;

Pope writes:

Most WOMEN have no CHARACTER at all.

It is tedious to copy out the puerilities of such parallelisms. Thus Bacon:

If we simply looked to the fabric of the world;

Shakespeare:

And, like the baseless fabric of a vision.

Bacon:

The intellectual light in the top and consummation of thy workmanship;

Shakespeare:

Like eyasses that cry out on the top of the question.

Myriads of pages of such matter would carry no proof. Probably the hugest collection of such 'parallels' is that preserved by Mrs. Pott in Bacon's 'Promus,' a book of 628 pages. Mrs. Pott's 'sole object' in publishing 'was to confirm the growing belief in Bacon's authorship of the plays.' Having acquired the opinion, she laboured to strengthen herself and others in the faith. The so-called 'Promus' is a manuscript set of notes, quotations, formulae, and proverbs. As Mr. Spedding says, there are 'forms of compliment, application, excuse, repartee, etc.' 'The collection is from books which were then in every scholar's hands.' 'The proverbs may all, or nearly all, be found in the common collections.' Mrs. Pott remarks that in 'Promus' are 'several hundreds of notes of which no trace has been discovered in the acknowledged writings of Bacon, or of any other contemporary writer but Shakespeare.' She adds that the theory of 'close intercourse' between the two men is 'contrary to all evidence.' She then infers that 'Bacon alone wrote all the plays and sonnets which are attributed to Shakespeare.' So Bacon entrusted his plays, and the dread secret of his authorship, to a boorish cabotin with whom he had no 'close intercourse'! This is lady's logic, a contradiction in terms. The theory that Bacon wrote the plays and sonnets inevitably implies the closest intercourse between him and Shakespeare. They must have been in constant connection. But, as Mrs. Pott truly says, this is 'contrary to all evidence.'

Perhaps the best way to deal with Mrs. Pott is to cite the author of her preface, Dr. Abbott. He is not convinced, but he is much struck by a very exquisite argument of the lady's. Bacon in 'Promus' is writing down 'Formularies and Elegancies,' modes of salutation. He begins with 'Good morrow!' This original remark, Mrs. Pott reckons, 'occurs in the plays nearly a hundred times. In the list of upwards of six thousand words in Appendix E, "Good morrow" has been noted thirty-one times. . . . "Good morrow" may have become familiar merely by means of "Romeo and Juliet."' Dr. Abbott is so struck by this valuable statement that he writes: 'There remains the question, Why did Bacon think it worth while to write down in a notebook the phrase "Good morrow" if it was at that time in common use?'

Bacon wrote down 'Good morrow' just because it WAS in common use. All the formulae were in common use; probably 'Golden sleepe' was a regular wish, like 'Good rest.' Bacon is making a list of commonplaces about beginning the day, about getting out of bed, about sleep. Some are in English, some in various other languages. He is not, as in Mrs. Pott's ingenious theory, making notes of novelties to be introduced through his plays. He is cataloguing the commonplace. It is Mrs. Pott's astonishing contention, as we have seen, that Bacon probably introduced the phrase 'Good morrow!' Mr. Bucke, following her in a magazine article, says: 'These forms of salutation were not in use in England before Bacon's time, and it was his entry of them in the "Promus" and use of them in the plays that makes them current coin day by day with us in the nineteenth century.' This is ignorant nonsense. 'Good morrow' and 'Good night' were as familiar before Bacon or Shakespeare wrote as 'Good morning' and 'Good night' are to-day. This we can demonstrate. The very first Elizabethan handbook of phrases which we consult shows that 'Good morrow' was the stock phrase in regular use in 1583. The book is 'The French Littelton, A most Easie, Perfect, and Absolute way to learne the Frenche Tongue. Set forth by Claudius Holyband. Imprinted at London by Thomas Vautrollier, dwelling in the blacke- Friers. 1583.' (There is an edition of 1566.)

On page 10 we read: -

'Of Scholars and Schoole.

'God give you good morrow, Sir! Good morrow gossip: good morrow my she gossip: God give you a good morrow and a good year.'

Thus the familiar salutation was not introduced by Bacon; it was, on the other hand, the very first formula which a writer of an English-French phrase-book translated into French ten years before Bacon made his notes. Presently he comes to 'Good evening, good night, good rest,' and so on.

This fact annihilates Mrs. Pott's contention that Bacon introduced 'Good morrow' through the plays falsely attributed to Shakespeare. There follows, in 'Promus,' a string of proverbs, salutations, and quotations, about sleep and waking. Among these occur 'Golden Sleepe' (No. 1207) and (No. 1215) 'Uprouse. You are up.' Now Friar Laurence says to Romeo: -

> But where unbruised youth with unstuffed brain
> Doth couch his limbs, there GOLDEN SLEEP doth reign:
> Therefore thy earliness doth me assure,
> Thou art UP-ROUSED by some distemperature.

Dr. Abbott writes: 'Mrs. Pott's belief is that the play is indebted for these expressions to the "Promus;" mine is that the "Promus" is borrowed from the play.' And why should either owe anything to the other? The phrase 'Uprouse' or 'Uprose' is familiar in Chaucer, from one of his best-known lines. 'Golden' is a natural poetic adjective of excellence, from Homer to Tennyson. Yet in Dr. Abbott's opinion 'TWO of these entries constitute a coincidence amounting almost to a demonstration' that either Shakespeare or Bacon borrowed from the other. And this because each writer, one in making notes of commonplaces on sleep, the other in a speech about sleep, uses the regular expression 'Uprouse,' and the poetical commonplace 'Golden sleep' for 'Good rest.' There was no originality in the matter.

We have chosen Dr. Abbott's selected examples of Mrs. Pott's triumphs. Here is another of her parallels.

Bacon gives the formula, 'I pray God your early rising does you no hurt.' Shakespeare writes: -

Go, you cot-quean, go,
Get you to bed; faith, you'll be sick to-morrow
For this night's watching.

Here Bacon notes a morning salutation, 'I hope you are none the worse for early rising,' while Shakespeare tells somebody not to sit up late. Therefore, and for similar reasons, Bacon is Shakespeare.

We are not surprised to find Mr. Bucke adopting Mrs. Pott's theory of the novelty of 'Good morrow.' He writes in the Christmas number of an illustrated sixpenny magazine, and his article, a really masterly compendium of the whole Baconian delirium, addresses its natural public. But we are amazed to find Dr. Abbott looking not too unkindly on such imbecilities, and marching at least in the direction of Coventry with such a regiment. He is 'on one point a convert' to Mrs. Pott, and that point is the business of 'Good morrow,' 'Uprouse,' and 'Golden sleepe.' It need hardly be added that the intrepid Mr. Donnelly is also a firm adherent of Mrs. Pott.

'Some idea,' he says, 'may be formed of the marvellous industry of this remarkable lady when I state that to prove that we are indebted to Bacon for having enriched the English language, through the plays, with these beautiful courtesies of speech, 'Good morrow,' 'Good day,' etc., she carefully examined SIX THOUSAND WORKS ANTERIOR TO OR CONTEMPORARY WITH BACON.'

Dr. Abbott thought it judicious to 'hedge' about these

six thousand works, and await 'the all-knowing dictionary' of Dr. Murray and the Clarendon Press. We have deemed it simpler to go to the first Elizabethan phrase-book on our shelves, and that tiny volume, in its very first phrase, shatters the mare's-nest of Mrs. Pott, Mr. Donnelly, and Mr. Bucke.

But why, being a great poet, should Bacon conceal the fact, and choose as a mask a man whom, on the hypothesis of his ignorance, every one that knew him must have detected as an impostor? Now, one great author did choose to conceal his identity, though he never shifted the burden of the 'Waverley Novels' on to Terry the actor. Bacon may, conceivably, have had Scott's pleasure in secrecy, but Bacon selected a mask much more impossible (on the theory) than Terry would have been for Scott. Again, Sir Walter Scott took pains to make his identity certain, by an arrangement with Constable, and by preserving his manuscripts, and he finally confessed. Bacon never confessed, and no documentary traces of his authorship survive. Scott, writing anonymously, quoted his own poems in the novels, an obvious 'blind.' Bacon, less crafty, never (as far as we are aware) mentions Shakespeare.

It is arguable, of course, that to write plays might seem dangerous to Bacon's professional and social position. The reasons which might make a lawyer keep his dramatic works a secret could not apply to 'Lucrece.' A lawyer, of good birth, if he wrote plays at all, would certainly not vamp up old stock pieces. That was the work of a 'Johannes Factotum,' of a 'Shakescene,' as Greene says, of a man who occupied the same position in his theatrical company as Nicholas Nickleby did in that of Mr. Crummles. Nicholas had to bring in the vulgar pony, the Phenomenon, the buckets, and so forth. So, in early years, the author of the plays (Bacon, by the theory) had to work over old pieces. All this is the work of the hack of a playing company; it is not work to which a man in Bacon's position could stoop. Why should he? What had he to gain by patching and vamping? Certainly not money, if the wealth of Shakespeare is a dark mystery to the Baconian theorists. We are asked to believe that Bacon, for the sake of some five or six pounds, toiled at refashioning old plays, and handed the fair manuscripts to Shakespeare, who passed them off, among the actors who knew him intimately, as his own. THEY detected no incongruity between the player who was their Johannes Factotum and the plays which he gave in to the manager. They seemed to be just the kind of work which Shakespeare would be likely to write. BE LIKELY TO WRITE, but 'the father of the rest,' Mr. Smith, believed that Shakespeare COULD NOT WRITE AT ALL.

We live in the Ages of Faith, of faith in fudge. Mr. Smith was certain, and Mr. Bucke is inclined to suspect, that when Bacon wanted a mask he chose, as a plausible author of the plays, a man who could not write. Mr. Smith was certain, and Mr. Bucke must deem it possible, that Shakespeare's enemy, Greene, that his friends, Jonson, Burbage, Heming, and the other actors, and that his critics and admirers, Francis Meres and others, accepted, as author of the pieces which they played in or applauded, a man who could write no more than his name. Such was the tool whom Bacon found eligible, and so easily gulled was the literary world of Eliza and our James. And Bacon took all this trouble for what reason? To gain five or six pounds, or as much of that sum as Shakespeare would let him keep. Had Bacon been possessed by the ambition to write plays he would always have written original dramas, he would not have assumed the part of Nicholas Nickleby.

There is no human nature in this nonsense. An ambitious lawyer passes his nights in retouching stock pieces, from which he can reap neither fame nor profit. He gives his work to a second-rate illiterate actor, who adopts it as his own. Bacon is so enamoured of this method that he publishes 'Venus and Adonis' and 'Lucrece' under the name of his actor friend. Finally, he commits to the actor's care all his sonnets to the Queen, to Gloriana, and for years these manuscript poems are handed about by Shakespeare, as his own, among the actors, hack scribblers, and gay young nobles of his acquaintance. They 'chaff' Shakespeare about his affection for his 'sovereign;' great Gloriana's praises are stained with sack in taverns, and perfumed with the Indian weed. And Bacon, careful toiler after Court favour, 'thinks it all wery capital,' in the words of Mr. Weller père. Moreover, nobody who hears Shakespeare talk and sees him smile has any doubt that he is the author of the plays and amorous fancies of Bacon.

It is needless to dwell on the pother made about the missing manuscripts of Shakespeare. 'The original manuscripts, of course, Bacon would take care to destroy,' says Mr. Holmes, 'if determined that the secret should die with him.' If he was so determined, for what earthly reason did he pass his valuable time in vamping up old plays and writing new ones? 'There was no money in it,' and there was no reason. But, if he was not determined that the secret should die with him, why did not he, like Scott, preserve the manuscripts?

The manuscripts are where Marlowe's and where Moliere's are, by virtue of a like neglect. Where are the MSS. of any of the great Elizabethans? We really cannot waste time over Mr. Donnelly's theory of a Great Cryptogram, inserted by Bacon, as proof of his claim, in the multitudinous errors of the Folio. Mr. Bucke, too, has his Anagram, the deathless discovery of Dr. Platt, of Lakewood, New Jersey. By manipulating the scraps of Latin in 'Love's Labour's Lost,' he extracts 'Hi Ludi tuiti sibi Fr. Bacono nati': 'These plays, entrusted to themselves, proceeded from Fr. Bacon.' It is magnificent, but it is not Latin. Had Bacon sent in such Latin at school, he would never have survived to write the 'Novum Organon' and his sonnets to Queen Elizabeth. In that stern age they would have 'killed him - with wopping.' That Bacon should be a vamper and a playwright for no appreciable profit, that, having produced his deathless works, he should make no sign, has, in fact, staggered even the great credulity of Baconians. He MUST, they think, have made a sign in cipher. Out of the mass of the plays, anagrams and cryptograms can be fashioned a plaisir, and the world has heard too much of Mrs. Gallup, while the hunt for hints in contemporary frontispieces led to mistaking the porcupine of Sidney's crest for 'a hanged hog' (Bacon).

The theory of the Baconian authorship of Shakespeare's plays and poems has its most notable and recent British advocate in His Honour Judge Webb, sometime Fellow of Trinity College, Dublin, Regius Professor of Laws, and Public Orator in the University of Dublin. Judge Webb, as a scholar and a man used to weighing evidence, puts the case at its strongest. His work, 'The Mystery of William Shakespeare' (1902), rests much on the old argument about the supposed ignorance of Shakespeare, and the supposed learning of the author of the plays. Judge Webb, like his predecessors, does not take into account the wide diffusion of a kind of classical and pseudo-scientific knowledge among all Elizabethan writers, and bases theories on manifest misconceptions of Shakespearean and other texts. His book, however, has affected the opinions of some readers who do not verify his references and examine the mass of Elizabethan literature for themselves.

Judge Webb, in his 'Proem,' refers to Mr. Holmes and Mr. Donnelly as 'distinguished writers,' who 'have received but scant consideration from the accredited organs of opinion on this side of the Atlantic.' Their theories have not been more favourably considered by Shakespearean scholars on the other side of the Atlantic, and how much consideration they deserve we have tried to show. The Irish Judge opens his case by noting an essential distinction between 'Shakspere,' the actor, and 'Shakespeare,' the playwright. The name, referring to the man who was both actor and author, is spelled both 'Shakspeare' and 'Shakespeare' in the 'Returne from Parnassus' (1602).* The 'school of critics' which divides the substance of Shakespeare on the strength of the spelling of a proper name, in the casual times of great Elizabeth, need not detain the inquirer.

* The Returne from Parnassus, pp. 56,57,138. Oxford, 1886.

As to Shakespeare's education, Judge Webb admits that 'there was a grammar school in the place.' As its registers of pupils have not survived, we cannot prove that Shakespeare went to the school. Mr. Collins shows that the Headmaster was a Fellow of Corpus Christi College, Oxford, and describes the nature of the education, mainly in Latin, as, according to the standard of the period, it ought to have been.* There is no doubt that if Shakespeare attended the school (the age of entry was eight), minded his book, and had 'a good sprag memory,' he might have learned Latin. Mr. Collins commends the Latin of two Stratford contemporaries and friends of Shakespeare, Sturley and Quiney, who probably were educated at the Grammar School. Judge Webb disparages their lore, and, on the evidence of the epistles, says that Sturley and Quiney 'were not men of education.' If Judge Webb had compared the original letters of distinguished Elizabethan officials and diplomatists - say, Sir William Drury, the Commandant of Berwick - he would have found that Sturley and Quiney were at least on the ordinary level of education in the upper classes. But the whole method of the Baconians rests on neglecting such comparisons.

* Fortnightly Review, April 1903.

In a letter of Sturley's, eximiae is spelled eximie, without the digraph, a thing then most usual, and no disproof of Sturley's Latinity.* The Shakspearean hypothesis is that Shakespeare was rather a cleverer man than Quiney and Sturley, and, consequently, that, if he went to school, he probably learned more by a great deal than they did. There was no reason why he should not acquire Latin enough to astonish modern reviewers, who have often none at all.

*Webb, p. 14. Phillipps's Outlines of the Life of Shakespeare, i. p. 150, ii. p. 57.

Judge Webb then discusses the learning of Shakespeare, and easily shows that he was full of mythological lore. So was all Elizabethan literature. Every English scribbler then knew what most men have forgotten now. Nobody was forced to go to the original authorities say, Plato, Herodotus, and Plutarch - for what was accessible in translations, or had long before been copiously decanted into English prose and poetry. Shakespeare could get Rhodope, not from Pliny, but from B. R.'s lively translation (1584) of the first two books of Herodotus. 'Even Launcelot Gobbo talks of Scylla and Charybdis,' says Judge Webb. Who did not? Had the Gobbos not known about Scylla and Charybdis, Shakespeare would not have lent them the knowledge.

The mythological legends were 'in the air,' familiar to all the Elizabethan world. These allusions are certainly no proof 'of trained scholarship or scientific education.' In five years of contact with the stage, with wits, with writers for the stage, with older plays, with patrons of the stage, with Templars, and so on, a man of talent could easily pick up the 'general information' - now caviare to the general - which a genius like Shakespeare inevitably absorbed.

We naturally come to Greene's allusion to 'Shakescene' (1592), concerning which a schoolboy said, in an examination, 'We are tired to death with hearing about it.' Greene conspicuously insults 'Shakescene' both as a writer and an actor. Judge Webb says: 'As Mr. Phillipps justly observes, it' (one of Greene's allusions) 'merely conveys that Shakspere was one who acted in the plays of which Greene and his three friends were the authors (ii. 269).'

It is necessary to verify the Judge's reference. Mr. Phillipps writes: 'Taking Greene's words in their contextual and natural sense, he first alludes to Shakespeare as an actor, one "beautified with our feathers," that is, one who acts in their plays; THEN TO THE POET as a writer just commencing to try his hand at blank verse, and, finally, to him as not only engaged in both those capacities, but in any other in which he might be useful to the company.' Mr. Phillipps adds that Greene's quotation of the line 'TYGER'S HEART WRAPT IN A PLAYER'S HIDE' 'is a decisive proof of Shakespeare's authorship of the line.'*

* Webb, p. 57. Phillipps, ii. p. 269.

Judge Webb has manifestly succeeded in not appreciating Mr. Phillipps's plain English. He says, with obvious truth, that Greene attacks Shakespeare both as actor and poet, but Judge Webb puts the matter thus: 'The language of Greene. . . as Mr. Phillipps justly observes, merely conveys that Shakspere was one who acted in the plays of which Greene and his three friends were authors.'

The language of Greene IN ONE PART OF HIS TIRADE, 'an upstart crow beautified in our feathers,' probably refers to Shakespeare as an actor only, but Greene goes on to insult him as a writer. Judge Webb will not recognise him as a writer, and omits that part of Mr. Phillipps's opinion.

There followed Chettle's well-known apology (1592), as editor of Greene's sally, to Shakespeare. Chettle speaks of his excellence 'in the quality he professes,' and of his 'facetious grace in writing, that approves his art,' this on the authority of 'the report of divers of worship.'

This proves, of course, that Shakespeare was a writer as well as an actor, and Judge Webb can only murmur that 'we are "left to guess " who divers of worship' were, and 'what motive' they had for praising his 'facetious grace in writing.' The obvious motive was approval of the work, for work there WAS, and, as to who the 'divers' were, nobody knows.

The evidence that, IN THE OPINION OF GREENE, CHETTLE, AND 'DIVERS OF WORSHIP,' Shakespeare was a writer as well as an actor is absolutely irrefragable. Had Shakespeare been the ignorant lout of the Baconian theorists, these men would not have credited him, for example, with his first signed and printed piece, 'Venus and Adonis.' It appeared early in 1593, and Greene and Chettle wrote in 1592. 'Divers of worship,' according to the custom of the time, may have seen 'Venus and Adonis' in manuscript. It was printed by Richard Field, a Stratford-on-Avon man, as was natural, a Stratford-on-Avon man being the author.* It was dedicated, in stately but not servile courtesy, to the Earl of Southampton, by 'William Shakespeare.'

* Phillipps, i. p. 101.

Judge Webb asks: 'Was it a pseudonym, or was it the real name of the author of the poem?' Well, Shakespeare signs 'Shakspere' in two deeds, in which the draftsman throughout calls him 'Shakespeare:' obviously taking no difference.* People were not particular, Shakespeare let them spell his name as best pleased them.

* Phillipps, ii. pp. 34, 36.

Judge Webb argues that Southampton 'took no notice' of the dedication. How can he know? Ben Jonson dedicated to Lady Wroth and many others. Does Judge Webb know what 'notice' they took? He says that on various occasions 'Southampton did not recognise the existence of the Player.' How can he know? I have dedicated books to dozens of people. Probably they 'took notice,' but no record thereof exists. The use of arguments of this kind demonstrates the feebleness of the case.

That Southampton, however, DID 'take notice' may be safely inferred from the fact that Shakespeare, in 1594, dedicated to him 'The Rape of Lucrece.' Had the Earl been an ungrateful patron, had he taken no notice, Shakespeare had Latin enough to act on the motto Invenies alium si te hic fastidit Alexin. He speaks of 'the warrant I have of your honourable disposition,' which makes the poem 'assured of acceptance.' This could never have been written had the dedication of 'Venus and Adonis' been disdained. 'The client never acknowledged his obligation to the patron,' says Judge Webb. The dedication of 'Lucrece' is acknowledgment enough. The Judge ought to think so, for he speaks, with needless vigour, of 'the protestations, warm and gushing as a geyser, of "The Rape."' There is nothing 'warm,' and nothing 'gushing,' in the dedication of 'Lucrece' (granting the style of the age), but, if it were as the Judge says, here, indeed, would be the client's 'acknowledgment,' which, the Judge says, was never made.* To argue against such logic seems needless, and even cruel, but judicial contentions appear to deserve a reply.

* Webb, p. 67.

We now come to the evidence of the Rev. Francis Meres, in 'Palladis Tamia' (1598). Meres makes 'Shakespeare among the English' the rival, in comedy and tragedy, of Plautus and Seneca 'among the Latines.' He names twelve plays, of which 'Love's Labour's Won' is unknown. 'The soul of Ovid' lives in his 'Venus and Adonis,' his 'Lucrece,' and his 'sugred sonnets among his private friends.' Meres also mentions Sidney, Spenser, Daniel, Drayton, and so forth, a long string of English poetic names, ending with 'Samuel Page, sometime Fellow of C.C.C. in Oxford, Churchyard, Bretton.'*

* Phillipps, ii. pp. 149,150.

Undeniably Meres, in 1598, recognises Shakespeare as both playwright and poet. So Judge Webb can only reply: 'But who this mellifluous and honey-tongued Shakespeare was he does not say, AND HE DOES NOT PRETEND TO KNOW.'* He does not 'pretend to know' 'who' any of the poets was - except Samuel Page, and he was a Fellow of Corpus. He speaks of Shakespeare just as he does of Marlowe, Kid, Chapman, and the others whom he mentions. He 'does not pretend to know who' they were. Every reader knew who they all were. If I write of Mr. Swinburne or Mr. Pinero, of Mr. Browning or of Mr. Henry Jones, I do not say 'who they were,' I do not 'pretend to know.' There was no Shakespeare in the literary world of London but the one Shakespeare, 'Burbage's deserving man.'

*Webb, p. 71.

The next difficulty is that Shakespeare's company, by request of theEssex conspirators (who paid 2 pounds), acted 'Richard II.' just before their foolish attempt (February 7, 1601). 'If Coke,' says the Judge, 'had the faintest idea that the player' (Shakespeare) 'was the author of "Richard II.," he would not have hesitated a moment to lay him by the heels.' Why, the fact of Shakespeare's authorship had been announced, in print, by Meres, in 1598. Coke knew, if he cared to know. Judge Webb goes on: 'And that the Player' (Shakespeare) 'was not regarded as the author by the Queen is proved by the fact that, with his company, he performed before the Court at Richmond, on the evening before the execution of the Earl.'*

* Webb, pp. 72, 73.

Nothing of the kind is proved. The guilt, if any, lay, not in writing the drama - by 1601 'olde and outworne' - but in acting it, on the eve of an intended revolution. This error Elizabeth overlooked, and with it the innocent authorship of the piece, 'now olde and outworne.'* It is not even certain, in Mr. Phillipps's opinion, that the 'olde and outworne' play was that of Shakespeare. It is perfectly certain that, as Elizabeth overlooked the fault of the players, she would not attack the author of a play written years before Essex's plot, with no political intentions.

* Phillipps, ii. pp. 359-362.

We now come to evidence of which Judge Webb says very little, that of the two plays acted at St. John's College, Cambridge, in 1600-1601, known as 'The Returne from Parnassus.' These pieces prove that Shakespeare the poet was identified with Shakespeare the player. They also prove that Shakespeare's scholarship and art were held very cheaply by the University wits, who, as always, were disdainful of non-University men. His popularity is undisputed, but his admirer in the piece, Gullio, is a vapouring ignoramus, who pretends to have been at the University of Padua, but knows no more Latin than many modern critics. Gullio rants thus: 'Pardon, faire lady, though sicke-thoughted Gullio makes amaine unto thee, and LIKE A BOULD-FACED SUTOR 'GINS TO WOO THEE.' This, of course, is from 'Venus and Adonis.' Ingenioso says, aside: 'We shall have nothinge but pure Shakespeare and shreds of poetry that he hath gathered at the theaters.' Gullio next mouths a reminiscence of 'Romeo and Juliet,' and Ingenioso whispers, 'Marke, Romeo and Juliet, O monstrous theft;' however, aloud, he says 'Sweete Mr. Shakspeare!' - the spelling varies. Gullio continues to praise sweete Mr. Shakspeare above Spenser and Chaucer. 'Let mee heare Mr. Shakspear's veyne.' Judge Webb does not cite these passages, which identify Shakspeare (or Shakespeare) with the poet of 'Venus and Adonis' and 'Romeo and Juliet.'

In the second 'Returne,' Burbage and Kemp, the noted morrice dancer and clown of Shakespeare's company, are introduced. 'Few of the University men pen plays well,' says Kemp; 'they smack too much of that writer Ovid, and that writer Metamorphosis, and talke too much of Proserpina and Jupiter. Why here's our fellow Shakespeare' (fellow is used in the sense of companion), 'puts them all downe, ay, and Ben Jonson too. O that Ben Jonson is a pestilent fellow; he brought up Horace giving the Poets a pill, but our fellow Shakespeare hath given him a purge that made him bewray his credit.' At Burbage's request, one of the

University men then recites two lines of 'Richard III.,' by the poet of his company.

Ben, according to Judge Webb, 'bewrayed his credit' in 'The Poetaster,' 1601-1602, where Pantalabus 'was meant for Shakspere.'* If so, Pantalabus is described as one who 'pens high, lofty, and in a new stalking strain,' and if Shakespeare is the Poet Ape of Jonson's epigram, why then Jonson regards him as a writer, not merely as an actor. No amount of evil that angry Ben could utter about the plays, while Shakespeare lived, and, perhaps, was for a time at odds with him, can obliterate the praises which the same Ben wrote in his milder mood. The charge against Poet Ape is a charge of plagiarism, such as unpopular authors usually make against those who are popular. Judge Webb has to suppose that Jonson, when he storms, raves against some 'works' at that time somehow associated with Shakespeare; and that, when he praises, he praises the divine masterpieces of Bacon. But we know what plays really were attributed to Shakespeare, then as now, while no other 'works' of a contemptible character, attributed to Shakespeare, are to be heard of anywhere. Judge Webb does not pretend to know what the things were to which the angry Jonson referred.** If he really aimed his stupid epigram at Shakespeare, he obviously alluded to the works which were then, and now are, recognised as Shakespeare's; but in his wrath he denounced them. 'Potter is jealous of potter, poet of poet' - it is an old saying of the Greek. There was perhaps some bitterness between Jonson and Shakespeare about 1601; Ben made an angry epigram, perhaps against Shakespeare, and thought it good enough to appear in his collected epigrams in 1616, the year of Shakespeare's death. By that time the application to Shakespeare, if to him the epigram applied, might, in Ben's opinion perhaps, be forgotten by readers. In any case, Ben, according to Drummond of Hawthornden, was one who preferred his jest to his friend.

* Webb, pp. 114-116.

** Webb, pp. 116-119.

Judge Webb's hypothesis is that Ben, in Shakespeare's lifetime, especially in 1600-1601, spoke evil of his works, though he allowed that they might endure to 'after-times' -

Aftertimes
May judge it to be his, as well as ours.

But these works (wholly unknown) were not (on the Judge's theory) the works which, after Shakespeare's death, Ben praised, as his, in verse; and, more critically, praised in prose: the works, that is, which the world has always regarded as Shakespeare's. THESE were Bacon's, and Ben knew it on Judge Webb's theory. Here Judge Webb has, of course, to deal with Ben's explicit declarations, in the First Folio, that the works which he praises are by Shakespeare. The portrait, says Ben,

Was for gentle Shakespeare cut.

Judge Webb then assures us, to escape this quandary, that 'in the Sonnets "the gentle Shakespeare himself informs us that Shakespeare was not his real name, but the "noted weed" in which he "kept invention."'* The author of the Sonnets does nothing of the kind. Judge Webb has merely misconstrued his text. The passage which he so quaintly misinterprets occurs in Sonnet lxxvi.:

> Why is my verse so barren of new pride?
> So far from variation or quick change?
> Why, with the time, do I not glance aside
> To new-found methods, and to compounds strange?
> WHY WRITE I STILL ALL ONE, EVER THE
> SAME,
> AND KEEP INVENTION IN A NOTED WEED,
> THAT EVERY WORD DOES ALMOST TELL MY
> NAME,
> SHOWING THEIR BIRTH AND WHENCE
> THEY DO PROCEED?
> Oh, know, sweet love, I always write of you,
> And you and love are still my argument;
> So all my best is dressing old words new,
> Spending again what is already spent:
> For as the sun is daily new and old,
> So is my love still telling what is told.

*Webb, pp. 125,156,235,264. Judge Webb is fond of his discovery.

The lines capitalised are thus explained by the Judge: 'Here the author certainly intimates that Shakespeare is not his real name, and that he was fearful lest his real name should be discovered.' The author says nothing about Shakespeare not being his real name, nor about his fear lest his real name should be discovered. He even 'quibbles on his own Christian name,' WILL, as Mr. Phillipps and everyone else have noted. What he means is: 'Why am I so monotonous that every word almost tells my name?' 'To keep invention in a noted weed' means, of course, to present his genius always in the same well-known attire. There is nothing about disguise of a name, or of anything else, in the sonnet.*

* Webb, pp. 64,156.

But Judge Webb assures us that Shakespeare himself informs us in the sonnets that 'Shakespeare was not his real name, but the noted weed in which he kept invention.' As this is most undeniably not the case, it cannot aid his effort to make out that, in the Folio, by the name of Shakespeare, Ben Jonson means another person.

In the Folio verses, 'To the Memory of my Beloved, Mr. William Shakespeare, and What he has Left Us,' Judge Webb finds many mysterious problems.

> Soul of the Age,
> The applause, delight, the wonder of our stage,
> My Shakespeare, rise!

By a pun, Ben speaks of Shakespeare as

> shaking a lance
> As brandish't at the eyes of Ignorance.

The pun does not fit the name of - Bacon! The apostrophe to 'sweet Swan of Avon' hardly applies to Bacon either; he was not a Swan of Avon. It were a sight, says Ben, to see the Swan 'in our waters yet appear,' and Judge Webb actually argues that Shakespeare was dead, and could not appear, so somebody else must be meant! 'No poet that ever lived would be mad enough to talk of a swan as YET appearing, and resuming its flights, upon the river some seven or eight years after it was dead.'* The Judge is like the Scottish gentleman who when Lamb, invited to meet Burns's sons, said he wished it were their father, solemnly replied that this could not be, for Burns was dead. Wordsworth, in a sonnet, like Glengarry at Sheriffmuir, sighed for 'one hour of Dundee!' The poet, and the chief, must have been mad, in Judge Webb's opinion, for Dundee had fallen long ago, in the arms of victory. A theory which not only rests on such arguments as Judge Webb's, but takes it for granted that Bacon might be addressed as 'sweet Swan of Avon,' is conspicuously impossible.

* Webb, p. 134.

Another of the Judge's arguments reposes on a misconception which has been exposed again and again. In his Memorial verses Ben gives to Shakespeare the palm for POETRY: to Bacon for ELOQUENCE, in the 'Discoveries.' Both may stand the comparison with 'insolent Greece or haughty Rome.' Shakespeare is not mentioned with Bacon in the 'Scriptorum Catalogus' of the 'Discoveries': but no more is any dramatic author or any poet, as a poet. Hooker, Essex, Egerton, Sandys, Sir Nicholas Bacon are chosen, not Spenser, Marlowe, or Shakespeare. All this does not go far to prove that when Ben praised 'the wonder of our stage,' 'sweet Swan of Avon,' he meant Bacon, not Shakespeare.

When Judge Webb argued that in matters of science ('falsely so called') Bacon and Shakespeare were identical, Professor Tyrrell, of Trinity College, Dublin, was shaken, and said so, in 'The Pilot.' Professor Dowden then proved, in 'The National Review,' that both Shakespeare and Bacon used the widely spread pseudo-scientific ideas of their time (as is conspicuously the case), and Mr. Tyrrell confessed that he was sorry he had spoken. 'When I read Professor Dowden's article, I would gladly have recalled my own, but it was too late.' Mr. Tyrrell adds, with an honourable naivete, 'I AM NOT VERSED IN THE LITERATURE OF THE SHAKESPEAREAN ERA, and I assumed that the Baconians who put forward the parallelisms had satisfied themselves that the coincidences were peculiar to the writings of the philosopher and the poet. Professor Dowden has proved that this is not so. . . .' Professor Dowden has indeed proved, in copious and minute detail, what was already obvious to every student who knew even such ordinary Elizabethan books as Lyly's 'Euphues' and Phil Holland's 'Pliny,' and the speculations of such earlier writers as Paracelsus. Bacon and Shakespeare, like other Elizabethans, accepted the popular science of their period, and decorated their pages with queer ideas about beasts, and stones, and plants; which were mere folklore. A sensible friend of my own was staggered, if not converted, by the parallelisms adduced in Judge Webb's chapter 'Of Bacon as a Man of Science.' I told him that the parallelisms were Elizabethan commonplaces, and were not peculiar to Bacon and Shakespeare. Professor Dowden, out of the fulness of his reading, corroborated this obiter dictum, and his article (in 'The National Review,' vol. xxxix., 1902) absolutely disposes of the Judge's argument.

Mr. Tyrrell went on: 'The evidence of Ben Jonson alone seems decisive of the question; the other' (the Judge, for one) 'persuades himself (how, I cannot understand) that it may be explained away.'*

* Pilot, August 30, 1902, p. 220.

We have seen how Judge Webb ' explains away' the

evidence of Ben. But while people 'not versed in the literature of the Shakespearean era' assume that the Baconians have examined it, to discover whether Shakespearo-Baconian parallelisms are peculiar to these two writers or not, these people may fall into the error confessed by Mr. Tyrrell.

Some excuse is needed for arguing on the Baconian doctrine. 'There is much doubt and misgiving on the subject among serious men,' says Judge Webb, and if a humble author can, by luck, allay the doubts of a single serious man, he should not regret his labour.